I0213660

PHOENIX ROAD

PHOENIX ROAD

THE TRUE STORY

OF HOW GOD SHATTERED ALL FORMS
AND BOUNDARIES OF MY EXISTENCE

A *MEMOIR AND APOLOGIA* BY

JON KELLY

LIVING
STONE
PUBLISHING

LIVINGSTONE PUBLISHING

Unless otherwise indicated, all Scripture quotations are taken from the New King James Version®. Copyright © 1982 by Thomas Nelson, Inc. Used by permission. All rights reserved.

Verses marked KJV are taken from the King James Version, 1769.

Verses marked ESV are taken from the Holy Bible, English Standard Version, copyright © 2001 by Crossway Bibles, a division of Good News Publishers. Used by Permission. All rights reserved.

Verses marked NASB are taken from the NEW AMERICAN STANDARD BIBLE®, Copyright © 1960, 1962, 1963, 1968, 1971, 1972, 1973, 1975, 1977, 1995 by The Lockman Foundation. Used by permission.

Verses marked NIV are taken from the HOLY BIBLE, NEW INTERNATIONAL VERSION®, NIV®. Copyright © 1973, 1978, 1984, 2011, by Biblica, Inc.™ Used by permission of Zondervan. All rights reserved worldwide.

All emphasis in Scripture quotations is added by the author.

The lyrics quoted by The Promise Ring are used with permission.

Cover photo © Bob Sacha / Corbis of Solaris Gregory, artistry by Tony Gregory, is used with permission.

Cover design by Dave Bricker (TheWorldsGreatestBook.com).

The websites, articles, books, music, and all other sources cited throughout this book are for reference only. Neither the author nor the publisher guarantees their retrieval, nor do they endorse the content of the sources.

PHOENIX ROAD
Copyright © 2014 by Jon Kelly
Published by LivingStone Publishing
Los Angeles, California

Library of Congress Control Number: 2013939503

ISBN: 978-0-9889590-0-2

All rights reserved. No part of this publication may be reproduced, stored in a retrieval system, or transmitted in any form or by any means—electronic, mechanical, digital, photocopy, recording, or any other—except for brief quotations in printed reviews, without the prior permission of the publisher.

To all the people I've ever known,
And, all the people I ever will…
This is *why*.

ACKNOWLEDGMENTS

THIS CHRONICLE COULD NOT HAVE BEEN SCRIBBLED DOWN if it were not for the support and steadfastness of my loving wife—I, and *we*, are blessed…"Still"…thank you, Alisa. My daughter, though she knew it not, was merciful and forgiving as the nights waxed long and my wits wore thin, not to mention my hairs! Thank you, Olivia—you are *a new generation*—I love you and I believe in you. We did it!

My gratitude to my family is without compromise. Thank you, Mom, for your fierce prayers and unyielding faith. Dad, your wisdom has guided my steps. And to my sister, whose passion always ignited my fire—thank you for blazing a trail!

My friends… Nate, Chad, Andrew, Jason, Freddie, Matt, Ryan, Falcon, and others… have strengthened my soul and sharpened my sword. I'm honored to know and be known by you.

Thanks to all the musicians, authors, teachers, pastors,

artists, editors, actors, and actresses, athletes, and individuals who have, and still do, inspire me. Where the flame rises up, the breath of God is near...

Thanks to bicycles, Mediterranean harbors, coffee and baristas, long stretches of Midwestern highway, Triumph motorbikes, the San Juan Mountains, sunsets, solitude, and Jesus—making the journey what it is... the *whos*, the *whats*, the *wheres*, the *whys*, the "*why nots*," the invitation to redemption, the promise of rest, the hope of a new creation, and the peace at the end of the day. Thank you for beginning before I start and continuing where I end... Thank you.

Thanks to my readers... whomever you are, wherever you are, and for whatever reason our paths have crossed—thank you for taking a chance on *Phoenix Road*. I pray it finds a unique place in your heart... that my words would fade out, and His would burn bright.

And lastly, I want to humbly thank the author—and that sullied group—who, as a writer, circumnavigated the unknown, shared sleep with aloneness, and clashed with fear, fatigue, his self, and God... You stayed the course; you championed your road. Thank you!

CONTENTS

Acknowledgments   vii
Author's Note   xiii
Introduction   1

1   The Call to Write   5

GROWING UP IS HARD TO DO   15
2   Younger Years   19
3   Things Were Not Always as They Appeared   31
4   All Hell Broke Loose   45

A NOT-SO-NEW AGE   65
5   Spiraling Out of Control   67
6   Higher Power   89
7   Go West My Son   113
8   Coming Home   133
9   A Great Fire   157
10   Calvary Road   189
11   Planes, Trains, and Bicycles   209

CONTENTS

HIGH DESERT YEARS   251
12   Colorado Still Calling   253
13   A New Generation   279

Afterword: Where Now?   295
Postscript   303

Chronology of Travels   305
Songs from Phoenix Road   307
Readings for The Road   309
Index   311
About the Author   327

"That this may be a sign among you
when your children ask in time to come, saying,
'What do these stones mean to you?'
…And these stones shall be for a memorial
to the children of Israel forever."
Joshua 4:6-7

RECORDED AND EDITED: WINTER 2009—SPRING 2014

This is my heap of stones.

AUTHOR'S NOTE

MORE THAN A ROADSIDE MEMOIR, *Phoenix Road* is what I have titled a "living apologia." I'm not certain a genre exists as such, nor if mine does so properly. (Perhaps, it hints at what others have titled a spiritual theology.) In setting out to record my story of redemption, however, I often found myself seated in the chair of commentator. Naturally, as a student of apologetics and defender of the faith, I could not recount my story without framing it in the Christian worldview. *Phoenix Road's* format is unique in this sense, engaging its reader through lush narrative *and* theological discourse—hence, *Phoenix Road* is my story and my defense (or reason for believing).

Likewise, in the day-to-day of life I often find myself longing for a deeper reality in Christian culture, on the radio, or in a good book. My intention as an author is to be real. *Phoenix Road* is a real-life portrait offering an authentic look at how the gospel plays out in a broken life. No guise was employed in crafting this tale; I simply wrote my story as it unfolded and cast light as I was moved. And, I suppose, redemption as it is—and as it did fall upon Saul of Tarsus on the road to Damascus[1]—only unfolds in the light and on the road. Thus, my road to truth revealed and brokenness restored is my *living apologia.*

Today, I invite you to travel *Phoenix Road* with me as we explore its vivid landscapes, perch on epic vistas, and reflect in deep solitary pools. As we navigate my climactic topography together, I believe some of the complexities we face in the twenty-first century will be unveiled. Perhaps you will stumble into an old friend, a spouse, or *another you* strolling nearby. But, what if somewhere along the way, you were to encounter the Christ? How would your life be transformed? How might your road change course?

Before you set out, let me pause and say that I hope the format of *Phoenix Road* proves to handle friendly along your journey and resourceful into the future. As a narrator and apologist, I've labored to cultivate a middle ground. Footnotes have been made easily accessible within the text, or you can pass them by. An index of subject matter is located at the end of the book for quick reference "on the road." In addition, I've included a few lists and resources for your enjoyment. At last, I want to personally thank you for your interest in my *living apologia,* and I wish you blessed travels… May your spirit rise and your heart burn! This is *Phoenix Road.*

—Jon Kelly

---

[1] The apostle Paul was converted on the road to Damascus as a light shone down from heaven—Acts 9:3-4 (see also footnote 202).

INTRODUCTION

I MUST CONFESS MY GREAT NEED for courage as I begin this journey with the Holy Spirit to rightly glorify the Lord and His work in drawing me to Calvary. The mind of man would suppose recording past events into a book was really of easy matter; however, this is not my case. I have found myself at great odds with the comfortable, harmonious, championing over life common in today's Christian marketplace. I have found something much more common to the depths and dregs of man and his base experience of suffering. I have and I am, still dying.[2]

I suppose, as I labor in the local cemetery, meditate on Bonhoeffer's *Cost of Discipleship*, and allow God to search my heart that He might illuminate these pages for His glory, I should expect nothing else. But, when Jesus bids you to come and die at His cross, His invitation to enter His crucible is always new, full of unknown, violent,

---

[2] 1 Cor 15:31.

horrific, by faith, and least of all absolutely miraculous. And yet, there is peace; as it is written, "He Himself is our peace" (Ephesians 2:14).

Meanwhile, a sparrow picks away at some seed from the lawn in the quiet coastal sunset. He hops and pecks and flickers a bit. He is happy bouncing about between the spattered daisy flowers near the long grass at the park's edge of the wood. Those two in first service this morning at The Barn (church in a barn) were full of twitter and talk, not to mention swoop. They were a delight also... reminding me of how Saint Francis of Assisi's San Damiano must have been.

Today, it is mid April at seven p.m. on Fidalgo Island. I'm sitting at one of four vacant, weathered picnic tables along the western shore of Washington Park. Pink-orange water gleams of the distant sun. The sky blots out in a matte-purple, rosy hue and hangs short over the neighboring San Juans. Clouds shoot off to the north and south running fast and thin. There's no barge or boat in sight; only a few gulls and ducks lit here and there, and a buoy or two nodding off. Farther down the coast to the southwest, the Olympic Mountains blanket-in with the cool Pacific air. A fresh chilly breeze stirring in the evergreens behind me just pricked my nose. It is evening now. This is God's land.

"But not yet, not yet!" The sun fights back and penetrates the hazy air. Its light burns yellow for a moment at its last blaze and glare. Soon it will relinquish to rest. Night shall fall. And this, too, shall be God's world. "But not yet, not yet!"

Old and young have begun to gather with child and camera. A sloop slides up the channel between Guemes from the north. Another great boast will adorn the San Juan Islands tonight—almost as glorious as the alpenglow of my San Juan Mountains back home. My ink isn't flowing quite as well, and my paper is a bit damp now. My solitude has escaped. I will give them their sunset; they can have their nightfall. I have already had mine, and I'm having it still…

In the morning, the sun will rise again. From somewhere over Bellingham and beyond the Cascades, it will dawn upon Anacortes. The old trestle will swim in the lucid golden water as the fog burns off in the marina. A mirage of undulating masts will shine and sparkle above the neighboring evergreens. As my fingertips roll open the blinds to the aroma of brewing coffee, a gull will announce the beginning of a new day. The sun and God will rise,[3] "with healing in His wings" (Malachi 4:2).

🐚   🐚   🐚

An ancient eastern legend tells of a precarious Phoenician bird that lends itself to a great fire, only to rise up immortal from its ashes. Similarly, *Phoenix Road* is my story of the times and events as they unfolded in my conversion to faith in Jesus Christ. My testimony is true and accurate—to the *best* of my knowledge. My road to "phoenix" is not a legend, and the Christ I serve is above and beyond anything any legend could ever imagine or

---

[3] Jesus is the Bright and Morning Star: Rev 22:16, 2:28; 2 Pet 1:19 (…until the day dawns and the morning star rises in your hearts).

dream of being. On October 31, 1997, Jesus of Nazareth, the holy and anointed Son of God, became my *Savior*. Today, He continues to become the *Lord* of my life. All praise, honor, and glory be to Him who is unchanging,[4] everlasting,[5] and most highly exalted[6] above every other existing thing, and being—Jesus, my consuming fire.

Understandably, I realize my metaphor could potentially become obnoxious, therefore, I have purposed not to litter the roadside with excessive signposts. However, I must inform you now that I did make the journey to Finix, or was it Phonix? And, "Yes," a great fire did burn somewhere along a Midwestern highway. And yet, as most of life's stories go—mine certainly not exempt—I am still resurrecting... Regardless, this is God's day! This is *Phoenix Road*.

---

[4] Mal 3:6; James 1:17.

[5] Ps 90:2; Isa 9:6, 40:28; Hab 1:12; Rev 4:8-11 (Who [Jesus] was, and is, and is to come...who lives forever and ever).

[6] Eph 1:10, 1:20-23; Col 1:15-19; Heb 1:2-4; Rev 5:12-14.

1

THE CALL TO WRITE

ALISA AND I RETURNED TO KAUAI less than six months after honeymooning in Hanalei on the North Shore. We considered downsizing from two houses to four suitcases, a trunk, and two bicycles—a great adventure! God's radar screen had a few channels we didn't get in too clearly. But, living "by faith"[7] seems to always require faith, married or not! Nearly six months later, I sat at our teak dining room table looking out the sun porch at the dense green mountainous fin hovering above the inland cloud cover. They say the wettest place on the planet is up there, but I wouldn't know; its cloudy umbrella never lifts long enough to catch a peek.

It was April, the plumerias were blooming, and our backyard was a garden of flowers and fragrance. Lox sat on the picnic table licking his old goldy-locks coat, and Boots rolled around on the deck, stretching her back under the

---

[7] The believer is called to live by faith: Rom 1:17, 5:1; 2 Cor 5:7; Gal 2:16, 2:20, 3:11, 3:22, 3:24; Phil 3:9; Heb 10:38; 11; James 2:24.

orchids. She was bored; no lizards had been out to play today. Our plantation cottage came fully furnished with amenities, and cats. Meanwhile, my classes were wrapping up, and I was seeking God for what He had in store next as my final semester of Bible college approached. It was one of those Father and son moments where He sits you down at the table and looks you directly in the eyes, so to speak. I felt as if we were in a final hand of poker, the stakes were high, and my hand wasn't the top dog, if you know what I mean! Somehow, I had secretly hoped for another draw, just one more card! And then, He spoke.

For quite some time, a year or more, maybe three, a Scripture verse had been popping up with an anxious little pull attached to it. It was kind of like a scratch, or an itch, or any sort of obnoxious little irritant. God's funny like that sometimes, isn't He? He told me He was concerned with me once, so I did a word study and found that part of the definition of being concerned includes being disturbed or made uneasy (Webster, 1910). Well, I guess He was inviting me to be *concerned* with His question: "What do you want Me to do for you, Jon?"[8] And the thing about it is, when you know that the Almighty God of Eternity is asking what you want Him to do for you, the mood shifts a bit. Because really, how does one respond to that question? It's a loaded question, right? I mean, He's going to answer it; He will bring it to pass. So, as I said, some time went by while I thought about it, probably more like three years on a low simmer.

---

[8] Mark 10:46-52 (51); Luke 18:35-43 (41); Matt 20:32—"Jon" was obviously an addition!

I had just finished a study through the books of 1 and 2 Kings when this little "concern" popped up again, this time in the Old Testament unrelated to the many previous gospel references. And if I didn't see it the first time, it just happened to be quoted twice in chapter 4 of 2 Kings.[9] It is quite ironic, in view today, how the Shunammite woman's concern for Elisha fueled an identical response from him: "What can I do for you?"

Needless to say, my disturbance was climaxing and I knew an answer would be required from me soon. My low simmer had begun to boil... In fact, I had an answer, and I believed God had planted it in my heart.

The final showdown had arrived. There we sat, God holding His winning hand, and me still hoping for some table scraps, a few leftovers, or a wild card. My mind was busy: *Could it be so easy? I mean, just ask, and You will do it? But You're not some kind of genie, is it even right? How can I even expect You to do it? I mean, where is the money going to come from, and what about Alisa? What will she do? And, why all the way from Kauai, anyway? I'm clear on the other side of the globe. Am I crazy thinking this up? Could You really want me to "go up to Jerusalem" to meet with You?*

So, what happened? I squared my shoulders, looked Him in the eyes, and laid my cards down straight. He looked at me, glanced down at my cards, and smiled a little, nodding His head as He looked back at me and said,

---

[9] 2 Kings 4:2 (Elisha questions a widow), 4:13 (and the Shunammite: "Look, you have been concerned with us for all this care, 'What can I do for you?'").

"Okay then, if that's what you got. Meet me in Jerusalem."
And the rest, as they say, is history!

THE LORD IS THERE

My time in Jerusalem was nearing its end. I rose early again
to sneak out to the streets in my running shoes before
the town awoke. I stretched and tied my shoes in the
third-story window of our back-alley dormitory on North
Hillel. The nearby Knesset park trail was a sanctuary of
fresh breath welcoming each day. As I made my way down
to the street and loosened up, preparing for my run with
Yeshua, deep thoughts and wonders still surfaced about
His calling me to "meet with Him here," in His holy city.

There is an expectation with God, that when He calls
you somewhere or to something, He is going to meet you
in that place and speak with you there: YHWH Shammah—THE LORD IS THERE (Ezekiel 48:35). My trip to
Jerusalem was one of those times. I was expecting God to
meet with me and speak something directive, life changing,
or reveal something I wouldn't otherwise have known, but
needed to know to fulfill His will and purpose in my life.
This divine speaking can take on any form He chooses obviously, but the one thing it is not, is ordinary, or common.
And for me, being in Jerusalem for the month was not
common. And, my expectation of being met by Him who
brought me there was to have a significant encounter with
Him, at His time, in His way, and at His chosen place.[10]

---

[10] Deut 12:5.

Yes, the Temple Mount was intense with conflict, and He moved me with compassion at the Western (wailing) Wall. The Mount of Olives, the Garden of Gethsemane, and the empty Garden Tomb all offered a unique encounter with the Lord of Glory. Hummus and halvah, saffron and za'atar filled the suq (Arabic for market). The Sea of Galilee was spectacular, teaming with life and fruitfulness. My studies, tours, and friendships were all blessed indeed. My cup runneth over… not to mention the coffee at Aroma! Should you "go up to Jerusalem?" Yes, definitely. Actually, maybe we could meet at Aroma on Hillel; the last red booth on the left… I'll save you a seat!

Every day had been packed full with learning and new experiences as Yeshua taught me more about Himself, His people, His culture and history. Yet this expectancy was beyond every day, and my spirit still questioned: "Why did You call me here?" I was still patiently waiting upon His time, and His place… This was the backbone of my early morning thoughts rising up within me as I awoke to one of my last morning runs in the City of my King.

Heading south on the trail through the Knesset drops you down past Saint John's of the Cross Monastery nestled into a glorious sun-filled meadow of olive trees and rock outcroppings. If you continue up the hill to the left, you can weave your way back up to the area of the King David Hotel. And not too far from there, a beautiful park parallels the Hinnom Valley. To the south, the park ends at an old Dutch-looking windmill and a tiered square named Casals Corner. Standing in this limestone square, one can view an outstanding portrait of the sun rising in the east over Zion—the Old City. This common park, on one of my everyday morning runs, was the place the King of Kings sought me out and desired to meet with me. This was my "Jehovah Shammah"—THE LORD IS THERE—experience. Interestingly enough, Ezekiel penned this verse as the name of the Old City Jerusalem after detailing the city gates and ending with the west side (Ezekiel 48:34), the wall I happened to be looking upon!

My journal records the day as June 26, 2008. A red Jewish prayer-string marks the page of my black leather pocketbook. I wrote:

6/26) Morning Run: I ran down to the Music Center Garden near King David Hotel. Looking east at the sunrise and Old City, west wall. Not my normal run route, I've been through twice before—God leading me here this a.m. for a purpose.

I stopped running abruptly, in the middle of the limestone roof-square, shinning bright in the sun. Staring directly into the sun, my heart began welling up in His nearness. I began to cry and give thanks— thanking Him for bringing me here to His city, His people—Yerushalayim. Remembering His goodness toward me, the past ten years stood at a head. Today, the dawning of a new day, a new hour, a new era! All had been coming to THIS DAY—this head!

I was broken and undone before Him (had the thought of Isaiah seeing the Lord[11]), crying, deeply

---

[11] Isa 6:1-9.

aching in pain, my inner man broken. His nearness was so potent and weighty upon me, yet still light. A dove hopped around in the morning light from pillar to pillar along the square's edge! I could only give thanks to Him for His bringing me here to Jerusalem and His goodness being reflected over the past decade.

He then spoke to me through His goodness and nearness as His Spirit pressed closer. He was smiling. *"Jon, you are in Jerusalem.* I did what you asked. I answered your request."[12] This revelation of exactly what HE HAS DONE allowed me to come to a place where I knew He wanted me to respond: "What do You want me to do for You, LORD?" I knew what I had to ask, but I couldn't get the words out…

He just waited for me in His nearness. I was in pain, having to die. His nearness was bringing my death.[13] Fears were also coming up. I'm not sure what they were, but they, or it, were intense to move through—possibly fear of what He might ask, or require of me? Or, just afraid to ask, placing myself totally at His will. Maybe this was the fear, letting go totally of my will and ideas concerning what I should or would do?

His nearness continued. He pressed in upon me. I broke more. He ministered to me through His dove

---

[12] The italics was an inner, verbal speaking—a still small voice (1 Kings 19:12); the non-italicized was spoken through an inner knowledge (1 Cor 12:8).

[13] 1 Cor 1:29.

hopping off the short pillars: hop, hop, "Take a leap of faith!" My soul was encouraged and my breathing relaxed. His peace came over me and I asked Him simply: "Jesus, what would You have me do for You?" And now, I wait.

This is truly why He brought me to Israel, to Jerusalem. He wanted me to ask Him what He wanted *me* to do for Him—here, here in His holy city Jerusalem. Here, where His first followers did the same.[14] Here, where He did with His Father.[15] Thy will be done. Amen, so be it (see footnote 351).

I will always remember this time, this trip, this day—TODAY! And Alisa, too, will give testimony of her experience of waiting on Him while I sought His face here in Yerushalayim.

—*Love Strengthened.*

❀　❀　❀

I returned to Kauai a week later after a short stop in Turkey to catch my breath and cool off in the Aegean at Bodrum—a highly anticipated excursion! I was blessed to retrace a few of Paul's steps and explore the ruins at Ephesus. "No," I didn't get an immediate answer from Him. Alisa welcomed me back to the lush beauty of the Garden Island in Hawaiian tradition with a kiss and lei! Her gifts and treasures I stored up along the way swept her up into the awe and wonder of the journey. The village of

---

[14] Luke 24:49; Acts 1:12-14, 2:1.

[15] John 12:12, 12:27, 18:1; Luke 22:39-44; Mark 14:32-36; Matt 26:36-39, 26:42.

Nazareth offers a lavender olive oil lotion that is purely *au naturel.* The clouds still part, and I drift off to green Galilean fields every time she glides it on. It seems to be running out; I told her it may be near time for *us* to return to replenish her supply. The thought hasn't escaped my mind yet!

The rest of our time in Kauai went by fairly quick. I was finishing up some Bible classes and discipling a local brother God had divinely paired me with. He was a *rare bird*, a true godsend from my heavenly Father. Our friendship helped me transition back from my time in Israel—he kept my own wings grounded. It was during this time of study and meditation that the Lord began to stir within me what He would have me "do" for Him.

Nearly a year has passed and a short stay in Washington since that time. Alisa and I have covered a lot of ground visiting friends up the coast from San Diego to Seattle. One thing has continued to grow louder and more constant: His calling me to write… He has been relentless! Insistently, He continues to confirm His desire for me to record the testimony of *His work* in my life. He has not stopped pursuing me! It has recently come down to a simple decision of obedience. And so, today, I write. Well, I suppose there's a bit more to it than that. But today, sitting in the gateway to my San Juan Mountains back home in Colorado, I do what Yeshua has asked me to do for Him. I write.

GROWING UP IS HARD TO DO

I WAS NEARLY TWENTY-TWO YEARS OLD on October 31, 1997. This day marked the beginning and end of a long life. It is perhaps necessary to color in a little background to show the panorama of God's glorious workmanship.[16] Similar to Paul's gospel (good news) to the Romans, the backdrop of the black night must fall before the rising of the Bright and Morning Star.[17] So, let me rewind a bit and give you a glimpse into the days and years preceding that "Great and Terrible Day!" Taking a journey is always exciting, isn't it? Or at the least, it is an opportunity to expand one's faith and enjoy vast discovery—however untraveled the path becomes... Besides, I'm not absolutely certain it was curiosity that killed the cat; it could have been the neighbor's son?

---

[16] Workmanship (Grk., *poiema*; Eng., poem): Eph 2:10; Rom 1:20 (things that are made).

[17] John 8:12; Rev 22:16, 22:5, 21:23, 21:25; John 1:4-5, 1:7-9; 1 John 1:5-7; Luke 1:78-79; 2 Sam 22:13; Heb 1:3; James 1:17.

I suppose, growing up under a rather well-to-do roof provides one with a certain measure of security. It does not, however, guarantee one's admission into heaven, nor a peaceable nurturing childhood within the confines of a healthy family unit. My story is really nothing so out of the ordinary; it could have been a handful of my friends', or any number of yours down the street in your town. One element set my story apart. This is the picture I hope to identify as I explore my younger years. So come along and sing along with me: "One of These Kids Is Doing His Own Thing…"[18]

The Bible isn't exactly clear why demonic possession occurs. Nor does it give straightforward guidelines as to how, when, or by what means Satan enters into a human life. One thing it is certain about, demonic possession[19] is real, and its occurrence is common and at hand. Again, the form it takes on, or he (Satan) assumes, is not quite so obvious. It is said, "Hindsight vision is always twenty-twenty." Well, that is not always true, and in some cases, it is far too behind to boast in. My hopes are that

[18] Sesame Street Sing-along "One of These Kids (Is Doing His Own Thing)" by Joe Raposo and Jeff Moss is a version of the song "One of These Things (Is Not Like The Others)" by Joe Raposo, Jon Stone, and Bruce Hart (more info at: http://muppet.wikia.com/wiki/One_of_These_Things).

[19] Demonic Possession or Influence: Matt 4:24, 8:16, 8:28-33, 9:32-33, 12:22, 15:22-28, 17:18; Mark 1:23-27, 1:32, 5:2-19, 7:25-30, 9:17-29, Luke 4:33-36, 8:27-36, 9:38-43, 11:14; John 6:70, 8:44, 13:2; Acts 8:9-10, 10:38, 13:6-10, 16:16-18, 19:11-16; Ex 7:11, 7:22, 8:18-19; 1 Sam 16:14-15, 16:23; Dan 4:33-34, 4:36. Common Language Usage: Matt 9:34, 11:18, 12:24, 12:26-29, 12:43; Mark 3:22, 3:30; Luke 7:33, 11:15, 11:18-20, 11:24-25; John 7:20, 8:48-49, 8:52, 10:20-21; James 3:15; Rev 18:2; Deut 18:10.

you and I will become more aware of the spiritual conditions existent in those we love and interact with daily.
Oftentimes the best place to begin is right at home, and
I don't mean across the sofa. So, let's see what The Great
Physician[20] has diagnosed in my person as we look back
onto His examination table over the years. And remember,
this is an exciting journey full of discovery!

Is your bag packed and your passport handy; are your
shoes tied?

Let's get moving!

---

[20] Matt 9:12; Mark 2:17; Luke 5:31; Isa 61:1.

2

YOUNGER YEARS

I GREW UP IN A SMALL AFFLUENT COMMUNITY located on the shores of Lake Winnebago. If you look down at the manhole cover in your street, or the iron tree-grate in your city sidewalk downtown, chances are they were stamped in our foundry. But more notably, the town is known for its paper industry; I suppose trees and water might have had something to do with that. Lake Winnebago boasts a great depth of twenty-five feet, yet at forty miles long and six to eight miles wide it is the largest inland lake in the Midwest. Twenty minutes to an hour will get you across, depending on which boat you take: either the fourteen-foot, aluminum Lund fishing boat, or the twenty-one-foot, glass Sea Ray ski boat. Both will serve their purpose just fine; I would recommend, however, not using the skiff or John Boat used for duck hunting, or a canoe borrowed from a friend, for that matter. The whitecaps that roar up the middle when the wind shifts might be a bit more than you bargained for. Also, be sure to trim your prop, especially if you're running a three-blade stainless steel—those cost a lot of "lawn mows" to pay back!

The winter is another world altogether. Imagine one of George Lucas' Stormtroopers walking out of the distant white, and you're almost there. Thirty feet of ice can stack up in jagged twelve-inch thick plates, like miniature mountain ranges shoved up beyond the shore into front lawns or jutting out of living rooms on occasion. Tip-ups and ice shanties dapple the lake as fishermen huddle around in snowmobile suits and Sorrels while their kids ice skate or roast hot dogs over a coffee can. Walleyes and perch (local fish) make a great meal, but an eleven-foot sturgeon lying on the ice makes you wonder whom you were swimming with all summer. Not to mention, the twelve-prong spear the lady from the gas station down on the corner thrust through its bony prehistoric-looking back. Ice boats, motocross bikes, snowmobiles, and just about anything with studded wheels race up and down the lake. Even a bicycle with a hockey skate rigged up to the front fork will do. Withered Christmas trees mark the boundaries of temporary roads and signify bridges over cracks and exposed water. You can still cross over "the pond" if you've got the nerve… Cram into the back of your buddy's pick-up and trade in your water ski for a snowboard—the county park rope-tow runs every school night, just don't forget your leather mittens!

The Wilds of Wisconsin

Wisconsin is a land of sportsmen (a word I have never really understood). There are several other stereotypes besides hunting and fishing characterizing America's Dairyland, and for the most part they are true: the "Packer Backers" in Green Bay, Milwaukee's home of Harley Davidson, Harley bars, cheese heads, cheese curds and string cheese, Germans, Lutherans and Catholics, mosquitoes, bratwurst and beer—cheap cold beer. According to Alisa, who sprouted in Ohio, but grew up primarily in Boulder, Colorado, it can tend to be a little "rough and wild." This is where I grew up, in the wilds of Wisconsin!

I've traveled about a bit by now, and as I said before, the term "sportsman" has always remained a little lucid. I've also had the chance to observe other qualified men and the environs in which they "sport." What I've come to understand is that my own father is Der Meister Sportler! Undoubtedly, hands down, he is The Master Sportsman. Don't get me wrong; he is a top-notch Doc! And, I would trust my care to his hands and eyes over anyone else. I suppose the price has always been right too, but when I refer to his sportsman-like nobility, there is really no competition.

Today, my dad lives in one of the various smaller cottages along the lake. What the neighbors know however, that many passersby in boats do not, is that across the road behind the house is the Grand Cathedral—his very own Sportsman's Warehouse. Have you ever passed through the Gateway to the West Archway (I won't comment) on I-80 in central Nebraska? Well, I'm pretty certain he'd give Cabela's a run for their money by now. All kidding aside, every true sportsman needs a well-organized garage for his fishing rods and tackle, guns and ammunition, decoys, outerwear, and don't forget the bird dogs.

Alisa and I have recently rented a house with our very first garage with four walls and a roof, and what a joy it is to get our bicycles and gear out of the house. I would add, however, that if you have just received your first leak-free garage, you might want to erect a flashing neon sign that says: "Hello, Bike Antlers?" On second thought, I was kidding; no one ever forgets his bike is still on the roof rack! (A random quote from an old California preacher often springs to mind at such moments: "Praise the Lord Hibiscus!") And true enough, in keeping step with Paul's "good news," God's existence and attributes are clearly seen through the natural world.[21] But, I'm sure by now your subconscious has begun to prod, "What's your point?"

My point is this: I stood in a tree-stand (elevated platform used for hunting deer) in the solitude of the wilderness for weekends at a time. From a young age, I sat in the bow of a boat jigging away (fishing technique), or listening to the rhythm of the river wading to the next pool. I lived and breathed in the outdoors. If I wasn't fishing or hunting in it, I was playing… building forts in the surrounding fields, sneaking through the corn, or hiding in a tree. I enjoyed most all sports, as long as I was outside cutting loose! I only had one Nintendo game, well actually two, Duck Hunt and Downhill Skiing (but that was Atari). The outdoors was my safe haven. I belonged; and I understood the order of things. The solitude was

---

[21] Rom 1:20; Ps 19:1-6.

my serenity—my freedom, or in some very real sense, my freeness of life and being.

The question that arises is, "Why did I need a safe haven?" Or by default of receiving or seeking such an environment, "Why was I finding shelter within it? What was I being sheltered from?" Honestly, I don't have all the answers to that question today. I do have enough clarity to know that as a young boy I was very troubled by the spiritual climate or condition of my family, and potentially my own self. I was not ignorant of the discord and lack of peace that I innately knew ought to exist in a family and marriage. Even at that young age, I was aware that my parents were going to go through a divorce someday, a road that did eventually follow.

As I reflect today, I can see Satan busy at work in the shadows, lurking in wait around every corner. Being left alone in a large house, often for long periods, was extremely frightening. Suspicious noises and the knowledge of previous burglaries led me to hide behind the couch with a pencil gripped in terror, or shout to the other military men with me (imaginary) as I descended into the basement. These were not playtimes of self-made weaponry! I also experienced a short season of manipulation and sexual abuse. More and more I've continued to learn about the generational[22] effects of Satan's stronghold over my family. And it is good to know, and in certain cases liberating, that oftentimes sound reasons exist for these occurrences and behaviors.

---

[22] Ex 34:7; Num 14:18; Ps 78:7-8; Joel 1:3; Luke 1:50; Heb 3:10; 1 Pet 2:9.

Overall, there is one word that I come back to. I am very grateful for my family, and I truly believe my mother and father, and even my sister did everything they could with the knowledge and resources they had. Or at least, they did their best to care for our lives and family. Simply defined, however, neglect means to fail to care for *properly*. I'm aware that there are numerous types and severities of neglect. But please understand, I am not interested in pinpointing or finger-pointing. A few general relational areas lacked: communication, quality time, and accountability.

Does it take time to be a master sportsman and medical professional, or a competitive ballroom dancer and instructor, or to live on the run with your punk-rock friends? Yes; time is still *of the essence*. Was my family governed by selfish motives? Yes. Does the Bible speak into man's self-governed will?[23] Yes. It must also be stated that some of this neglect could have been self-warranted. I was not one to easily and openly receive intimate care and nurture, which, I'm sure, can be explained by a whole series of psychological theories. On occasion my frustration boiled over into an outbreak of: rage, violence, a scare of my sister with kitchen knives, or a fistfight with a bully at school. These acts were normally reactions of anger beyond my control, as far as I was aware or able. Not that they were

---

[23] The Bible and gospel message deal explicitly with man's independent, self-governed will: Satan's Fall: Isa 14:12-17; Ezek 28:12-19. Man's Fall: Gen 3:6-7, 3:17-24, 4:6-12; Rom 5:12-14. Man's Condition: Ps 51:1-17; Rom 1:18, 3:10-18, 3:23, 5:12. Messiah's Cure: Isa 7:14, 53:4-6, 53:12, 61:1-2 (Luke 4:14-21); Jer 33: 31-34; John 3:14-21; Rom 3:22; Eph 2:4-9. Man's Reconciliation: Rom 5:1-11, 8:14-17; Gal 4:3-7.

always unjustified or morally wrong, but my anger was a problem. Again, my purpose is not to point a finger but to frame a realistic portrait of my life. Hopefully, this basic framework will begin to create a context for viewing and discerning my spiritual journey. I'm trusting the Great Physician's diagnostics!

As my story unfolds, the extensive time I spent living in the meditation of the wilderness would become very relevant to my spiritual condition. Whether I, or any other single person, knew it, or not? Which of course, I've learned now, there have always been those certain onlookers watching with God's awareness from afar and engaged in prayer[24] for my eternal soul. Why? Well, isn't that just like a loving Father[25] who did, and does "so love the world that He gave His only begotten Son, that whoever believes in Him should not perish but have everlasting life" (John 3:16).

My own father was a very compassionate and patient man, and I've been blessed to inherit that training and quality from him. As I stood quiet and patient with my ears open in the stillness of nature all those years, I wonder what I was hearing…

The flicker of poplar leaves, cattails, and reeds brush and sway dancing in the breeze, golden corn stalks rustle; geese set their wings cutting through the air overhead; old oaks chatter with squirrels' talk; the

---

[24] Gen 18:20-33 (Abraham intercedes for the righteous); Isa 53:12; Heb 7:25; Rom 8:26-27, 8:34.

[25] Gal 4:4-7; Rom 8:14-15; Heb 12:5-9.

crack of a branch from a hoof or paw; a black-and-white spotted Downey pecking a neighboring limb for dinner; a Chickadee hopping from branch to branch with a flicker and a twitch; the marsh buzzing with crickets and frogs, a snort and a splash and slosh of stepping into water by something of great weight as it ruts around in the marsh grass heavily breathing, "What's out there?"

I always closed my eyes and turned my head forty-five degrees when I really wanted to hear; I found this posture allowed me to enter into my listening. Hearing things you cannot see takes a little practice, but I've learned that ninety-nine percent of the time my inner ear does not lie. There is a difference between listening and hearing, however. The writer of Hebrews[26] makes that explicitly clear, especially in light of James' exhortation not to be mere listeners of God's Word, but those who truly hear and by virtue of doing so must, by necessity, and will, respond in appropriate action (James 1:19-25). Christ's exhortation to "take heed how you hear,"[27] still penetrates the listener's ear today.

I wonder if I ever listened to anything else out in nature? Did I ever hear and obey, what or whom, I might have been listening to? Interestingly, wasn't it the serpent of old[28]

---

[26] Heb 3:7-19.

[27] Luke 8:18.

[28] Rev 12:9, 20:2.

who came to Eve in the garden[29] and spoke to her? Didn't Paul proclaim the necessity of the Helmet of Salvation[30] for the spiritual battle, and the practice of "bringing every thought into the captivity of Christ"?[31] Or, wasn't it Peter who described the Devil in the wild "walking about like a roaring lion, seeking whom he may devour" (1 Peter 5:8)? Paul also declared to the Ephesians that they were "once dead in trespasses and sins, walking according to the course of this world, according to the prince of the power of the air, the *spirit* who now works in the sons of disobedience."[32] The Ephesians were both hearing and walking, or patterning a lifestyle after that prince who held authority over their ears and lives.

According to Dietrich Bonhoeffer, however, "He [Christ] is the only pattern we must follow."[33] Like the Ephesians, there is really no doubt that much is being said in this world, but the question is: whom are you listening to, and what are you walking after? And truly, that makes each of us a *follower* (as seen in Bonhoeffer's statement also), even if it is our self. So, whom are you hearing; whom are you following? And if I might add, whom are you leading others to follow? Who?

---

[29] Gen 3:1-24.

[30] Eph 6:13-18 (16, 17); 1 Thes 5:8; Isa 59:17 (referencing the Messiah).

[31] 2 Cor 10:5.

[32] Eph 2:1-10.

[33] Dietrich Bonhoeffer, *The Cost of Discipleship* (Simon & Schuster Inc.: Touchstone; New York, NY, 1995), p. 304.

Quasi City Life

Wisconsin ain't all country, though. The Valley was somewhat of a quasi city life. To the north was a large independent seat known for its wealth in the paper industry. Academia and culture were secured by its liberal arts university. In the late 1870s the famed magician Harry Houdini appeared there (if it be of any consequence). Ironically, the entire Bible was read from cover to cover at his memorial square downtown a few years back. Cradling Winnebago to the south rests a thriving historical community dating beyond the EAA (Experimental Aircraft Association), B'gosh overalls, and its state university, to the sawmill and loggers. And as an early entrepreneur pioneering a workingman's land, its "native" renowned beer bubbled out of its brewery into national spotlight in 1900.

Somewhere in-between rested my home. One commonality besides the river valley joins these communities; they're named after American Indians. And, as I would later learn, there's a significant spiritual reality still existent behind their obvious origin of names, and their strategic locations controlling the local waterways. The Bible gives us clear insight into the spiritual battle, which has always existed over dominion between various principalities.[34] And, as most of us are aware, power and the love of money still remain to be a root of all kinds of evil (1 Timothy 6:10).

---

[34] Eph 3:10, 6:12; Col 1:16, 2:15; Rom 8:38.

❧   ❧   ❧

I was still in grade school when the punk rock and hard-core music scene of the eighties filtered over from the East Coast, spreading down from Green Bay and up from Milwaukee. I watched as my four-year-older sister used a permanent black marker to cross out the Converse logo on her purple high-tops with an anarchy symbol. The UK's *Never Mind the Bollocks, Here's the Sex Pistols* twelve-inch lay on the floor—Generation X was here!

Early punk and Independent rock (before there was "indie") became a strong influence in shaping my life, attitude, and thought. My first original, non-dubbed tape was the Ramones' album *Too Tough Too Die*, which was wearing out around the song "Mama's Boy." Mama now droned on in a deep low tempo, but I was ready to move on anyway... The Dead Kennedys' *Give Me Convenience or Give Me Death* with their remake of "I Fought the Law" was my new fix! In school, Social Studies got replaced with studying Thrasher Magazine and drawing Zorlac skulls. Skateboards, mosh pits, and fire engine red hair—the philosophy of rebellion appeared to be full of hope, and revolutionary. The suburbian ideal we had inherited was not ours. However, I would have to admit, the boys my sister hung out with in combat boots and Mohawks, skateboarding on top of a graffitied car, were a little scary.

Things were not okay in our world of friends, school, neighborhoods, and families. This we knew, and we did what we could. After all, with a name like Billy Idol, spiked hair, and a fist wrapped in steel, what young boy couldn't agree, and so, we also "Rebel Yelled!" Interestingly, God equates rebellion to witchcraft.[35] I suppose my "philosophy" was more deeply rooted than I had known, or perhaps it would be more accurate to say it was quickly rooting deeper than I was aware… Again, this was the wild Wisconsin I grew up in. But actually, MTV was broadcast from coast to coast!

[35] 1 Sam 15:23.

3

THINGS WERE NOT ALWAYS AS THEY APPEARED

LOOKING BACK, IT ALL HAPPENED SO QUICK. Summers flew by. Tennis lessons had long become uncool. The candy store in the little white house around the corner from the courts became the place to hang out. Soon, the chain-link gate where we leaned our bicycles would be locked tight and his door shut for good. The word on the street was that the "candy man" got busted at the supermarket swiping lunchmeat in the trap door of his homemade shopping crate, to stock his own store! I was beginning to learn that things were not always as they appeared to be, and I wasn't sure I liked it. But this new world I had longed for didn't seem to care much about what I liked. I guess there was a reason he always seemed a little creepy when we skipped tennis and spent our change on *Bottle Caps*.

Tennis lessons weren't the only thing that became uncool. I don't know who the cool guy was that made the rule, but he must have only lived a few blocks from the junior high, because walking five miles to school took a lot longer than riding my bike. Who knows, it was probably my own sister a few years earlier. Either way, the seventh grade was another world entirely. One word says it all, girls! Or, maybe two: girls, boys, and cigarettes. After all, the candy store was out of business.

THE OUTCASTS

I still remember tight rolling bleached Levis and my favorite pair of worn-out Vans (sneakers). Looking cool and impressing all the new girls was really *all* that mattered. I wonder what I was wearing the day that ninth grader grabbed my butt when I was bent over at the bubbler between classes? I was definitely in another world, and I had a lot to catch up on, and quick. Not too mention, she was a headbanger!

Well, in my world there were three types of people: the jocks and preps, the skaters and punks, and the grits and headbangers. The 1985 film *The Breakfast Club* could have been produced in our school. Unfortunately, or fortunately, I think there was a fourth group as well; they just didn't get a classification in our divine order. The outcasts were really quite noble, even righteous in many ways. This is the peculiar[36] group Christ would probably have chosen[37]

---

[36] Peculiar people (KJV): Ex 19:5; Deut 14:2, 26:18; Ps 135:4; Titus 2:14; 1 Pet 2:9.

[37] Isa 53:3; 1 Cor 1:28; Isa 60:14; Jer 30:17; Mic 4:6-7; Neh 4:4; Ps 22:6, 119:141.

to walk amongst and to call His disciples from. The words of God's prophet still resonate: "In that day, says the LORD, I will assemble the lame, I will gather the outcast… I will make the lame a remnant, and the outcast a strong nation" (Micah 4:6-7, c. 750–686 BC).

Which group did I belong to? That's a good question, and still open for debate—I could travel relatively freely between them all. Of course, there were those certain moments, like when the toughest ninth grader on the football team slam-dunked me into a trashcan in study hall while the teacher, my neighbor, just stood by and watched. But overall, I had an in with just about everybody, and yes, even the outcasts. For some reason, there always seemed to be a few located near my locker, or maybe it was I who kept getting lockers near them.

Speaking of lockers, it was a few years later in high school when I interrupted a grit beating a punk's head into hamburger as he punched it back and forth into the metal lockers (I guess I was the *outcast*). Isn't He like that with us? Didn't He take on our sinful flesh[38] and humble Himself[39] in our likeness? Paul the apostle spoke like Christ when he said: "To the weak I became as weak, that I might win the weak. I have become all things to all men, that I might by all means save some" (1 Corinthians 9:22). It really is difficult to believe sometimes that God Himself

---

[38] Rom 8:3.

[39] Phil 2:8.

desires[40] to be acquainted[41] with me. But as I said, the world isn't always as it appears!

COMING OF AGE

As I mentioned above, girls were the real reason behind attending junior high, other than it was mandatory. However, that would only be partly true—a more honest evaluation would be: sex. I suppose we could blame the media, our parents, our declining nation, the grade school principal who tied me hand in hand to a young girl with a jump rope as a "learning lesson" for provoking one another on the playground, or the poster on the back of a friend's bedroom door, but pornography[42] in some form had satiated the sexual appetite of nearly all youth, or so it seemed. Testosterone didn't care which group it coursed through; there were young heated males on each and every side of the tracks, and fence.

The order of events and relationships is a bit foggy, but I suppose the content is what is of importance. I might first

---

[40] 1 Tim 2:3-6—who [God] desires all men [/women] to be saved and to come to the knowledge of the truth... who [Jesus] gave Himself a ransom for all...

[41] John 17:20-26 uniquely characterizes the intimate oneness Jesus has with His Father and desires to have with His followers: "that they [believers] all may be one, as You, Father, [are] in Me [Jesus], and I in You; that they also may be one in Us..." "I in them, and You in Me..." "that the love with which You loved Me may be in them, and I in them."

[42] Pornography (from harlot—Grk. root, *porne*), and fornication (Grk., *porneia, porneuo*): Matt 15:19; Mark 7:21; Acts 15:29; Rom 1:29; 1 Cor 5:1, 6:13, 6:18, 7:2; 10:8; 2 Cor 12:21; Gal 5:19; Eph 5:3; Col 3:5; 1 Thes 4:3; Jude 1:7; Rev 2:14, 2:20-21, 9:21, 14:8, 18:3, 19:2.

admit to having an isolated encounter of homosexuality.[43] I'm not sure how to explain it really, other than it was an odd circumstance involving outward pressure by the peer desiring the interaction, and I succumbed to his tactics, or should I say his *moves*. Was I a victim? Well, that's the way I felt, and deeply disturbed also, so much so that I lost that childhood friendship for good. Thinking back now, it was a very similar situation and context to the manipulative circumstances of the sexually abusive occurrences at an earlier age. Yes, I was definitely prone to that form of abuse. But, as with nearly all of life's struggles, I played my role. So, that was that, it never happened again.

The horrible thing about it, however, was not the time it took to get over the feeling of being dirty or the inner shame and embarrassment, but the knowledge that this pattern was probably continuing with other guys I, or he, knew. That made me angry. But, I kept it to myself. What are you supposed to do when you're in seventh grade, who do you tell a thing like that; who do you trust? And greater yet, How do you tell someone? Definitely, things and people were not always as they appeared. Masks were being torn off, and the truth was not always so beautiful.

The Wonderful Counselor[44] is beautiful, however, clothed in the radiance[45] of "grace and truth,"[46] and He

---

[43] A biblical perspective of human sexuality can be seen in Genesis 1:26-28, 1:31, 2:18, 2:21-25.

[44] Isa 9:6.

[45] Ps 45:2-8—You [king and/or Christ] are fairer than the sons of men... (Messianic according to Heb 1:8-9).

[46] John 1:14.

comes bearing life and that more abundantly.[47] He declared Himself this way: "I am the way, the truth, and the life."[48] Today, I can personally say that "He who the Son makes free, shall be free indeed."[49] I've also watched that truth set others free[50] from various strangleholds of sexuality. No matter the lifestyle, addiction, or sin, the Wonderful Counselor stands at our side advocating for our forgiveness and freedom. So, take hope with me! Christ's redeeming hand can restore the road to beauty[51] and abundant life!

❧ ❧ ❧

Now, where did we leave off? "GIRLS!" Oh yes, I almost forgot. Let's get back to them!

I had several girlfriends throughout seventh and eighth grade, none of which I "went with" for over a month. *Going together* was the hot topic on every football shaped note being passed around class. Who, when, where, what, at the next dance, after the football game... what else could have been more important? Except that is, a slow dance or a walk to McDonald's with so-and-so afterward. Supposedly, young women mature quicker than men. I'm

---

[47] John 10:10—I [Jesus] have come that they may have life, and that they may have it more abundantly.

[48] John 14:6.

[49] John 8:36.

[50] John 8:32—And you [disciples] shall know the truth, and the truth shall make you free.

[51] "He has sent Me to heal the brokenhearted, to proclaim liberty to the captives, and the opening of the prison to those who are bound... to give them beauty for ashes..." (Isa 61:1-3; see also Luke 4:17-19— Christ's Messianic fulfillment).

not sure that is justification for diving down the hall to grab a guy in the crotch with nailed claws. A female jock—maybe she was still daydreaming about sliding into home base and scoring one for the team at her softball game the night before? Or maybe, the Postmodern Era was already way underway. "Like, no way, Dude, the girls on TV always wear the pants!"

The 60s *Leave It to Beaver* sitcom was history. *Three's Company*, with its live-in guy-girl relationships, gay comedy, and sexual innuendos, ruled the air. Interestingly enough, its theme song was composed by one of the same artists as the preschool sing-along I referenced in chapter 2. And, if the media and arts were moving on, why should things have been any different at school, or after school, for that matter? Or, in our community, culture, and country...

"Free Love" truly was revolutionary. Bras were not the only thing young women had flung off. Dresses waved on clotheslines while local foundries saw a whole other side of pressed blue trousers! And so, girls led the way—in kissing, making out, oral sex, and just about every aspect of relationships. Boundaries, what boundaries? Guys like myself, who had learned very little about the man's role in initiating and leadership, were enabled. But, in the heat of the moment I don't think we cared too much. Passion, pimples, hormones, and horny girls were the coming-of-age saga. We just sat back on cruise control, while they kicked it into overdrive!

CONFIRMED

What would Martin Luther of Wittenberg have thought? If you're thinking *reformation*, so am I! Those years were not so different from the hypocrisy, and contradiction prevailing in sixteenth-century European Christendom. (On a side note, it was on October 31, 1517, when Luther posted his Ninety-Five Theses on the Castle Church door, igniting the Protestant Reformation.[52]) Wasn't it like that, though? At age thirteen, life was a roller coaster, and you just hung on as tight as you could. Well, there were also those moments when you stuck your hands up into the sky, fearlessly screaming until you nearly puked! Contradictions were everywhere; everywhere I looked I saw what was becoming my one and only truth—there was none, only lies. Luther, however, protested. He spoke and the church (Christ's body, not the "sacred" institution) heard, and the response was cataclysmic.

I did not hear, however. My cataclysm came much later. My family attended a local Lutheran church on holidays and a few other times throughout the year. Mostly, it was my mom's thing, and my sister enjoyed the stories a little. My dad would have rather been in a boat somewhere. But me, what did I think of church?

I hated going to church. I hated the uncomfortable clothes. I hated the awkward kids and close proximity of relational interactions. I hated the fluorescent light, cold

---

[52] See under "Initial Dissemination" at: http://en.wikipedia.org/wiki/The_Ninety-Five_Theses; or find more info at: www.orlutheran.com/html/facts95.html.

white tile, and the lime green painted cement block of the Sunday school rooms in the basement. I hated kneeling on that rug in the foyer singing those nursery songs, because that's what the kids had to do, and everybody else was doing it, so I *had* to too. I hated the pigtails, patent leather shoes, lacy dresses and tights. I hated the little white envelopes with our names printed on them. I hated my mom giving me a dollar that I folded up and put in the brass plate they sent by as everyone sat stiff and still. I hated the low-toned speaking, and not normal singing voice of the pastor in his flowing white robe, as if he were talking to the clouds on a dark gray day. I hated the old teachers who didn't "get me." I even hated the red punch and sugar cookies—they were such a lure, but I ate a few anyway. It was all fake to me. I hated fake. I hated being fake. I hated going to church. I hated church.

There was one punk rock guy who came to church, though. He wore his street clothes: a sleeveless torn jean jacket with a band patch on the back, Vans high-tops, spiked bleached hair, and spiked black leather bracelets. He was older, my sister's age or so. I didn't really get how it worked, or why he was there. He seemed pretty cool, though. I never talked to him, though. I still remember his name—it was a cool name, easy to remember. I'm not going to share it with you, though!

Thinking about it now, *dress* was the primary form of communication amongst punks. As a rather isolated minority group, and at an age of being totally self-absorbed, it makes sense that an outward form of communication was necessary, and the louder the better! It accomplished two things very well. One, it expressed to other potential like minds a similarity and acceptance, creating an immediate bond of trust. Second, a dog collar around one's neck warded off all those he didn't want to deal with—it set a boundary: you were in, or you were out (not too different from Christ when He said, "He who is not with me is against me."[53]). Perhaps Christ was punk, not *a* punk, but punk?

Why were the punks so adamant? Truth: raw fisted, white knuckle, in your face, say it and mean it, now—TRUTH. Ultimately, the punks had seen enough of the makeup, money, music videos, and my bright red punch in its Styrofoam cup. Or, was it polystyrene?[54] Only, they were going to do something about it. Because, the jocks weren't "Just Doing It," as Nike declared in its historical marketing meeting of 1988, even with $300 million invested in catchy advertising.[55] Punks took matters into their own hands—they owned it!

Back to Luther's "ism." Or more respectfully, Luther's followers' *ism*. Of this, I believe Martin would also agree, if not find cause or reason to tack on a few more Theses to his door! A most interesting thing happened at the "Lutheran" church when I was in junior high. I got confirmed. I'm still not sure what that meant to the church other than church membership and politics. I know what it meant to me—nothing. And, I would never have to

---

[53] Matt 12:30; Luke 11:23.

[54] A hint at Radiohead's iconic track "Fake Plastic Trees" referencing the 80s, off *The Bends* (EMI: London, 1995).

[55] www.cfar.com/Documents/nikecmp.pdf.

step foot in church again. I was "pow" (*pau*: Hawaiian for finished), and that was a good thing! And as someone rightly stated, "There ain't nothin' better than a darn good thing!" Because, if you showed up by parental force once a week for a month or two and copied other kids' work out of the trash, how important was that. So, I'm not exactly sure what they were confirming, but if those actions constituted loyalty and honor, so be it—more power to their *ism*. I cringe now, thinking how those "good works" are really not too far out of line with legalism's religiosity and hypocrisy's whitewashed tomb.[56] Today, I'm left wondering what Martin Luther of Wittenberg's response would have been.

The big day had come. It was time to appear before the entire church and receive a certificate and a Good News Bible. But, there was a catch. In order to wear the red gown, I had to drink "the punch," and write an essay. I waited till the day before I had to meet with the pastor to write it. I still distinctly remember my mom calling me in from outside playing, to get my butt in the house and do it!

I sat down at my wooden desk with a pencil and several clean white sheets of loose-leaf paper. Perturbed and procrastinating, I traced wood grain with my pencil lead while kicking my heels into the carpet. My mind consumed itself with every thought and idea I didn't agree with, finding every reason not to write their essay. And then, it was like something overcame me. I wrote nonstop, freely and effortlessly all the way through! I answered all the

---

[56] Matt 23:27; Acts 23:3.

questions in a snap with great confidence, and I was done, just like that (which never happened again I might add, on any other homework)! I truly believe now that God moved me with His grace, and a part of me even found some fulfillment in writing the essay. The only problem was, even though I knew the answers sufficiently, I didn't fully comprehend or believe in what I was saying.

One topic I do remember: "What does Christianity mean to me?" And, though I never clearly learned the gospel message of Jesus' saving grace through faith, which reformed Martin Luther while lecturing through Romans and Galatians, I do remember having some natural insight of my own. Apparently, my paper was so honest and truthful that a Sunday school teacher, a patient of my dad's, applauded me to him, referencing my essay as "One of the best they had ever read." When he told me, I thought to myself in his traditional manner, "Well, it isn't rocket science!" Unfortunately, since I had just faked my way through their test and won their praise it just *confirmed* my view that it (church) and they (members) were all a sham. I guess it never crossed my mind that I might be the phony. But again, things were not always as they seemed.

Ten years later (1999) at a Methodist church in town, I was asked to share my testimony for the first time, publicly, in the church. The house was full and God did a great work that Pentecost Sunday (celebrating the outpouring of the Holy Spirit—Acts 2). Afterward I was in tears, as God had moved powerfully with great love and conviction. An older white-haired woman appeared before me out of the crowd at the stage and said, "You probably don't remember me..." I knew as clear as day that it was the Sunday school teacher from the Lutheran church who had spoken highly of my paper; I remembered her name and addressed her positively. She sparkled and smiled with several tears as she said something to the effect of: "I always knew this day would come." We hugged and she disappeared, and I haven't seen her since. I'm not sure how or why she was at that Methodist church that Sunday morning. I do know, however, that that morning was instrumental in *confirming* my vision to pursue Bible college for God's greater use.

God's Spirit sparked another memory that day! He reminded me of my eighth grade Confirmation Essay. So, I visited the old Lutheran church, and there in my "member file" in a dusty metal cabinet, it sat waiting. As I read it, I was amazed at how much of what I had written actually came to pass in my own life. Similarly, God moved the apostle John's pen on the island of Patmos when he wrote: "The testimony of Jesus is the spirit of prophecy" (Revelation[57] 19:10). Likewise, the apostle Paul characterized the God whom Abraham believed: "God, who gives life to the dead and calls those things which do not exist as though they did" (Romans 4:17). Perhaps, God had seen beyond my appearance: "For the LORD does not see as man sees; for man looks at the outward appearance, but the LORD looks at the heart" (1 Samuel 16:7). Most assuredly, with this, Martin Luther would not, nay, could not, recant!

In a sense, it was as if God had been waiting there for

---

[57] Revelation or apocalypse (from Grk., *apokalupsis*): a disclosure of truth presently unseen or unknown.

a decade, waiting for my return, not to an "ism," but to Himself.[58] And, could it be *He* had confirmed me after all? Certainly, God's grace is exceedingly abundant[59] and His foreknowledge[60] beyond finding out.[61] Most truly, things were not always as they appeared!

---

[58] Matt 11:28-30—Come to Me all you who labor and are heavy laden, and I will give you rest...

[59] 1 Tim 1:14 (The grace of our Lord was exceedingly abundant); Ps 86:15, 103:8; Ex 34:6; Neh 9:17; John 1:16, 4:2; 1 Pet 1:3.

[60] Rom 8:29, 11:2; Eph 1:5, 1:11; 1 Pet 1:2.

[61] Isa 55:8-9; Ps 92:5; Job 36:26.

4

ALL HELL BROKE LOOSE

THE BERLIN WALL TUMBLED in November of 1989. I was fourteen years old. One year later I was a freshman in high school, and unlike the end of the Cold War, my own life was just beginning to heat up. In nine short months my world began to tear and fray at the seams.

Where do I begin?

The ruble and smoke of another lifetime still lingers in the not-so-distant past. My own Iron Curtain would soon rent in two.[62] I remember a shot of Bono on the nightly news; his microphone wasn't "Rattling with Hum" tonight; he was chiseling out communism one block at a time. I can almost taste the concrete in the air today… *Pungent dust gags and chokes my lungs. My fingertips are worn raw from throwing block. Adrenaline courses hard. Day and night blur. Wreckage towers swallowing blank stares.* When the dust settles and the smoke clears, What is left standing? Is

---

[62] Matt 27:51—upon Christ's death the temple curtain into the holiest place tore from the top down, the earth quaked, and the rocks split.

anything recognizable? Am I standing? Where do I begin? How do I begin?

I just begin. Here, and now, I begin.

      ❧   ❧   ❧

As a freshman housed under the same roof with the seventh and eighth grade at the junior high, I didn't belong. True, maybe the roof had little to do with it, but it didn't help the capitulation between the ever-increasing divide. Besides, there was no white flag; there were only four black bars and one Black Flag (hardcore band).[63] Not to mention, the Stars and Stripes of an appointment to flag duty in the sixth grade were no longer waving. I might also add that "Coolidge" (song by the Descendents), had nothing on the Coolidge Cardinals at my elementary school! But, if punk rock's raucous *"Oi!"* is too deafening, not to worry... Another sibling was singing barefoot in the streets.

Punk rock met its rival in his hippie sister of a passing era. Really, no different from skateboarders and rollerbladers, they both had similar agendas, only their approaches were different, and one wore fruit boots! My own sister returned from boarding school with her "One Love" Rastafari bumper sticker and a tie-dyed T-shirt. Teen angst was exchanged for a political zeal. Birkenstocks (sandals) were *in*, and so was a hippie re-awakening...

My German ancestors brought more to the New Land than sauerkraut and sausages. Pagan beliefs and philosophies of nature were deeply rooted in their "barbarian"

---

[63] Early (1977) hardcore-punk band whose symbol was four black bars: www.ipass.net/jthrush/flaghist.htm.

tribal land.[64] The early twentieth-century immigrants to the United States planted their roots and sowed the seeds of a back-to-nature movement that began to sprout in the early 60s. San Francisco's Summer of Love in 1967 and New York's White Lake, Aquarian Exposition of '69 (Woodstock) helped clear the brush for postmodernity.

As I said in chapter 1, I grew up in Wisconsin, which was very heavily populated by Germans. One look at my name would tell you I am Irish; however, "Things are not always as they appear." My family name is robustly German, but after rebirth into Christ and adoption by my heavenly Father[65] it too was transformed. I will expound on this change down the road.[66]

In the United States, the back-to-nature movement of the Hippies and their Rastafarian practices can be traced back to Germany and the UK (late nineteenth century).[67] It is interesting to note that early punk and hardcore also found their origin in Europe. Today, with Europe's descent into post-Christianity and the United State's slippery diversion into postmodernism, one has to ask, "What is in store for a deteriorating America?" What costs have our harlotries incurred, and at whose expense? As I peer out my window, I can't help but see the generations of

---

[64] Bruce Shelley, *Church History in Plain Language* (Nashville, TN: Thomas Nelson, 1995), p.153.

[65] Rom 8:14-17.

[66] Isa 45:4-6; God used this passage and a mission trip to Ireland to confirm my name change.

[67] http://en.wikipedia.org/wiki/History_of_the_hippie_movement/temp; p. 2.

regret in the eyes of today's youth. Hopefully, my own past has made me more nearsighted than I've observed. Time will tell.

BACK TO NATURE

My adventurous "free spirit"[68] and my sister's footsteps led me down a grassy path into deeper harmony with my back-to-nature roots. As I said in chapter 3, I was now confirmed, and in some actual sense I was released from God's (the Holy Spirit's) overarching arm of sovereignty to do as I pleased (or so it seemed). I did just that. I remember sitting down in Advanced Mathematics one particular afternoon, pulling my sweatshirt hood over my head, and deciding not to care any longer. So, I slept instead. And that was that; it was as if I had just turned off the light switch. I managed to "just get by" in all my schoolwork applying little or no effort. I opted to skip classes and enjoy a cruise on my skateboard through the park along the river. The plush green grass caught me daydreaming and smoking cigarettes while the clouds rolled by through the towering oaks. My retreat back-to-nature had begun.

I was in nature the first time I experimented with fermented beverages.[69] No, I'm not referring to Kombucha Tea; Wisconians were not that green! But, I had planned

---

[68] With what irony the world clothes *bondage* in, or blissful ignorance rather. Galatians 4:3 applies—When we were children, we were in bondage under the elements of the world.

[69] The National Youth Anti-Drug Media Campaign: www.abovetheinfluence.com/facts/drugs-alcohol.aspx?id=search_properAlcohol#.

a midnight affair with a bottle of Irish cream liqueur, an enormously large cigar I had won at a carnival, and an old wool army blanket. My companions of secrecy awaited my arrival, reclining in a quiet open field bathed in the moon's light. The field was a distance from my house, farther than many other fields I could have chosen. I must have just liked that spot—beyond the white split-rail fence, off the trail, nestled in the grass near the sumacs. I used to walk past it on my way to school, and that particular morning I snuck out the booze wrapped in the blanket and hid it in the bushes for later that night. Deliberate, decisive, and daring!

There were probably many reasons why I began to drink, one of which was simply boredom. Another was the challenge and secrecy of a solitary practice: "I was doing my own thing," and I liked it. As the adventure wore off, however, it truly became a practice of isolation. I withdrew deeper into myself and drowned out the noise of life, tucking myself in with depression's warm, thick blanket.

How did I acquire alcohol and cigarettes at age fifteen? I stole them. I suppose this truly was the beginning of thievery for me. Stealing from parents, alcohol from my own, and cigarettes from friends'. How else does a minor get what he wants from the high society of adulthood? He brings it down to his level—he takes it! Six months later I landed my first official job working at a supermarket. Coincidentally, I had to stock the beer. And, as these things go, the stealing led to theft (mostly breaking into cars), and several attempts at burglary followed. Leading others into these practices[70] was perhaps the worse evil.

I remember a specific incident of shoplifting an expensive jacket from a vintage store. Sometime later, a man at an AA meeting in the same town questioned me about it. I never felt more ashamed, or more busted! Years later, after giving my life to Christ, I donated jacket upon jacket from my personal collection to a local vintage shop. Likewise, I have had vehicles broken into several times over the years since, and I can only thank God for His merciful hand in my life. "The law entered that the offense might abound. But where sin abounded, grace abounded much more" (Romans 5:20). God's *much more* grace has proved to be sufficient in transforming my guilt and shame into innocence and liberty.[71] His grace truly is sufficient.[72]

Another tangled web I got caught in, as a freshman, was a very serious romance. Looking back now, the emotional depth and intensity was far greater and more involved than any kid needed. But, we were not kids; we were maturing adolescents. We had all the parts to show for it and an accompanying attitude of independence! Beginning rather playful with grass stains on our knees after a football game, soon the doors opened to the darkness of our heavily consumed hearts. My back-to-nature journey continued as we looked within ourselves and explored philosophies and traded daily muses. Along these lines, suicidal thinking began to surface and take root in my

---

[70] Rom 1:32—practicing and approving of others' unrighteousness and sinful behaviors.

[71] 2 Cor 3:17—where the Spirit of the Lord is, there is liberty.

[72] 2 Cor 9:8, 12:9.

psyche. The exchange of secret notes by mysterious hands and evil psychological games, like a dead rabbit left in the abandoned "exchange locker," proved to be too much. Our adolescence, and romance, came to an abrupt halt.

SONS OF SATAN

Where did I get the name for my newfound social group? What compelled me to create such a group? Why did I choose to publicize it hiding in the shadows? Was I the one leading it? If not, who was leading me?

I suppose those are all relevant questions the janitor at the junior high was probably asking as he cleaned the black graffitied letters off the walls throughout the school (primarily bathrooms). But, these weren't *text* messages! And, as far as being a social group, maybe that's a stretch, unless one member and I constitute such. But, where did the idea come from? Truthfully, I'm not quite sure. I have a good idea, though. Satan.

Yes, it can be that simple. Consider Scripture's portrayal of the pre-redeemed: "And you He made alive, who were dead in trespasses and sins, in which you once walked according to the course of this world, according to the prince of the power of the air, the spirit who now works in the sons of disobedience" (Ephesians 2:1-2). The first time I came across this phrase in the Bible—the sons of disobedience—after being "saved," I was struck with awe. And, all the more, I was busted! God reminded me of my former lifestyle by shinning His light on this specific act of rebellion—the Sons of Satan. Beyond a catchy title, and in contrast to a holy God, my actions were truly satanic. So, yes, it *can* be that simple! Yet, isn't it truly amazing how He (Almighty God—El Shaddai[73]) is intimately acquainted with every moment and memory of our lives?[74]

Paul's letter to the Ephesians continues: "[W]e all once conducted ourselves in the lusts of our flesh, fulfilling the desires of the flesh and of the mind, and were by nature *children of wrath...*" (2:3, emphasis). It is of interest to note that the Bible references the "sons of disobedience" two more times,[75] and in all three cases there is a greater context dealing with the wrath of God. Similarly, John 3:36 states that "the wrath of God abides on him" who does not believe in the Son (Jesus). And, Revelation culminates with Christ treading the winepress of God's wrath[76] as final judge and victor over "spirits of demons"[77] and the nations possessed and governed by Satan. I would also add that this is good insight if you're in the business of starting up your own "Sons of Satan Social Club," or the like.

Fortunately for me, there remains to be good news, as Romans 5:9 (emphasis) declares: "[H]aving now been justified by His [Jesus'] blood, we shall be *saved from wrath* through Him." El Shaddai's intent was, and still remains, to be a fruitful life lived in union with Himself. "For God *did not appoint us to wrath*, but to obtain salvation through

---

[73] El Shaddai (Hb.), Gen 17:1.

[74] Ps 139:13; Isa 44:2, 49:5; Jer 1:5, 17:10; Matt 9:4; John 1:48; Eph 3:19.

[75] Eph 5:6; Col 3:6.

[76] Rev 19:15.

[77] Rev 16:14.

our Lord Jesus Christ."[78] In the end, there is really only one choice: Christ or wrath? As for me, I have chosen Christ.[79]

What about you, my friend; what have you chosen? I'm not kidding about this one… I'd set that smoke down for a minute, and think about it.

I know, I left you hanging, and you're still wondering, "What did the Sons of Satan do exactly?" Truthfully, not much. But, I suppose a few clips might shed some more light on the examination table. So, for better or for worse, let's role the tape!

❦   ❦   ❦

The Rolling Stones recorded Mick Jagger's "Sympathy for the Devil" in June of 1968 in London. Twenty-one years later I was dubbing it repeatedly on blank tapes and supplanting them around the junior high. We used the track as a sort of theme song for our charade. I also typed out various letters that were placed neatly in envelopes alongside the tapes. I don't recall what they said any longer; but, I'm certain they were the musings of anti-normal ethics trying to penetrate a disillusioned status quo! (Not that we were seeing clearly,[80] nonetheless, Were they immune from blindness? or bias?). Undoubtedly, the Lord Himself spoke with clarity when He said, "For judgment I have come into this world, that those who do not see may

---

[78] 1 The 5:9-10, emphasis.

[79] Col 3:3-4—Christ who is our life (1 John 5:20); Josh 24:15—As for me and my house, we will serve the LORD.

[80] Ex 4:11; Isa 29:18, 35:5, 42:7; Matt 11:5; Luke 4:18, 7:21-22; John 9:25.

see, and that those who see may be made blind" (John 9:39). Apparently, we would have made a greater impact by supplanting the Word of God, yet as things stand today, none less criminal!

Shock value was definitely a major player in our marketing scheme. The grand finale in our escapade of "sympathy with the Devil" was quite sick and demented in my mind today. I believe it was truly demonic, especially in light of the many premeditated factors, and it invoked the taking of life. In a very real sense, this was my true introduction to a back-to-nature spirituality: I shot and killed three blackbirds with my Daisy Rider and hung them from ceiling pipes in the school hallways. I used red scarlet ribbons as nooses around the blackbirds' heads. I'm not sure why I chose three blackbirds. It is interesting that blackbirds, or "birds of the air" in Scripture,[81] commonly refer to Satan. And it is of even greater interest that in the final leg of my spiritual journey (seven years later) I worshiped and sought the power associated with the crow common to animalism.

In Mel Gibson's *The Passion of the Christ* (2004), you might recall the black raven that landed above the cross of the unrepentant criminal[82] during the crucifixion scene. Or, you might be familiar with the 1994 film *The Crow*, in which Brandon Lee died during the last weeks of filming

---

[81] Mark 4:4, 4:13, 4: 15; Luke 8:5, 8:12; Matt 13:32 (Mark 4:13, key to parables and surrounding context); Jer 5:26-27 (wicked, deceiver); Dan 4:14, 4:21, 4:33 (Nebuchadnezzar's demon possession/lunacy); Deut 28:26, 28:45 (cursed); Gen 40:17, 40:19 (death); Rev 19:17-21 (birds eat the flesh of the beast, false prophet, and the damned).

[82] Luke 23:32-33, 23:39-43.

when a dummy bullet was shot into his gut. Lee played the lead role of a rock star seeking revenge for the murder of his fiancée and himself (who were to be married on Halloween) after coming back from the dead and taking on the illusory characteristics of the crow. I was one of the curious moviegoers adding to the $94,000,000 worldwide box office revenue.[83] Today, my question is, "Was Lee's death symbolic in regards to the nature of his film?" One thing is evident, symbolism is real, and both God and Satan use it to communicate good and evil in the world. Whether one's eyes can see, one's heart believes, and one's mind rightly interprets such symbolism is another matter. The Bible clearly reveals, however, that the natural man (un-regenerated) cannot receive or know the things of the Spirit of God, for they are spiritually discerned (1 Corinthians 2:14). I trust this symbolism will become evident in my own life farther down the road…

Until then, what did the Sons of Satan's three blackbirds symbolize? I think it would be safe to say that Satan's three dead birds represented Nietzsche's groundbreaking shift into Europe's post-Christian paradigm: "God is dead."[84] Metaphorically speaking, the act was a challenge to authority, of which there is none higher than God. In actuality,

---

[83] http://en.wikipedia.org/wiki/The_Crow_(1994_film).

[84] Nietzsche; *The Gay Science*, 2nd ed.; 1887; Book 5, section 343: "The greatest recent event—that God is dead, that the belief in the Christian God has become unbelievable…" (http://atheism.about.com/library/weekly/aa042600a.htm).

The Holy Trinity[85] of the Father, Son, and Holy Spirit is the only symbolic group of three I would have known or comprehended. And, just as Lucifer asserted himself to replace, or be, God by receiving worship unto himself,[86] so Satan continues to exalt himself[87] today wherever and by whatever clever means he can[88]—even rebellious boys, blackbirds, and scarlet twine.

Was I a victim? Maybe. Was I ignorant? Certainly. But, does that change my willingness to hear and obey? No. The verdict remains: guilty as charged! "But God…" those two simple words cannot be overstated![89] "But God demonstrates His own love toward us, in that while we were still sinners, Christ died for us" (Romans 5:8). What type of Being rescues *sons of disobedience* (undeserving sinners) and welcomes them into His holy family to be united, share, and dwell with His own glorious Son forever?[90]

---

[85] Gen 1:1 ("God": *Elohiym*—Hb., potential plural); Gen 1:3 ("said": Jesus the Word created: John 1:1-3, 1:14; Eph 3:9; Col 1:16, 3:10; Heb 1:2, 2:10; Rev 3:14; Ps 104:30 [Spirit creates]); Gen 1:26 ("us," "our": plural); John 17:21-22 ("one" singular, referencing "Us" plural); Heb 1:2-3 (Jesus one with God); Matt 3:16-17 (Jesus, Spirit, Father); Gal 4:6 ("God, Spirit, Son": working and willing in unison); Matt 28:19 ("name of" singular, referencing plural: "Father, Son, Holy Spirit"); Isa 44:6; Rev 1:11 ("First and the Last" references God and Jesus, revealing oneness).

[86] Isa 14:12-15; Ezek 28:6-8, 12-19.

[87] 2 Cor 10:3-6 (5).

[88] 2 Cor 11:3, 11:14; Matt 10:16; Ezek 28:3-5, 28:12, 28:17.

[89] "But God…": Rom 6:17; 1 Cor 1:27, 2:10, 10:13; Gal 6:14; Eph 2:4.

[90] Rom 8:29—that He [His Son- Jesus] might be the firstborn of many brethren. Heb 12:10— that we [sons] may be partakers of His holiness. 2 Pet 1:4—that… you may be partakers of the divine nature, having escaped the corruption that is in the world through lust.

Such mercy is unprecedented; such a Being is unrivaled in every possible way! By God's mercy a new verdict stands: I have been received into His body,[91] the "church of the firstborn who are registered in heaven, to God the Judge of all, to the spirits of just men made perfect, to Jesus the Mediator of the new covenant…" (Hebrews 12:23-24). Furthermore, the writer admonishes: "See that you do not refuse Him who speaks… For our God is a consuming fire (12:25, 29).

In the end, the books will be opened.[92] And having been signed and sealed by the Lamb of God,[93] they will read: "Once a Son of Satan, BUT NOW a son of God!" Amen.

THE GREAT DIVIDE

Freshman year wasn't the only thing called to a halt early. Two weeks before summer break my right knee broke for the second time in two years. Soccer season was over before it began. I can see him now, flying through midair with the toe of his cleat thrusting forward in full hacking force straight into my leg, directly below my kneecap. I still managed to punch the highflying ball crossed over from the left corner (my left, not yours). My defense cleared the net—another challenger shut down!

The only thing I knew for sure was the Grand Canyon didn't belong where my kneecap was supposed to be. I

---

[91] 1 Cor 12:12-14, 12:27; Col 1:24.

[92] Rev 20:12, 20:15, 21:27.

[93] John 1:29, 1:36; Rev 13:8, 22:1, 22:3.

was quickly going into shock as I rolled around on the ground *slightly* screaming every one-syllable word I knew. What seemed an eternity later, the referee finally blew the whistle, stopping play. And, another lifetime passed before my dad got his Suburban out on the field and they loaded me up across the backseat. From the home team's goal box to our hometown hospital was slightly under thirty minutes driving slightly over the speed limit. You know those nice straight lines they cut in the concrete on the Interstate so the road can expand and contract with the temperature? Well, we jumped, jammed, and slammed over thirty trillion of those jolting limestone cliffs (Niagara Escarpment)[94] as the Burban raced home!

They began screwing the pieces of my shattered growth plate back together as soon as we arrived. I awoke to my doctor explaining that he was going to remove the drainage tube running down my cast from my hip into my knee; he said it might hurt a bit. He pulled, ripped, and tore as I rubbed the sleep out of my eyes to another summer without two legs.

The previous summer, my knee decided to twist and roll in opposite directions as two female acrobats landed on either side of it jumping on a trampoline. I never liked my first doctor; I never trusted him either. Not that he was at fault this time; nevertheless, there I stood on the sidelines, hunched over my crutches with a full leg cast. I missed the rest of school too, which, unbeknownst to

---

[94] The escarpment circles from Chicago around the great lakes to New York, forming the Niagara Falls—see red line on map at: http://commons.wikimedia.org/wiki/File:Niagara_Escarpment_map.png.

anyone else, was probably in my best interest. I had been officially benched! I was helpless.

❦   ❦   ❦

I suppose it was bound to happen, and actually I knew it would. Even still, when it finally came, I was shocked and spun by its reality. I was outside shooting hoops with my neighbor when they called me inside. As I said, I knew what was happening, but even so, like a detached observer, I pulled up my stool to their midst on either side of the kitchen island. I watched it all from a distant shore. Perhaps there was some denial that flooded in momentarily, or I had been drowning in it unaware for many years. Either way, the great day of awakening had come, and with it a great divide.

When lightning strikes a tree it crashes to the ground, cracking and splintering into thousands of gnarly fragmented strands of wood fiber. It's kind of like snapping a green stick and then twisting it round and round until it finally brakes in two. The wood fibers explode into a splintered chaos. Like the stick, like the tree, it became impossible to fit twenty-five years of marriage back together. No amount of titanium plates and screws can fix everything. Despite what *they* say, sometimes it is too late. And, I suppose that is why it has been written, "Today, if you will hear His voice, Do not harden your hearts as in the rebellion."[95] Because, again, what they say doesn't

---

[95] Heb 3:7-8 (15); Ps 95:7-8. Also of relevance, in Matthew 19:8 Jesus wisely answered the Pharisees that it was because of their *hardness of hearts* that Moses had permitted divorce for infidelity (19:9).

really mean a bucket load of dung, and needless to say, that bucket doesn't hold much water either. Besides, I've seen trees struck by lightning, and do you know what "they" do with the half lying in the road? They run it through a chipper and spit it out into a dump truck with a zillion other pieces. Tell your Sadducee friends to go figure that one out![96]

The only thing that didn't divide that summer was the loyalty of several friends. Amazingly enough, we managed to rig up an old two-wheeled garden cart to my friend's road bike, and he selflessly hauled me around town every night to all the hot spots where the girls were hanging out. He benefitted too, I suppose, you know, as the "compassionate" one! Life wasn't so bad, I guess. However, the drinking continued, and along with it the violence.

Near that time, my right hand shattered as it broke upon the eye bone of a neighborhood adversary. "He hit me with a garden hoe first!" I exclaimed (as I hid my hand behind my back). That was my justification to the police officer who came to my door a day later to investigate his medical bills. I wasn't smiling politely, however, when my grandfather, an old Navy Doc, towered over me at the kitchen counter two weeks later, holding my broken, crooked hand firmly with his large thumbs. "This might hurt a bit," he said as he thrust my hand into the counter and reset my bone. "Almost, one more time." I took a deep breath and turned my head as I grit my teeth. "That'll teach you your lesson!" Somehow, I didn't learn that easy.

---

[96] Matt 22:23-34 (Sadducees don't believe in the resurrection; issues of physical nature become problematic in their limited scope.).

Other fights, and other nights would prove otherwise.

As the summer waned, I was back on the streets on my own bicycle. The human body is truly a miraculous creation—with its ability to heal (far above any evolved system of chaos could ever be). When the doctor cut my cast off I wept as I sat on the floor, writhing in sweat, clenching with all my might but to no avail. It wouldn't budge; I could not lift my own leg! To my amazement, however, after several agonizing weeks at therapy I was back on my feet! And, my wheels! Before long, I was covering the entire city as I raced home to beat curfew.

One particular night, I didn't make it. The local PD intercepted me as I quickly pedaled away from a fight scene. I wasn't even in the fight, but my temper and the alcohol on my breath were enough to book me for the night. Eventually, after they couldn't reach my parents from the jail, they drove me home with my bike in the trunk. The driveway rolled on forever as the red and blue lights flashed off the house with a "For Sale" sign in the front yard.

House For Sale

The summer ended when the four red letters S-O-L-D were hung above our For Sale sign. My sister took the sold sign down and I hid it in my bedroom while she was out Drivin' n' Cryin'. Kevin Kinney's 1989 album *Mystery Road*, with its track "House for Sale," was no longer a mystery. The house was sold. My mom eventually moved across town to the duplexes near the high school, where other divorced neighbors had found themselves. Ironically, a few years later, the very purchasers of our house were divorced, and the ex-husband moved across town two doors down from my mom. Two doors in the other direction lived another divorced neighbor; only she had beaten my mom to the "other side of suburbia." My dad moved just a few blocks to the lake. My sister returned to college. And me, well, I moved wherever, and whenever, I wanted to.

Three houses and two parents? Hmm... I'm free! For a few final weeks while the banks were closing and my mom was preparing to move, I had three homes to work my shenanigans with. I hammered it hard and got my money's worth! Well actually, as I mentioned earlier, I was mostly thieving that as spare change from cars. Now, I even had my own police issued "jimmy bar"; I have no idea where I got it, though, other than a friend of a friend... My friendships had moved that way too. I was finding myself in a lot of dark, smoky basements of kids I didn't entirely know. Most of these kids were being more influenced by the Hippie Era, and some with parents who had never quite left its practices behind. Some of these parents were arrested for growing or selling drugs; divorce, alcohol, domestic violence, and suicide affected others. I even remember having a crush on a lesbian who had been kicked out of her home and was living on the run. There wasn't much I wouldn't have done to win her affection. I was truly lost. I had opened myself, both willingly and unconsciously, to host all numerous activities, and thinking.

Looking at the timeline of my life, my freshman year

marked a great cataclysmic shift. Ultimately, that tremor tumbled the building blocks of my ideology; my life lay in ruins at ground zero. Immediately, I was standing in a new world. Definitions were stripped of meaning. Principles had been challenged. Relationships were tested beyond thresholds. And above all, "Who, or what, was worthy of trust?" Even greater yet, as I reflect today, was the reassurance that confirmed my doubts and unbelief in: truth, family, society, humanity, and God. These underpinnings became the deeply rooted questions and lies that comprised my "existence issues" of later years. Most certainly, as far as I knew, or cared, all hell had broken loose!

A NOT-SO-NEW AGE

THERE IS NO NEW AGE, just as there is no Post Age or Neo-middle Age, or any other Other Age! Nor is there an Age for the Aquarians! "Is there anything of which it may be said, 'See, this is new?' It has already been in ancient times before us."—the Preacher has well spoke (Ecclesiastes 1:10). And, let us say Protagoras was the first relativist (fifth century BC),[97] "Has much changed?" Has anything new (ideologically) been discovered recently or now for the first time?[98] Was A. W. Tozer defending the faith against anything new in 1948?[99] Is twenty-first-century postmodernism new?

Well, I'm certain there is much to be said concerning

---

[97] Paul Copan, *True For You But Not For Me*, 2009, pp. 20-21: Plato cited Protagoras as having said: "Man is the measure of all things."

[98] New: not existing before; made, introduced, or discovered recently or now for the first time (from: Oxford American Dictionary, online through Apple, 2011).

[99] A. W. Tozer, *The Pursuit of God* (Wing Spread Publishers 2006 [1948]), chap. 4, pp. 50-55.

said matter… However, this is hardly the place for exalting such new ideas! There is time, however, and I suppose one could say there is a Church Age, but that's beside the point. Time will tell what time has told.

In the meantime, I was in hot pursuit of a desperate New Age! Stripped of any remaining morally objective truth, I was "back-to-nature" and ripe for a blossoming new age. Carousing till daybreak with spirituality and fine spirits, my being was awakened to every sort of enchanting whoredom. I ran fast and furious with my eyes wide open; blindness to reality never fools illusion, or her elusive seduction.

I, on the other hand, was fooled, not to mention duped, deceived, hackled, haunted, and horrified. It just took a bit of time… Although moments ticked-and-tocked, which I believed would scarcely end, I suppose it truly was "just a bit." But, I'll let Father Time[100] tell time's tale.

---

[100] Everlasting Father: Isa 9:6, 63:16; Gen 1:1, 1:14, Ps 8:3; Heb 1:10 (*in the beginning* God created days and years); Job 38:4 (God questions Job concerning creation); Prov 8:22-30 (wisdom resided with God *from the beginning, from everlasting* while God created); John 1:1-3, 1:14; 1 John 1:1; Col 1:19, 2:9; Heb 1:2-3 (*in the beginning* was the Word, who is God, who created, who became flesh [Christ] the fullness of God bodily); Col 1:15-19; John 17:5 (Christ is *before all things* and creator of); Heb 5:9, 12:2 (Christ *authors eternal* salvation); Heb 1:10-12 (*since the beginning* Christ *has remained* and His *years will never fail*); Rev 1:8, 1:11, 21:6, 22:13 (Christ is the *Alpha and Omega, First and Last, Beginning and End—who was, is, and is to come*).

5

SPIRALING OUT OF CONTROL

THE FIRST DAY OF HIGH SCHOOL was a blur. We had to leave a friend's basement at last. The doomed day had come, and inevitably the dead had to rise. Intoxicating revelries and new discoveries had been escalating exponentially the last few weeks of my freshman summer. Conveniently, I gravitated toward my mother's house near the high school. The school year was off to a grand start! It seemed summer had never ended. *I never knew the school year didn't have to come.* One thing was certain; my life was spiraling out of control. I was barely keeping it together, or I guess it had become obvious that I wasn't. Drinking, soccer, and U.S. Government were difficult for me to manage.

Perhaps my parents didn't know what to do. Or, they thought they had a workable solution for me, or us, or themselves. Interestingly, however, I was not part of it. Well, I was, and directly, just not the informative and legislative process. But, I knew something was up. My mom and dad had been talking on the phone quite a bit, and it wasn't a rekindling of their romance. Finally, I overheard a phone conversation with my sister who was at college; actually, I listened in on another phone line upstairs. Back in the day of landlines and multiple phones, do you remember that trick of holding down the receiver and being a spy, or a secret detective on a covert mission? Well, on this particular mission I learned that my hunch was correct. I was being shipped off to boarding school like my sister had; that was not going to fly with me, however!

It all happened in a flash. My mom told me to pack my bags… my dad would be coming to pick me up soon! Apparently it was all arranged, even a position on the soccer team, because I was to pack my cleats too. My sister called to share her concern and affirm their good intentions, trying to be vague and not allude to where I was actually being taken. While she was talking, my mind began to race through my "escape flight!" and I immediately started stuffing a backpack with my essentials: Walkman cassette player, Leatherman multi-tool, Maglite mini flashlight, and my parachute! I had practiced this "bag packing" several times throughout my life as a youngster, but now it was time to actualize!

With my suitcases packed and ready to go in the upstairs hallway, my dad would be arriving shortly. I turned on the shower in the bathroom across the hall from my bedroom and locked the door behind me as I exited back to my bedroom and locked its door. I removed the window screen, grabbed my backpack, and climbed out onto the roof of the duplex. I remember looking into the neighbor's bedroom window as I ran by and thinking to myself, *So, this is where she sleeps...* I saw myself in the glass one last time before I launched off and tumbled across her lawn, dodged the fence, and wove my way through several back-yards and neighborhood streets to the nearby wooded park.

I hid out in the woods until after school, when I hitched a ride to a friend's candlelit tent at the back of his rainy, forested yard. His dad was on to us, however. So, when my smokes had ceased to comfort me with their warmth and companionship, he delivered me to another friend's basement. Which in turn, the alcohol in his dad believed I was an outlaw, and he kicked me out. Finally, the fol-lowing night I was secure in the warmth of yet another friend's basement, where I remained until I could make my negotiations. Basement hopping, by the way, is not all it's cracked up to be! I never took so much comfort in basements before, nor had as much paranoia as I peered up over my shoulder at those little sliding windows.

Ironically, the following day I tried to attend class. But, my math teacher said I was no longer a student and sent me to the office, where the secretary informed me I had been dis-enrolled. So, I slung my backpack over my shoulder and walked out the front door of the very place I wanted to be, though had always tried to escape. I did continue to go to soccer practice as if nothing ever hap-pened, and my coaches never knew; I suppose there was some disconnect there. I think it was my way of trying to have some say in my life. I tried to hang on to whatever little control was slipping out of my fingers, even if it was something I disliked such as school.

In the end, I negotiated with my dad to have me re-enrolled at school and to move in with him. I think I even cleaned up my act for a bit too. Most importantly, my point had been made. I had a say in my life, and I wasn't going to run away from my (or our) life without a fight. I wasn't going to abandon some deeper reality of what ought to be in a family, even if everyone else had (in my eyes). When my sister attended boarding school years earlier, I felt deserted. I was angry with her for abandoning me, even though I knew it truly was in her best interest at the time. But, I was not my sister. And, I was driven by a different fight; one that I was not altogether aware of, nor understood. I just knew I was committed—to not give up, to fight this fight!

WORTH FIGHTING FOR

The apostle Paul emphasized another fight in his letters to Timothy, whom he encouraged to "Fight the good fight of the faith. Take hold of the eternal life to which you were called…" The apostle's last words to a beloved son and co-laborer in the gospel were penned from prison in Rome, where he awaited execution by Nero. His proclamation still sears believers' hearts like iron forged in fire: "I have fought the good fight, I have finished the race, I have kept the faith."[101] Paul's unyielding resolve to follow hard after the Lord is a true testament. Praise God there is a true faith worth fighting for, and a victory (crown of

---

[101] 1 Tim 6:12; 2 Tim 4:7, respectively.

righteousness)[102] for all those who fight bravely and persevere till death! Today, I am encouraged by Paul's words to Timothy, as I continue to tape up my gloves, step out into the ring, and fight the good fight of faith—a faith worth fighting for.

What are you fighting for friend? If it's that dirty old hat hangin' over your eyes, is it cuttin' it? Is it a faith *worth* fighting for? Maybe it's time to hang up that old hat and get on with it?

❧   ❧   ❧

Inevitably, as spirals do, I continued to spiral—downward, and quickly, very quickly thanks to centripetal acceleration. My world was hurling into a tailspin. Centrifugal force reeked great havoc on my brain, blurring my memory somewhere between tailspin and splat! A few key events of those high school years have endured the great fight. But, I just have to ask, "Who was I fighting?"

Isn't survival mode like that? You fight, fight, fight just to survive, just to barely stay alive. Just to begin the cycle of death all over again. Never finding rest, never finding peace, and never finding victory. It angers me thinking about it now, the unbreakable bondage of the old man (sinful man), stuck within himself, his conscience seared by guilt and sin—always fighting, and never coming to an end, never coming to victory's crown. It's like a bad tattoo, saturated and stuck in your own skin, never fading, never forgotten. Or, like Job, scraping at the boils on his flesh

---

[102] 2 Tim 4:8; 1 Cor 9:25; James 1:12; 1 Pet 5:4; Rev 2:10, 3:11.

with pottery shards.[103] Or, a man on a bicycle, pedaling around Ireland for weeks, in the cold winter rain, lost in the dark night, ready to throw himself off the black cliffs and tear his flesh off with his bicycle crank once he dashes to the rocks below. Woops! I'm crisscrossing stories now!

Before I continue, I would have you know, I am not so cruel… Therefore, I must say: there is hope. And yet, the realist within beckons: "There is no hope in your *self*." And, that is true, of course. And yet, the mercy of God never ceases to abound:[104] "[A]ccording to His abundant mercy [God] has begotten us again to a *living hope* through the resurrection of Jesus Christ from the dead" (1 Peter 1:3, emphasis). This hope found in the resurrection of Jesus Christ is alive. It is the very heartbeat of Christianity. The very life and blood the "old man" needs to set him free. Jesus, who was dead, is alive again!

"What?" Yes, I know, it's nearly unbelievable. A man was alive, then that man died, then that man breathed again, stood up, and walked out of his own tomb? Yes.

"Well, how does a man do that?" He doesn't; men don't do that. God does.

❧　❧　❧

Jesus spoke candidly to Martha in John 11 regarding her brother Lazarus, who had died four days prior. In reality, Jesus was peering into Martha's heart, and He used this

---

[103] Job 2:7-8; not to infer Job's suffering was a consequence for sin.

[104] Sufficiency of God's mercy and grace: 2 Cor 3:5, 9:8, 12:9; Heb 4:16; John 1:14; Acts 20:32; Eph 1:6-7, 2:4; 2 Tim 1:9; Titus 2:11, 3:5, 3:7; 1 Pet 2:10, 5:10; James 2:13, 3:17; 2 John 1:3.

unique window to address her deepest heart matter—belief. "Jesus said to her, 'I am the resurrection and the life. He who believes in Me, though he may die, he shall live.' 'And whoever lives and believes in Me shall never die. Do you believe this?'"[105] The resurrection is the hope[106] living and breathing in the soul surrendered to Jesus Christ. *Christ* is the living hope! Furthermore, "To them [saints or believers] God willed to make known what are the riches of the glory of this mystery among the Gentiles: which is Christ in you, the hope of glory."[107]

True, it is nearly unbelievable. And true, it is a mystery. Also true, man or woman's work is to simply believe in Him (the Son) whom God (the Father) sent.[108] This is the question the gospel seeks to penetrate every flesh-encapsulated heart with: *Do you believe?* The hope of a better reality, of a true rest, of triumph over sin, the world, and death is God breathed. It is a living hope for every hopeless man and woman. It is free, alive, glorious, and available to you right now! Jesus Christ is the living hope, risen, and victorious. The empty tomb still resounds with heaven's chorus today: *"Christ in you, the hope of glory!"*

Now, that's a hope worth fighting for! Better yet, worth living for!

Let's continue on and explore that centripetal, or was it centrifugal, force. Where was that "spiral" taking us?

---

[105] John 11:25-26.

[106] 1 Pet 3:15.

[107] Col 1:27.

[108] John 6:29.

❦   ❦   ❦

Negotiations; I had made negotiations to live with my dad. Soon after, I turned sixteen and things got really revved up. I could drive to school, to the park, to the fair with alcohol on my breath and get arrested, or even up to the U.P. to snowboard for the weekend. I drove forward, backward, smoked 'em in circles, sideways in the snow, sober, or drunk, and mostly racing buddies in the dark, in the wrong lane, or playing chicken out of control. My problem really was not my drinking (well, actually it was), but the blackouts that followed—somewhere in between hammering with the boys to waking in a yard or an unknown farm in the country, with beer cans littered through my truck, puke hurled down the driver's door and crusted in my beard, and no idea what had happened the previous eight hours. Obviously, this "out of control" activity can lead to problems, and all the more, when it is fueled by anger, violence, and self-destructive motives. It is only God's pure mercy that I am alive today, for there were those who did die: some from cars, some from guns, and several self-inflicted, but most involved drinking or drugs, and all were out of control.

Why did I escape death? Maybe you're reading this and asking the same question. Truly, there's only One who knows the answer to that question. Ask Him, "Why am I alive?" See what He says; maybe it's a question you should have asked long ago? Maybe you did? Maybe it's time to ask again? Either way, don't ask unless you want an answer. And if you do, you'd better be prepared to act upon it. Well, I'm no guidance counselor; do they still have those in high school? Not that I ever used one, who could have imagined such a thing back then? I could hardly see through all the fog; let alone tell somebody else where I was traveling, and stop long enough to let them identify *my* landmarks. As if they knew or cared, right? But, that's exactly it; all the anger, ego, and self-determination were covering up a whole fleet of scars and wounds, some of which were still festering and oozing uncontrollably.

FARTHER AWAY FROM HOME

Uncontrollably, or "out of control," simply means to not be in control. I think I can go ahead and give the green light on applying that term now, despite how *in* control I assumed I was of my own universe at sixteen. Before my truck was taken away and put up for sale in Green Bay, I had one unforgettable God happening. It wasn't quite a "June Carter love walk," but that scene, among others in *Walk the Line*, depicting Johnny Cash's struggles with addiction hit home, too close to home. Maybe angel would be correct, or perhaps Angel of the LORD; either way, I'm even more certain now that the God I have become intimately acquainted with today was there—The LORD Is There (Ezekiel 48:35)—despite how in control I was!

❧   ❧   ❧

I remember backing out of a driveway, and then I remember a thud, and the sound of beer cans clinking on the rear glass as cigarette butts and ashes flew past me. When I pushed the gas the engine just revved. When I went to get out, the door wouldn't open—gravity weighed too much. When it finally did, I fell out down to the rear wheel. The truck was standing on end in the bottom of a deep ditch. The fall night was cold, rainy, and muddy… through the window the party was still going on. I think I decided to flee for two reasons: fear of getting busted again (I knew the cops would be coming around soon), and the hosts of the party were a year or two older (I didn't need to hear about it from them). Regardless, it was fear. You never read about fear motivating God in the Bible, however. To the contrary, "perfect love casts out all fear" (1 John 4:18). Why? Because, "fear involves torment." And, "he who fears has not been made perfect in love," nor does "he abide in God, who is love" (4:16). Clearly, God was the farthest thing from my heart or mind; torment, on the other hand, was a close friend I walked with often. I'm certain Satan enjoyed my sin that night!

I wasn't exactly certain where I was, however. I had a good idea a friend's house was pretty much east through a forest and farm field, maybe a few miles. I knew if I got there I could make it home another few miles. Really, in a blackout consciousness, I had no idea how far I was from home or how long it would take me to walk there. I remember being fairly scared and cold as I started out through the swampy forest in my jeans and T-shirt. My teeth began to chatter, and my shivering grew violent as my wandering prolonged. It was well past midnight. My Vans (tennies) weren't doing me much good; I don't think my "coolness" was relevant any longer. The cornfield was plowed under for the year. The rows of mud and debris were deep, and turning into water-filled trenches before me. I sloshed, stammered, and dragged myself through those foxholes. I think I was going a little mad. No end was in sight as it thundered again, rumbling inside my brain. I remember running wildly as fast as I could—tripping, crawling, and stumbling over my own body. I remember an area of the field, more in the middle, sunken, where the furrows became really deep and the water was high. I remember it was too much; I was hitting my wall struggling to go on...

That was it. "Thus far and no farther!"[109] I'm not sure how long I passed out for, but the next thing I remember was my body plunging up out of the water and seeing my reflection on the surface as lightning crashed across the sky, electrifying my eyeballs and my lungs as I gasped for air. I was choking and coughing up water; I was scared. There was nobody there. *Who pulled me up from the water? Who grabbed me by the head and thrust me to my knees?*

Godly fear can be a healthy instinct driving one back to reality, or rationality. After all, "The fear of the LORD is the beginning of wisdom, and the knowledge of the Holy One is understanding" (Proverbs 9:10). I remember calling out to God, or whoever was not there! I don't recall what I yelled, but I have a feeling it was something to the effect of: "Why, why are You doing this to me?" The irony is amazing to me now—"whoever was not there," it could not be said more perfectly: Jehovah Shammah, The LORD Is There. Yes, even there, in the muck and mire of my

---

[109] Job 38:11—God discourses with Job out of the whirlwind (Job 38:1—40:2).

humanity, my addiction and sin—there, The LORD Was There! Even when everything in my universe had gotten *out of control*, God was not. God was in control.

A divine sense of the will to live must have catapulted me back to my feet and directed my way home. I do remember running through a neighborhood nearer to mine, crying and broken as a child, whaling as I ran. I stood at the front door; it was locked. I had to ring the bell and knock. My mom came to the door startled and scared. She turned on the porch light. I was home.

I awoke in my bed around seven a.m. warm and clean. I had some bangs and bruises, but nothing severe. I wasn't sure what had happened, or where my clothes had disappeared. I wandered downstairs and found them outside in a heap on the porch, ground with mud, ripped and torn with thorns and blood. Fear and awe struck me as I sat on the stoop in the sunshine starring at my own clothes, not wanting to touch them. Then, my mom pulled up into the driveway. She had been searching for my truck the past couple hours—whatever directions I gave her as she disrobed me and cleaned me a few hours earlier had not been accurate. Apparently, I was *farther away from home* than I realized, than they too had realized.

❦ ❦ ❦

There is one way to keep your child closer to home, and not driving drunk. Sell his car! And, that's exactly what my parents did. After all, it was theirs, they owned it, they had bought it, and now they were selling it. Somehow, though, as boys do, I got my hands on another set of wheels. Only this time, it only had two, and you couldn't roll up the windows. *Wow! My first motorcycle: fast, black, and dangerous!* Somehow, I made a promise to myself that I would not drive it after drinking. I kept that promise, I never did. Plenty of others did drive drunk, however, as I hitched along for the ride, to anywhere, farther away from home.

The Law Won

Truthfully, how it happened, I'm not exactly sure. It could have been my truck's mysterious disappearance from the towing yard after being impounded from the ditch incident? Or, that second arrest for speeding excessively on my second motorcycle, costing me my license? It might have been that tobacco incident in the school library; or, that fine for graffiti during homecoming? Then again, there was that after school fight and midnight car chase. Or perhaps there was something I purposed to forget… Certainly, I was being framed! Eventually, however, I had to face the music.

The local PD was easy, but the county court was not! I stood before the court in a shirt and tie betwixt my mom and dad. Every click of the transcriber's typewriter tightened that noose around my neck. It was the first time my parents had officially united since their separation, and I was the glorious center of their reunion. That's how I felt, and the judge was poking my buttons, just like the overweight bully in grade school who "poked, poked, poked" me every day until I beat him up at recess—I hated punching him in the face and holding him down, kneeling on his belly, but I couldn't take it anymore, and nobody would stop him. Maybe that was the tune in her head as she shuffled through my file and prodded around my psyche, hoping for my reaction—"Another One Bites the Dust…"[110] Well, she got it. I reacted.

"By the law is the knowledge of sin" (Romans 3:20). "For where there is no law there is no transgression."[111] Underneath all my anger and tenacity, there was a broken kid who needed to be fixed. My tape cassette finally wore out; my younger years' theme song, "I Fought the Law (And I Won)" by the Dead Kennedys, had come to an end. The law had won. And, *she* was pretty happy to do so! "The law entered that the offense might abound."[112] True, she had identified my sin, but in no way was she able to enact a change of my character—her authority was powerless. "For what the law could not do in that it was weak through the flesh, God did by sending His own Son in the likeness of sinful flesh… that the righteous requirement of the law might be fulfilled…"[113] What did she do then? What purpose does the "letter of the law" serve?

"The law was our tutor to bring us to Christ, that we might be justified by faith" (Galatians 3:24). Furthermore, "Before faith came, we were kept under guard by

---

[110] "Another One Bites the Dust," by Queen, off *The Game* (EMI, 1980).

[111] Rom 4:15. For a thorough application of "the law" see: Rom 2:11-29, 3:10-31, 4, 5:12-21, 6:14-18, 7, 8:1-5; Gal 2:16-21, 3, 5, 6:12-16.

[112] Rom 5:20.

[113] Rom 8:3-4.

the law… But after faith has come, we are no longer under a tutor" (Galatians 3:23, 25). That is the ultimate goal of the law, not to condemn and sentence the lawless, but to bring him or her to a powerful Savior who can save to the uttermost![114]

So, she brought me; she served me the big tutor! But, my time to fold had not quite come; it would be nice to say it had, but it hadn't. I still had chips on the table and another couple hands to be dealt before the "Man of the House" called my bluff. And, He definitely would, just not yet. Not yet.

The state of Wisconsin did drop the mallet, though! I was sentenced to mandatory alcohol treatment. The first white-walled rehab my mom brought me to was just about enough to make me go insane, or at least believe I was crazy. I found out I couldn't be admitted without my permission, since I was under eighteen, or some legality. Regardless, I had sneaked out to her red car I had been eyeballing through three or four corridors of white walls and soundproof glass; I was getting out one way or another! My mom must have sensed the program would never have worked, and after some negotiating I was permitted to attend outpatient rehab. Needless to say, when all the other guys were heading over to the locker room for soccer after school, I was not. I got to head off to treatment; I got to *bite her dust!*

---

[114] Heb 7:25 (or as often translated, to the gutter-most).

Twelve Steps

Every day after school I would go to treatment. Doesn't that sound a little odd? I suppose sometimes in various circles to those in the know, I would say group, as, "I have group today." But, treatment implies that just by attending these counseling sessions I was being treated, or, at the least, receiving treatment. Was I being treated? And, what was I being treated for? What was my condition? Alcoholism, I guess; I was addicted to using alcohol and other substances. So, that made me an alcoholic. And, if that's who I am (or was), it's practically genetic, or it might as well be, right? Well, I'm not so sure this classification properly identifies my nature or genetic make-up. But, did it work? Sure, I suppose it did, for a while... "And then what?" Exactly; my genes must have had a bad inseam or something.

Well, all kidding aside, my outpatient treatment program did help me recover from alcohol and substance abuse. Did I crash four years later? Yes. So, did my treatment cure me? No. Was my condition more behavioral than nature-genetic? Yes. Do I consider myself an alcoholic today? No. Am I a new creation in Christ Jesus—have the old things passed away, and have all things become new?[115] Yes. And, no. Yes, I am a new creation. Yes, the old things that used to control me no longer control me. Yes, my life has been cleansed and I've received a fresh start. Yes, I am no longer an "alcoholic!" But, on rare occasion, has

---

[115] 2 Cor 5:17.

the thought of bombing my brains out and escaping this reality ever occurred to me? Yes, it definitely has!

Do I? Definitely, I do not.

So, what's my point: one thing has not changed, and it's not whether or not I am an alcoholic; it is the simple truth that I am a sinner. (I speak here in the present as a Christian.) I am a human being living in a fallen world under the curse of sin and its plethora of temptations and consequences. As such, I have a body of flesh (Greek: *sarx*, see footnote 116), and thus I embody the potential to act upon its lusts. I can choose *to* sin. Or, I can choose *not* to sin. I choose how I behave. Or, I choose to forfeit that choice and let external forces and the "lust of my flesh" make my choices for me. In the latter, I choose sinful behavior; in the prior I choose righteousness (what is right in accordance with a holy God). Before I stray too far theologically,[116] let me just say that the Bible is very clear concerning sin: it is pleasurable for a season, but the wages of sin are death.[117]

The bottom line is this: no matter what sinful behavior a person is committing (drunkenness, sexual immorality, theft, lying, or gossip), the underlying "treatment" they need is not attachment to a group, philosophy, code of principles, or any other religious action. It is not what they need to do, but who they need to become! (I speak

---

[116] For a greater context see Gal 5:16-25; Rom 6:3-14, 22-23, 7:4-25, 8:1-14. My primary concern here is not to discourse on man's inherent sinfulness nor the flesh versus spirit; however, note the Greek usage of *sarx* for flesh in Paul's arguments, which opposes the NIV's modern (pre-2011) use of sinful "nature."

[117] Heb 11:25; Rom 6:23 (respectively).

here of the non-Christian.) What a sinner truly needs is salvation from his or her sin. This is the heart of the matter: "But God demonstrates His own love toward us, in that while we were still sinners, Christ died for us" (Romans 5:8). Isn't it wonderful to hear those simple words—But God—again? Yes, God meets us right where we're at, and frankly, that's the only place God meets sinful people (at the intersection of Christ's cross).

The next step for the recovering sinner is to be filled with the Holy Spirit. How can a man (or woman) overcome the "law of sin and death" (Romans 8:2)? By digging a hole in the ground, shouting his sins in anger, and trying to bury them with black earth?[118] Or, priestly confessions in a dark shadowy box? No, he must take possession of Christ's death and resurrection by faith. The old man *has died* and a new man *has risen* in new life through the Holy Spirit. Christ demonstrated His sovereignty over sin and death by His resurrection from the dead. Further yet, before He ascended to the Father, He promised to send a Helper to indwell the believer—the Holy Spirit.[119]

So, the Holy Spirit is as essential to the victorious Christian life as is salvation. The Holy Spirit is God. He

---

[118] A close friend had this experience while living in the forest near Williams, Oregon (summer 1999).

[119] Luke 24:49; John 14:16-20, 14:26, 15:26-27, 16:7; Acts 1:2-8, 2:1-4, 2:31-33 (see also footnote 270).

is personal,[120] holy, and active in glorifying the Father through our acceptance of, and obedience to the Son. The Holy Spirit releases the believer from the bondage of sin and empowers her to overcome sinful behaviors and addictions. The Spirit-filled believer is free to "walk in the Spirit, and not fulfill the lust of the flesh."[121] Sin no longer has power over us! As Romans 6:6-11 (emphasis) declares:

> Knowing this, that our old man *was crucified* with Him [Christ], that the body of sin might be done away with, that we should no longer be slaves of sin. For he who has died *has been freed* from sin. Now if we died with Christ, we believe that we shall also live with Him… For the death that He died, He died to sin once for all; but the life that He lives, He lives to God. Likewise you also, reckon yourselves *to be dead indeed to sin, but alive to God* in Christ Jesus our Lord.

Reckon: regard it as done! This ongoing practice the Christian exercises can be compared to working out, or staying fit. The believer's behavior is conditioned by a continual surrender and giving over of selfish and fleshy

---

[120] The Holy Spirit is a <u>person</u>: John 16:13-14 references the Spirit as "He" (masculine personal pronoun) eight times concerning His role in glorifying Christ. <u>Personal traits</u>: intellect/knowledge (1 Cor. 2:10-11), emotions (Eph 4:30), will and ability to make decisions (Acts 16:6), loves (Rom 15:30). <u>Personal actions</u>: teaches (John 14:26), comforts (John 14:26, 15:26), tells the truth (John 15:26), guides (John 16:3), convinces/convicts (John 16:8), prays/intercedes (Rom 8:26-27), commands (Acts 13:2) [from: www.theholyspirit.com/Holy-SpiritPerson.asp].

[121] Gal 5:16; Rom 8:1, 8:4.

(natural-ruled) desires to God. As Paul has instructed, the believer must "*work out* your own salvation [deliverance]."[122] Similarly, the mature have *exercised* their senses to discern both good and evil, *by reason of use* (Hebrews 5:14, emphasis). And again, this practice of reckoning is upheld by the work of the Holy Spirit through faith, not man's heavy labor (as seen further in Philippians 2:13).

So, in the end, it's really a heart matter. It is not a genes matter, or a treatment matter, or a twelve-step matter. Worthy of noting, the original Twelve-Steps of 1935 were vigorously Christian based,[123] but have since eroded under pluralism's hand. Victory over sin has not changed, however. It still begins with freedom inside the human heart, spirit, and mind, with the behaviors of the flesh and body following. Perhaps a more simplistic Three-Step method for success might be: (1) Salvation from sin, (2) Spirit-filled life, (3) Surrender self and reckon the flesh (see footnote 232). Regardless, it is God's creative work and man's cooperative obedience. My testimony is fifteen years and counting—humbly, I can say Jesus is truly Thee Great Physician[124] and *curer* of incurable behaviors!

❦ ❦ ❦

My downward spiral did not stop with the law or treatment,

---

[122] Phil 2:12, emphasis; note: this "salvation" (or deliverance) need not be eternal in nature, as Paul's prior context reveals being sanctified of vainglory or selfish motivations. Additionally, see 1 Tim 4:7 for a related reference to "exercise".

[123] See the original Twelve Steps at: http://en.wikipedia.org/wiki/Twelve-step_program.

[124] Mark 2:17; Luke 5:31.

however. As seemingly as it may have appeared that I was "spiraling higher *into* control," I was not. Nor had I begun to make my way "closer to home." My spiral was more of a double helix, or a two-step foxtrot. And, as little foxes do,[125] my age of discovery had just begun to begin… as I set out from the comfortable slumber and lowly den of tradition, peering higher beyond blue skies and a bright shinning sun.

---

[125] Song 2:15.

6

HIGHER POWER

THERE WAS MORE TO TREATMENT than confessions of brandy-filled oranges for lunch made with medical syringes in the basement. Or, a convenient supermarket job stocking the beer cooler, and one's private home supply (stored under the stairs, behind the flag, before the red light and hanging beads). As your mind races through your childhood secrecies of sin in attics and crawl spaces, and if not your own, then friends', neighbors', or cousins', it should be of no surprise. Sin is everywhere. And, sin is in everyone. "No, not one!" Yes, it is true, God's decree stands: "There is none righteous, no, not one… all have turned aside" (Romans 3:10-12).

As it is with most addictions, or addicts, one cannot simply remove X, Y, or Z and not replace it with something, someone, or some form of activity. The void is too big, temporarily anyway, and especially for the non-Christian without God's presence. I remember a skinny guy who became a compulsive smoker. Ironically, he had not smoked before? And now, he smoked more cigarettes, and drank more coffee than anyone had ever seen, and if he wasn't or couldn't, he talked about doing it! Another guy became angry, or angrier, as he pumped weights and got tough! An "innocent" girl became a mom. Others frequented AA and NA meetings, and dances, and played Frisbee golf, a lot... But, this book is not about them, nor barbecues.

So, what was my substitute? After all, I had not yet believed nor received Christ's substitutionary sacrifice,[126] nor applied its prescriptive "Three-Step" method. I suppose there were several substitutes, though, and two for sure. The first was a determined young girl coursing with strength and beauty, who, for the better part of high school, kept me stable. God's hand of mercy definitely overshadowed me through those fragile years. And the second, which was perhaps a close tie with the beautiful young girl, was spirituality.

By saying "spirituality," I'm implying all of the various forms of meditation, worship, philosophy, and my search to "find myself," as others often voiced. Mostly, however, my passionate pursuit and hunger was to devour every New Age book my primary treatment counselor suggested. Not that she was to blame for my intense interest and yearning for spiritual things, but she did have a monumental impact in my life over the next five years. In retrospect, it is what it is, and in a large way, her influence

---

[126] Substitution: Isa 53:4-6; Rom 4:25; 1 Cor 15:3; 2 Cor 5:21; Gal 1:4; Eph 5:2; 1 Pet 2:24. Propitiation: Rom 3:25; Heb 2:17; 1 John 2:2, 4:10.

had a reciprocal effect: she indirectly redirected the course of my ship, which would eventually find harbor in Christ. For that I am thankful, and even grateful today. Capsizing in tumultuous seas, however, I could have done without. Well, maybe I couldn't have done without my spiritual shipwreck, but I wouldn't wish it upon anyone, ever. At least—for the sake of retrospect, and regardless of the approaching storm—my ship was out at sea searching for port.

I find it interesting that this chapter happens to be number six. Biblical numerology has often depicted number six as symbolizing man. It has also been given the meaning of: "The constant battle between the spirit and the flesh."[127] I'd have to agree with coincidence—number six is appropriate for this chapter. My search for "higher power" was just that: My search! It was all about I, Me, and My... my preferences, my views, and my world as I knew it, saw it, and desired it. It really had little to do with anything "higher" than five feet ten inches! After all, the Zippo lighter I got engraved as a token of encouragement for a close friend in rehab read: "You Are Your Own God." That just about sums it up. I mean, one read through Hesse's *Siddhartha* and you've pretty much got that nailed. Well, I suppose believing it and "actualizing its being" takes a bit longer, but you've got a good start, anyway. A few more "I Am's," a couple "Om's," and you're well on your way... to the wonderful world of man. Or, should I say mantra?

---

[127] See Six: www.christian-resources-today.com/biblical-meaning-of-numbers.html.

If that were totally true, things would be better. However, there's quite a bit more at stake in the spiritual game of "finding oneself" than higher power or man. And, it must be noted that the use of *higher power* denotes God, for the all inclusive and unexclusive politically correct approach, or search rather. But, there is more to this game than God and man; there is another spiritual player. No, you cannot see him. Yes, he is real! And more than real, he is actively seeking to thread himself through any door, window, or loophole left open on one's path to enlightenment. Therefore, the following WARNING is in order: Keep an Eye on Your Peephole!

❧   ❧   ❧

As a side note, and in keeping step with my chronology, it was during my junior year that my dad got remarried. Despite the web of logistics that arise when one's father (or parent) remarries, involving other kids, too few bedrooms, peers at school, etc., perhaps the most challenging was his wife's religious commitment to the Mormon Church. And in time, as I became a born-again Christ follower, this presented new and more complex dynamics in my relationship with both my dad and stepmother. Two decades on, however, I am still confronted by the costs of my parents' divorce, and obviously I am not alone. An exceeding number of our country's youth are being ravaged by this plague today. Upon reflection, and regardless of how indebted I feel, our postmodern void clearly demands a response: please, STOP!

✵ ✵ ✵

Back to Satan: "Be sober, be vigilant; because your adversary the devil walks about like a roaring lion, seeking whom he may devour" (1 Peter 5:8). And actually, this spiritual game is really not a game at all. It's not a game of go-fish, karma and good works, or even tug-of-war. It's real and it's for keeps; winner takes all. You've got everything to lose, and even more to gain. But, one thing is certain; spirituality is not a game.

CREATURE RATHER THAN CREATOR

Therefore God also gave them up to uncleanness, in the lusts of their hearts… who exchanged the truth of God for the lie, and worshiped and served the creature rather than the Creator, who is blessed forever. Amen. (Romans 1:24-25)

Ultimately, this was my great terror. Did I say terror; I mean error! It seems obvious sitting here, on this side of the cross, behind my monitor! But out there, then, all things went, and "nothing didn't go." I pulled up every leaf-covered mossy log in hope of discovering the answer. My search inherently contained the paradox of life: I am living, yet I am not truly alive. I had a mystery on my hands to solve: *How can this be? How can I be alive and not have life? Why am I even living? What is the purpose of my life? Why do I exist? Do I exist? Does existence even exist?*

Yes, the geyser of self had erupted, and with its questions the quest began. So, like a detective, I turned over the logs, and rocks, and old fire pits with bloodied knees. I boxed-up fragments of glass and trash and sent them to the appropriate authorities. I thought they'd be good visual aids for their environmental class on "Going Green." I'm not sure if the high school biology department ever received my specimens or used them for their purposed intention, however. Similarly, my post-high school enrollment into a university environmental program was a little misguided; I'm not sure the Plant Biology professor was on my wavelength.

Speaking of the awesome and mysterious cosmos, Tozer compares the natural man to the God-believing man: "The man of earth kneels also, but not to worship. He kneels to examine, to search, to find the cause and the how of things."[128] True, my hands were digging deep, deep into the earth, and deeper into my earthy self. I was fumbling through the dark, however, from one question to the next, from one author (self) to the next, and my hands were coming up empty. My clues were only leading me in circles—always back to me.

Bound in the earth's horizon, man's reasoning tends to follow that course of his own accord. The Christian, however, is called to be "transformed by the renewing of his mind"[129] by God's Spirit (not his own will). Unfortunately, my search was less about transformation and more about reincarnation! Circular, or contradictory, it didn't really matter. I devoured all the New Age, metaphysical,

---

[128] A. W. Tozer, *The Pursuit of God* (Wing Spread: 2006), p. 73.

[129] Rom 12:2; Eph 4:23; Phil 2:5; 2 Tim 1:7; Heb 8:10; 1 Pet 4:1.

angels, light, Eastern, and Native American spirituality
books I could get my hands on. True, most of them were
written in the name of "healing," but what part of illusory denial is healthy? If self-realization realizes more of
self, or if creative visualization aims to create self's vision,
what part of healing does the human being experience?
Certainly, not a more complete or whole human being,
that is, the abundant life[130] that God intended (created)
for man and woman. It seems that self begets self, not a
remembrance of, or a reawakening into a more complete
and healthy being. Self is limited by the very nature that
characterizes it as such. In all the varying definitions of
self, the repetitive denominator is the singular: a, one,
individual, ego or I. Therefore, as it seems, is defined,
and as my own experience has confirmed, self is limited
to its nature.

Funny how man-ish this self stuff is, isn't it? I would also
add, that in addition to the whole and abundant life God
has desired, His image[131] is the standard for holistic being.
Speaking of the believer who loves God, the Bible states:
"For whom He [God] foreknew, He also predestined to
be conformed to *the image of His Son* [Jesus]" (Romans

---

[130] Abundant life: John 10:10; Jer 33:6; Ezek 20:6; Ps 36:8; Rom
5:17; Eph 3:20; Titus 3:6; 2 Pet 1:11. Healing: Isa 58:8; Mal 4:2; Matt
9:35; Luke 9:11; John 13:10; Acts 10:38; Rev 22:2. Health: Jer 30:17,
33:6; Prov 3:7-8, 4:22, 12:8, 16:24; 3 John 1:2. Completeness: John
17:21, 17:23; 2 Cor 13:9, 13:11; Phil 1:6; Col 2:10, 4:12; 2 Tim 3:17;
Heb 3:21; James 1:4; 1 John 4:12, 4:17. Fullness: John 1:16, 15:11,
16:24, 17:13, 17:21; Ps 16:11; Rom 15:29; Eph 1:23, 3:19, 4:13; 1
John 1:4.

[131] God's image is man's standard from Genesis to Revelation: Gen
1:26-27, 9:16; Rom 8:29; 1 Cor 11:7, 15:49; 2 Cor 3:18, 4:4; Col
1:15, 3:10; Heb1:3.

8:29, emphasis). I don't see a lot of room for self to glory there, do you? But, man has been bowing down to his shiny illusory mirror for ages, and I don't suppose he will stop worshiping himself anytime in the near future. Man loves *his* self, and *her* self, far too much!

Herein enters terror! For as I said, spirituality is not a game. Where does all this self-realization, self-help, and self-saving spirituality originate? When you take a step back and look at man's place in the universe, it's really quite preposterous, isn't it? But, it was never about what was logical, or even obvious, for that matter. Was it?

Logically, Lucifer could never be or become God. So, when God's most highly anointed cherub saw himself—in his own eyes and heart (self perspective)—as being fit to receive worship and usurp God's throne, he was cast out of heaven.[132] The idea of Lucifer becoming God is self-defeating. It simply cannot be. If God could be replaced, He never was God. There can only be one unique, omnipotent, uncaused, true God. If there were two, or a replacing of, both would lack, and thereby neither would be God (as defined). If a *created* being, such as Lucifer, could become the Creator, or even equal to the Creator, his very nature would have to change in such a way as to precede his nature. But how can that be? Can a created being *become* his own first cause (self-caused), or the First Cause—the uncaused cause: Can Lucifer *be* God?

Common man knows that the natures of created beings do not change or reproduce other natures (or beings) of

---

[132] Isa 14:12-22; Ezek 28:1-19.

their own accord. Genesis (God-breathed origins) clearly teaches that *like creatures reproduce after their kind*,[133] not any other way. I'll leave macroevolution to Darwin's origination of species and the likes of such creative scientists. Such created beings, who, by the way, have only reproduced "after their kind," and theories, I suppose. Theories: did I mention that? Oh, yes I did: Theories!

❧   ❧   ❧

My passion for apologetics (defending the faith) gets me fired up! Thank you for your patience! Most definitely, this journey we have embarked on would be void of revelation, if it were not for God's Spirit. As Scripture rightly declares:

> No one knows the things of God except the Spirit of God... Now we have received, *not the spirit of the world*, but the Spirit who is from God... These things we also speak, *not in words which man's wisdom teaches* but which the Holy Spirit teaches, comparing spiritual things with spiritual. But *the natural man does not receive the things of the Spirit of God*, for they are foolishness to him; nor can he know them, because they are spiritually discerned. (1 Corinthians 2:11-14, emphasis)

God's Spirit and Word are man and woman's only

---

[133] <u>Kind</u>: Gen 1:11-12, 1:21, 1:24-25. Man is unique from plant life/creatures in that he is created in the *likeness of God*, in God's image, and his reproductivity is assumed to follow suit *after its kind* (Gen 1:26-28).

instruments (or means) for navigating life. Likewise, if God's light ceases to illuminate my journey (these pages), my aim to give compass and to set direction amidst the labyrinth of reality perishes. My single hope remains: "Your ears shall hear a word behind you, saying, 'This is the way, walk in it,' whenever you turn to the right hand or whenever you turn to the left" (Isaiah 30:21). Similarly, whenever I've been lost in the illusive mirage of no-man's-land, or I've wandered through the distant haze to the outer fringe, it has been God's Spirit who has brought clarity to redirect my path and regain my focus on the destination. So again, as we continue on our journey, I want to thank you for your patience as I gather my thoughts, and we head back down *Phoenix Road...*

❧   ❧   ❧

The rocks of Mother Earth were crying out! The stones were alive! Animism is the basic belief that spirit inhabits all existing things. My animistic view was influenced heavily by my interest in Native American spirituality and practices. I worshiped the Great Spirit as I cast my prayers upward at creator Father Sky and bowed my knee to creatress Mother Earth. I purified my soul with the smoke of my smudging pot (a purification ritual performed by burning sage and cedar) and cleansed the energy and my environment with offerings of incense. Life was One, and everything had to be in balance as I pursued harmony within the Oneness of which I was, or was becoming!

Symbolically, I designed my first tattoo to represent this universal unity through a picture of the tree of life, the earth, and the sun all interconnected in full display of their creative colors. Sometimes today, onlookers are perplexed by my "blue onion or balloon" on my arm! I suppose the green blades of grass growing up my foot don't help their inquisitive, confused looks. But as I said, it was through Oneness that I was finding my place in the universe. I think it was the physical connectedness the American Indians had with creation that drew me deeper into animism. And remember, I was clean and sober; I wasn't experimenting with "recreational drugs" any longer.

Well, that concussion I took playing goalkeeper in soccer, and not wanting to "come back" to present consciousness after seeing some otherworldly light, could have influenced the sobriety of my psyche! But, the last of my paraphernalia had been a charitable donation to a classmate on his own journey to "find himself." What a great friend I was! I still remember the conviction I had while I was giving it to him; I just didn't have the backbone to throw it away. Perhaps that single uncut thread was what snared me down the road and reeled me back into addiction's perpetual spindle. I had gotten off the ride and even left the amusement park, but I never pulled the plug. The Ferris wheel was still a revolving attraction.

My need for a creative outlet didn't stop with tattooing, or green hair, likened to my favorite band's album, *Green Mind* (1991), by Dinosaur Jr. I still remember a line from "Quicksand"—a David Bowie rendition off *Whatever's Cool With Me* (Sire, 1991)—referencing not to deceive oneself with belief. Interestingly, as much as I tried to *not* conform to the traditions and culture around me, for reason of hypocritical views and lifestyles, I was actually creating my own system of belief—no matter how syncretistic it was. So, I hid away in my basement painting the alien-like subjects of Dinosaur Jr. album covers and wrote short stories for English and Creative Writing about "How to Be a Tree" in the afterlife or other spiritual subjects crafted into poetry. On one occasion, a deranged story involving death, sex, and spirituality, and a live classroom presentation, brought upon the disciplinary action of the principal. Worse yet was my influence[134] upon several other students who were *in* on the stunt. Needless to say, nonconforming behaviors and practices such as these don't receive the highest marks on Report Cards! But, "Who cared?" It wasn't like "higher education" was on my agenda toward transcendental enlightenment.

The Oak Grove

My dimly lit basement was not the only place I hid away, however. Nor was the loft of the abandoned barn in the woods at the edge of town, where I drummed and chanted fearfully hoping to raise up spirits or the hauntings of infamous ghosts. Others just smoked pot and crawled out broken windows running for cover from walkie-talkies and flashing "Cherries-n-Berries!" Ecclesiastes' view of the natural man toiling under the sun—"Vanity of vanities, all is vanity" (Ecclesiastes 1)—was an underlying thread

---

[134] God does not take lightly the approving of and leading others into sinful practices: Rom 1:32; Matt 18:6; Mark 9:42; Luke 17:2.

woven through every thought and belief I had.[135] And yet, the old barn and the park along the river were not the only places I hid away.

Isolating in nature was definitely on the top of my "Things To Do" list! I can only speak from experience, but too much of oneself is never a good thing. True, solitude is necessary, and even Christ ascended nightly to various mountains to seek His Father in prayer,[136] but He always descended to the community and entered back into fellowship with His disciples. *Isolation is dangerous!* Remember that lion roaming in the wilderness, or that angel of light, or Eve's deceiver, or the prince of the power of the air—one is never truly alone in isolation.

❧   ❧   ❧

I entered the oak grove on the backside of the woods nearly every afternoon. The oaks towered above the dense, overgrown woods I had to travel through. They stood loose and majestic as the crown of the wood in their own space and glory. The only thing standing between them and the Pacific was the sun and sky and thousands of miles. They had been around years before and would be telling stories long after the wood was a bygone tale. Every day I felt honored and welcomed to enter their circular space, embraced by their peaceful ambience and lasting

---

[135] A closer look at the *natural man's* underlying perspective in Ecclesiastes reveals great despair: hate of life (2:17), hate of work (2:18), turning of heart and despairing (2:20), desire to never have existed (4:2-3, 6:3, 7:1).

[136] Matt 14:23, 15:29, 17:1, 17:9; Mark 6:46, 9:2, 9:9; Luke 6:12, 9:28, 9:37, 21:37; John 6:3, 6:15.

strength. The evening light shone down through their canopy, casting shadows amid playful twirls of acorns and dancing leaves. Autumn's warmth comforted my spirit as I leaned back, propped up against the thick familiar bark of an old friend. Golden farm fields rolled out from my leather boots, hovering and emanating creation's glory before vanishing into the west. The horizon aglow, soon its ember would die out and smolder into night. The oak grove was my hiding place.

It is difficult to "go there" today. Because things happened there, thoughts happened. Mostly, that is all that happened, *thinking,* other than a few captivating experiences I will relate in the near future. In the meantime, I thought. I meditated on my life, my purpose, my quest, and existence. One thought pervaded my thinking in the oak grove more than any other: *I was not worthy to live.*

The Bible references oak groves more than once. Common to the idolatrous practices of the Ancient Near East was the worship and sacrifice to pagan deities under oaks[137] at high places. In every instance these acts were condemned by God as harlotry—Israel strayed after other lovers, denying their covenant with their First Love. Today, if you were to visit the ancient archaeological site of Tel Dan in northern Israel, you would find yourself standing under the canopy of an enormous oak tree. Interestingly, 1 Kings 12:29-31 records that Dan was where Jeroboam, the king of Israel (northern divided kingdom), set a gold calf upon a high place for worship and sacrifice. He also

---

[137] Ezek 6:13; Hos 4:13; 1 Kings 12:29-31, 13:14, 13:33-34, 14:22-24; 2 Chr 11:14-16, 13:8-11.

built temples and appointed priests. Jeroboam erected these high places not in accordance with the Levitical law God had ordained, but according to "his own heart."[138]

As glorious and beautiful as oak groves and high places are, and for this very reason, they are often the places men and women bow down and *worship and serve the creature rather than the Creator, who is blessed forever* (Romans 1:25).[139] Two similarities were present in my oak grove: (1) I was not worshiping Jehovah God of the Bible (I had many idolatrous lovers), and (2) The conviction I had of the *need for a sacrifice*. I would also add, for later reference, that there was a small hill just outside the grove that often served as a high place of prayer.

My "unworthiness to be alive" stemmed largely from my awareness that humanity was imperfect and the cause of great contention in the universe. And being that I was a human, I inherently was at guilt. This fact coupled with an animistic view of equality and a belief in Oneness, through which human superiority was decreased and other living forms (and things) were elevated, only secured my "unworthiness." Clearly, I did not believe in sin, or understand God's account of sin and its curse rampant in creation. Nor did I accept God's charge of dominion given to man.[140]

---

[138] 1 Kings 12:26, 12:33.

[139] Israel and Judah to be judged for <u>worshiping creation</u>: Jer 2:27 (Saying to a tree, 'You are my father,' And to a stone, 'You gave birth to me.'); 3:9 (she [Israel] committed harlotry with stones and trees); 3:23 (salvation is hoped for from the hills/mountains); 8:2 (Judah loved, served, walked after, sought, and worshiped the sun, moon, and host of heaven).

[140] Gen 1:26-29.

But, I was aware of a universal biblical truth—that there was an undeniable dissonance and chasm fragmenting through humanity—lying at the root of my humanness. It was this awareness that presented my need to make or offer a sacrifice for my imperfection and guilt.

Again, I did not believe in Christ's sacrifice for my sin, nor understand His finished work on the cross, once and for all.[141] I did not know that Christ died in my place, and that the death He died paid the penalty for my guilt, imperfection, and sin. I did not know that Christ came to set the captive free (Isaiah 61:1) from the rightful, legal sentence of death and separation from a holy and just Being for eternity. I did not know, but what I did know was that *I needed to make a sacrifice.*

Really, considering how often I lived and dwelt in that "place," it is amazing I survived. Daily, I stared at that fallen oak, leaning up high into its neighbor's branches. I saw myself climb it a hundred times with every foot and handhold by memory. I studied the limbs and sketched mental pictures of the rope, and knot, and the weight of my naked body upon the limb… I tried to imagine those I loved, and those who loved me, and how they would respond, and if they'd understand. I had pretty much determined there would be no note or explanation; my reasons were too personal. Daily, I visited my hidden place, and daily I contemplated, even longed for, the courage to be so brave…

Before I continue, I just have to say that if you need

---

[141] Heb 7:27, 9:12, 9:26, 10:10; 1 Pet 3:18; Jude 1:3.

to be reading these words, if you need to be hearing this story, then you really need to. You need to know that there is nothing valiant about suicide; there is nothing glorious about attempting to appease God's verdict by one's own sacrificial works, however noble, pious, full of good intention, or even giving of one's life. Nor is suicide an alternative for any other circumstance. Christ died for you; He died for me. That's the end of the story; there is *no* other choice. Period. And, if you need to vocalize your contemplative thoughts or plans to someone else, someone other than yourself, someone outside your mind, then that's what you need to do. You have to get help. You have to reach out. I'm praying you will; and more than that, Christ is praying[142] for you right now, and He died so you don't have to. You do *not* have to die. I did not have to die. Choose Christ's sacrifice today; do it, choose Christ. Choose Christ now!

I must confess, however, that after being a believer for a decade and a half I do not have any remembrances of suicidal thinking, that is, until the past year. Oops, and the memory I slipped in from Ireland (chapter 5), but that doesn't count! But yes, believers *can* have suicidal thoughts! My recent battles of the mind and thought life have resulted vaguely from many factors including: stress, anger, sleep deprivation, false expectations, marital conflict, finances, and others I'm unaware of I'm sure. And perhaps (and certainly), writing this book! I'm not exactly sure how or from where this thinking surfaces;

---

[142] Christ is interceding on your behalf: Heb 7:25; Rom 8:26-27, 8:34; Isa 53:12; John 17:20-26.

however, I do know Satan is intimately involved in its behind-the-scenes plotting. I'm also aware that there is always some sort of feeling of hitting a wall, having been pushed beyond my logical threshold, or being trapped in a corner. I have also realized that when "every next little thing" becomes a problem, red flags are waving! The imagery of this verse comes to mind: "[S]in is crouching at the door. Its desire is for you, but you must rule over it" (Genesis 4:7, ESV).

Most recently, God revealed to me that if I enter a black room and close the door, though I am blind and cannot see, the door still exists—there *is* an exit! There is always a way of escape:

> No temptation has overtaken you except such as is common to man; but God is faithful, who will not allow you to be tempted beyond what you are able, *but with the temptation will also make the way of escape*, that you may be able to bear it. (1 Corinthians 10:13, emphasis)

Similarly, and regardless of how or why these thoughts arise, and as difficult as it might be, they are sinful and need to be confessed as such. Your adversary lurks not far up this alley; don't give him a foothold, not even a whisper!

The spiritual battle the believer faces is real. As I've said, spirituality is not a game—both teams are shooting to win, not that Satan is in any way an equal opponent of God! But, as fleshy creatures exposed to sin's many consequences in the earth, man (and woman) stands as the central target.

And, the believer is the bull's-eye! Fortunately, God has equipped us with His spiritual armor and our helmet of salvation[143]—what else could be more important in battle than a sound mind? Well, yes, He gave us a double-edged sword too![144]

❧   ❧   ❧

Ironically, or not, it might be of cultural interest that I used to listen to a hardcore punk band in grade school—the Suicidal Tendencies (1983–). They always had the coolest skulls, like Zorlac designs and my original Powell-Peralta Tony Hawk skateboard deck (1983). Little did I know, however, that "suicidal tendencies" would be something I would wrestle with years later, and that I would become more than "Possessed to Skate" (song title, 1987). Of course, I just thought it was cool—skulls, being tougher than death, and "anti" slogans and attitudes. When I look back now I can almost muster a chuckle, but if I'm honest, there's really nothing funny about it. And, there's definitely nothing cool, or tough, about suicidal thinking!

On the contrary, tonight at church I heard a great sermon on hope. And, I suppose, this only affirms the necessity of placing oneself in community—fellowship within Christ's body (the church). God's promise refreshed my spirit: "Now hope does not disappoint, because the love of God has been poured out in our hearts by the Holy Spirit who was given to us" (Romans 5:5). Amen,

---

[143] Eph 6:10-(17); 1 Thes 5:8; Isa 59:17.

[144] The believer's spiritual sword is God's Word: Eph 6:17; Heb 4:12; Rev 1:16, 2:12.

our hope is not in ourselves! I was also comforted by an experience Paul related to the church in Corinth: "For we do not want you to be ignorant, brethren, of our trouble which came to us in Asia: that we were burdened beyond measure, above strength, so that we despaired even of life" (2 Corinthians 1:8). Yes, even the greatest of saints wrestled with utter hopelessness. And now that I think about it, Christ Himself was tempted by Satan in the wilderness to cast Himself off the pinnacle of the temple.[145] (I recognize the uniqueness of Christ and this circumstance; however, it still reveals Satan's motive to lie and murder.[146])

It must also be noted that even as the believer is armed with God's Word as his spiritual weapon, so Christ championed over Satan through standing on God's Word. That might tell us something about the importance of having God's Word hidden in our hearts[147] during the hour of battle, or the moment-by-moment attack of demonic arsenal that can wage relentlessly against our minds. It must never be forgotten, we have hope as an anchor for our soul;[148] our ship is moored to the buoy of God's presence—nothing can move us![149] The storm will soon pass… an eternal harbor awaits our arrival.

Well, we've made it through the oak grove! We have

---

[145] Matt 4:5-7; Luke 4:9-12.

[146] Speaking of the Devil: He was a murderer from the beginning… when he speaks a lie he speaks from his own resources (John 8:44).

[147] Ps 119:11; John 14:26.

[148] Heb 6:19.

[149] 1 Cor 15:58; Col 1:23; Heb 3:14, 6:19; 1 Pet 5:9; Ps 16:8, 62:6, 112:7.

not been moved, shaken a bit perhaps, but not moved! I think we're doing quite well. I think I'd rather talk about that skateboard stuff,[150] though. Let's ride with that a bit and see where it rolls…

SNOWBOARDING IS MY LIFE

I was eleven when my picture ran in the local paper for "sidewalk surfing" on my quarter pipe in the driveway. I secured the clipping in my desk drawer with another pressed, yellowed newspaper photo of my sister's boyfriend on a half pipe! My pink Bones Brigade T-shirt was worn out by seventh grade. That was just about the time I got my first snowboard—a Burton Performer Woody Elite 145. Skateboarding in Wisconsin was only a seasonal fix… the sun only shone five months out of the year and the The Turf indoor skateboard park[151] was two hours away in Milwaukee. But as the factories huffed and puffed and the gray settled in, the snow started to fly and local ski hills were being invaded by "snow surfers." Ski Brule was one of the first to let us hike up the runs after the lifts shut down; and once they let us on the lifts, it was all over! We bombed the moguls on Big Bear and tore up the sidewall on Log Jam as if we owned the place. And one thing was certain, in our minds anyway: we "Ruled the school!" And, we weren't going anywhere!

---

[150] I bumped into this rippin' skateboard blog/archive: http://the houseofsteam.com/category/4-years/1983/.

[151] Surfin' Turf Skateboard Park: 1979–82; The Turf Skateboard Park: 1987–96.

And now, I suppose, it's probably appropriate for me to make yet another confession: I did have another love besides the beautiful young girl, and spirituality. After all, as summer rolled around while I was still in treatment, I declared that I was going to Mt. Hood in Oregon to snowboard. That got challenged, just slightly, but I still got to ride those spring-session half pipes and drink huckleberry malts down at Government Camp! Snowboarding was progressing every day and I was in for the spin!

"Yeah Bro! Spin to Win!" My sister always despised the sticker on the back of my truck: Snowboarding Is My LIFE! Of course, my idol was shared by her previous boyfriend also. And, she was absolutely right; however, I didn't see it that way, nor would I for years. But as time unfolded, my snowboard had become a great golden idol, not unlike Jeroboam's calf.

So, what did I do when the sun came back out? That's simple, I found an old mattress and bedspring and strapped on my Woody! I hopped, and spun, and did "Method Airs" all afternoon. By my freshman year trampolines were popping up here and there, and I was fortunate enough to get my own. Now I could do flip tricks on my skateboard deck I could never do on the ground, and full flips and 720's on my snowboard. Every summer we duct-taped our edges and added another obstacle—"jibbin" was all the rage! I bungeed a drainpipe to the top of the fence, and we jibbed and bonked all night under the spotlight. As long as the boom box blared, we kept boarding! We even tried a few gutter slides along the back porch, and on rare occasion threw a few "Acid Drops" or one-footers off

the roof. And then, there was wakeboarding on the lake…
Ah summer! But it was really just all fun and games, to
keep our edges from getting rusty!

Winter was *all* business! I don't think I missed a weekend of shredding, ever! Even when I had forfeited my
license for "excessive miles gained in the per hour rating," a
buddy strapped an old Barrecrafter rack on his primer-gray
Chevy Citation, and we putted up to the U.P. puffing
smokes all the way! We usually rolled out of bed by four
a.m. and made it back by nine p.m. to catch a movie with
our ladies, and practice our new moves we'd learned on
the slopes! One friend, for various extracurricular reasons,
even slept in his boots and gear so he'd be ready when
we woke him up banging on his door. Ironically, he also
carried a neatly folded and methodical list of tricks he *had*
to master each time we rode. We worked just enough on
school nights to pay for boarding on the weekends! My
dad even hauled us out west a few times, which wrecked
me for good! Once I saw Colorado's I-70 corridor heading
up toward Summit County, there was no turning back.
My mind was set, and my heart was determined.

❧   ❧   ❧

It was only fitting that I wore my Dinosaur Jr. T-shirt
under my gown to graduation. And of course, who would
know but me! But, hadn't that been the whole point all
along? High school had finally come to an end; it was
time at last for my feet to follow my heart. For as every
grade school journal entry I wrote prophesied, I had no
choice but to pursue my dream. Only, I had laid down my

skis and hopes of becoming a professional skier, because *Snowboarding Is My LIFE!* And all I wanted to do was "Go Big or Go Home!" Besides, I was too young to settle down with the beautiful young girl, and the oak grove wasn't going anywhere anytime soon. And, the mountains held a wonder and awe that captivated my spirit with a freedom and sense of destiny that could only be one thing—my *Higher Power!* The Rockies were calling my name…

7

GO WEST MY SON

I WASTED NO TIME. Less than a week after I was handed my diploma I was on the road. I still remember when my moment of realization struck: High school was over and I didn't *ever* have to go back! That epic moment didn't last too long, though… the principle extended his hand, I lifted my head, the camera flashed, and the horizon stood aglow with dreams of a new life. I suppose, in many ways I had left home years ago, and it was only right for me to catch up to myself now.

Saying goodbye to friends and family was bittersweet. The relationships had cut deep, but the hope of discovery in a new time and place brought a long awaited release. The desire for a whole and complete life independent from years of shrapnel was greater than any heartfelt pressure or guilt to stay. I longed to create my own life, and to be free from others' desires to create it for me. So, a buddy and I packed and strapped everything we owned into and onto my Jeep. I raised the sails, cut the bow lines free, and we set the compass dead west: drive 1,000 miles, stop at the mountains, continue west 1,000 miles, stop at the sea!

That's exactly what we did. Except for a ninety-degree turn up to Montana and across the border into Canada, we stayed right on course! The windows were rolled down and the "Big Skies" kept getting bigger, and bluer! The farther we got from home the freer we felt. But somewhere beyond the Sierra Nevadas, our hearts groaned as their infant roots tore loose miles behind us in a forgotten land. A land I had once called home.

ROAD TRIP

The plan was to stop in Breckenridge, Colorado, and hook up with an older friend who was working at a resort. We were going to get jobs lined up and a place to stay, then bomb around the west coast, ride Hood, and circle back for winter. Well, aren't plans swell! I can see Jerry from *Seinfeld* snapping his fingers and waving his arms above his head: "Anyone can take reservations…"[152] I'm also reminded of the proverb: "A man's heart plans his way, but the LORD directs his steps" (Proverbs 16:9). Alas, it doesn't take a Bible scholar to know that a couple of kids, a couple thousand miles, and a couple months later everything is going to be smooth sailing from port to port!

We made it to Colorado worry free, other than a minor truck repair in Lincoln, Nebraska. All I remember now is the afternoon we spent surfing grocery carts in the parking

---

[152] *Seinfeld* "Reservation" episode: "The Alternate Side," Season 3, Episode 11, 1991.

lot listening to Green Day. A few days later we interviewed for Night Housemen (housekeeping) at the resort my friend had put a good word in for us. That was the gig we were hoping for: to work at night, get a discounted CAB pass (Copper, Arapahoe, Breckenridge), and ride *every* day! We checked out a few places, then decided to hold off on renting a pad knowing that we could always crash in employee housing. The upcoming season was looking good! So, we headed over to the Maroon Bells at Snowmass and did a little camping, mountain biking, and fishing. My friend caught all the nice fish, including a little snowboard "Betty" he had met on our previous trip the past winter. We attempted to hike over the pass heading to Crested Butte, only to get schooled! The alpine conditions proved to be more than our gear and feeble Midwest minds could handle—the Elk Mountains were full of untamed energy, not to mention snow!

With the U.S. atlas spread out on the hood and the whole world before us, we decided to do a tour of the National Parks. So, I pointed the ship north and we sailed on… We explored the Tetons, waited patiently for Old Faithful in Yellowstone, and even got a mouthful of brown fur. A moose strolled out three feet from our bumper, filling our lane like a house! No, nothing like a horse, a house! It was a close call, but the grill was still clean; we ate Top Ramen around the campfire another night. We rolled out our sleeping bags all the way to Missoula, and got an extended stay in Whitefish when we broke down in Kalispell. A day or so later, we finally climbed into Glacier sometime after 10:00 p.m.

It was hard to believe the sun was still shinning; "I guess it really is the Going-to-the-Sun Road!" But once the black curtain did fall, heaven's canopy enthroned us with stars and galaxies beyond our amazement. I had never seen such picturesque mountains or had been so awed by creation before. And to top it off, we got to hike a glacier and snowboard down, ollieing (jumping) over run-off creeks lined with mountain flowers, and airing off rock faces cascading like water falls! Glacier National Park won our blue ribbon "bomb" award! And, Pabst wasn't even in the contest!

It was hard for me to leave Glacier. Thinking back now, it reminds me of what Peter said after seeing the Lord transfigured on the mountain: "Lord, it is good for us to be here; if You wish, let us make here three tabernacles: one for You, one for Moses, and one for Elijah" (Matthew 17:4). Peter was so awestruck by his experience that he wanted to set up camp, and never venture on. There was nothing so physical about the encounter, however, in that he could permanently apprehend it and house it in a tent! So, once the mountain goats cleared the road, I hit the gas and we leapt over the border through Waterton up to Banff. And then we came to a breathless standstill—the turquoise waters of Lake Louise stole my gaze! One would only think that by now I'd be praising God for His glorious wonder and creative splendor. But I was still truly blind.[153] My eyes were stuck in the horizontal, I couldn't see vertically. Not yet, anyway!

---

[153] Ps 146:8; Isa 29:18, 35:5, 42:7; Matt 11:5; Luke 4:18, 7:22; John 9:25.

GO WEST MY SON

To be honest, I'm not sure if we made it to Jasper on that trip or not, but regardless, another trip a few years later would take me there. I'm also not quite sure what route we took back into the States and westward. But, eventually we had to come back down. For one reason only of course—so we could go back up!

❦   ❦   ❦

Mt. Hood was not an option. It was a sovereign and predetermined absolute chosen by the official high planning committee. Yes, I'll admit it, it's all my fault, poor us, we just had to session Hood while friends were swatting mosquitoes and smoking bowls at the quarry back home. No matter what the conditions, snowboarding in the summer was always epic! It was like being a rebel, and doing the very thing you loved, all at once. How insane is that? It's bomb-drop beyond insane, is what it is!

Yes, I know, I know… He wasn't rebellious. But, was He *a* rebel?

If you're thinking Burnside, so was I! As poor as a skateboarder as I was, if we were going anywhere near Portland, we had to skate Burnside Bridge! Wow! I got schooled again! That place was so gnarly, and the guys who skated it skated so fast. It was pure and controlled aggression! When some guy appeared through a hole in a concrete wall (neighboring parking ramp?), like ten feet up above a quarter pipe that already went to vert, and dropped in for his session, that was it, I was worked! But, we skated; we were at Burnside, and we ripped it up! Whether anyone else thought so, or knew it; we ripped it up! Because, we had rolled a lot of miles from Wisco, and I was even further from my first pink Executioner[154] board I mail ordered from Thrasher. *We made it this far... Who could stop us now?* We ripped it!

We continued down Coast Highway 101 to Coos Bay, where a local officer ripped me a nice little speeding ticket, and a few lone surf sharks braved the cold sea. We camped out on the beach somewhere near Crescent City, where I dreamt dreams under the stars. My heart merged with the beat of the cosmos whilst the rhythmic surf emanated through the sand: "We Are One... I Am One..." We awoke to the wind whirling in our ears sometime in the early dawn, so we jumped out of our sleeping bags into *our* dune buggy and spun out for the next destination, spitting, picking, and itching the sand from all of our cracks and crevices.

❦ ❦ ❦

I always smirk today when I see destination travel ads that glorify the traveler's experience in some fantastical way. Life is nothing like that! It's greater; it's real! Reality seldom unfolds in such an illusive time and space. Isn't that why the "Word becoming flesh" (Christ's incarnation: John 1:1-3, 14) penetrates our hearts? The spiritual inhabits the natural and our hearts resonate. His manifestation reveals that truth exists, what it is, and who[155] truth is found in. The believer's core resonates with conviction at

---

[154] Nash Executioner Skateboard (1985), pink with blue dragon; to see photos google: Nash Executioner.

[155] John 14:6—I am the way, the truth, the life.

the revealing of Christ's person and sacrifice. Truth illuminates deception. At once, our blind eyes are opened[156]—a vivid sense of depth and light penetrate the facade of sin's lustrous veneer—and the illusion is lifted.

We see this same transaction between the spiritual and the natural when Christ resurrects from the dead. The natural (Christ's flesh) is subordinate to the spiritual (the Holy Spirit). God's revelation of Himself is clearly seen in the Son of Man's[157] eternal-spirit-nature. Jesus authentically reveals and defines truth in reality. And, the spiritual makes known what the natural always knew: "For we know that the whole creation groans and labors with birth pangs together until now" (Romans 8:19-23). So, don't be fooled by fantastic script and imagery of salesmen, no matter how religious they sound, or how godly they look. And remember, if you book that trip to that Kauai paradise resort—life always happens. There's always a grain of sand to be found in an armpit or belly button!

❧   ❧   ❧

---

[156] Acts 9:18.

[157] Son of Man: *Messianic title* (Dan 7:13-14); Jesus referenced Himself under the *Messianic authority* this title declared to the Jewish hearer concerning: Authority Over Sin: Matt 9:6; Mark 2:10; Luke 5:24; John 5:27; Lord of Sabbath: Matt 12:8; Mark 2:28; Luke 6:5; Savior: Matt 18:11; Luke 19:10; John 6:27; Crucifixion: Matt 12:40, 20:18, 26:2; Mrk 8:31, 9:31, 10:33; Luke 9:22, 24:7; John 3:14, 8:28; Resurrection: Matt 17:19; Mark 9:9; Glory and Second Coming: Matt 16:27-28, 19:28, 24:30, 25:13, 25:31, 26:64; Mark 8:38, 13:26, 14:62; Luke 9:26, 21:27, 22:69; John 3:13, 13:31; Acts 7:56; Rev 1:13, 14:4.

My head spun higher as I rubbernecked out the window.[158] Sequoia National Park was out of this atmosphere! The redwoods were more than "generals" in my eyes; as Kings Canyon rightly declared, they were glorious majesties crowned in honor, marching in triumphal procession. I'm not sure it matters if General Sherman is bigger than General Grant, but I do find it interesting that President Eisenhower declared Grant as a National Shrine (only living shrine) memorializing veterans. The term "shrine" connotes a place as being holy, sacred, or divine. I guess my disillusionment with creation wasn't politically incorrect. Regardless, the Redwood Highway makes any man feel like a kid!

Like I said, somewhere beyond the Sierras our hearts began to uproot. Perhaps Peter Noone's schoolboy lovers tune—"What a Wonderful World"[159]—continued to muse from the boardwalk in Santa Cruz through my friend's groaning heart as we camped out in the loft at his dad's place in San Jose. "But what I did know..." was my friend's heart was still planted back home with his high school sweetheart in Wisconsin. I also knew that our *plans* were just about to change! And, I was no Bible scholar either! Nor still, I've just got my elbow sleeves worn in a bit!

After a week of late-night phone calls, I knew for certain

---

[158] Photo of "The Sun Shining Through General Sherman's Branches": http://en.wikipedia.org/wiki/File:Summer_2009_vacation _303.JPG.

[159] Peter Noone soloed Herman's Hermits' "(What a) Wonderful World" off *Wonderful World* (MGM, 1965). Original songwriters: Sam Cooke, Herb Alpert, Lou Adler (*The Wonderful World of Sam Cooke*, 1960, Keen Records).

that our plans were changing. I just waited. And inevitably, his heart's groans reached his lips… He still loved her, and he *had* to go home. I suppose us men would have little purpose if the "damsel" was never "in distress." So, after a last trip into San Francisco we packed it up and pointed our plates at America's Dairyland. The Golden Gate vanished into the sunset somewhere in our rearview mirror. For the most part, we just made a beeline back to his honey! With the exception of overheating in Utah's desert inferno, and having to crank up the heat as my naval pooled with sweat and ran like The Colorado, things were okay. I wasn't upset; I knew how the heart could ache. Besides, this was his trip too, and we were both just along for the ride. In some mystical way, I was actually excited to see what the journey had in store.

We flip-flopped our normal driving schedule so we could drive in the cool of the night. We hit our first wall about five a.m. when we crashed into a Motel 6 for a few early morning hours in Salt Lake. Glenwood Springs was our next stop. *Ahh, Colorado…* The hot mineral springs revived my spirit. It was great to be back *home*! My friend, on the other hand, had a late night of drinking and stumbled into a few bruises under a dark bridge. All things considered, he could have been "worse for the wear." But one thing was clear: he needed to get home! So, we anted up our spare change as we blew past Breckenridge, and we kept on trucking! A small piece of my heart sank with uncertainty, but I knew I'd be back. When or how, I wasn't sure, but I knew I would return.

Mountain Bound

It was a strange but familiar feeling when I pulled up to his apartment to drop him off. We unloaded his gear, said "Later!" and I drove off solo. Perhaps it was being alone with myself driving my truck for the first time all summer. Or, maybe it was as if we had never left home, and had just returned from a long weekend of snowboarding like the many years before. No, things were different; I was different. I wasn't exactly sure how or why, but I was not the same man.

My high school girlfriend was not the same person either. I suppose that's how those things go. But, being home again had stirred up some old feelings of my own. Yet, I knew my heart had already transplanted me a thousand miles away. And even if the Proclaimers had walked "500 Miles"[160] and *Benny and Joon* was a great film, my heart was in another land, burying itself in for a long anticipated winter. As the leaves began to change, I was fortunate to "luck" into a great month of painting. I was able to save up some cash and upgrade my traveling companion. Well, actually, it was a downgrade of one year, but I cut the odometer in half. Plus, it was a stick, jet-black, and had new tread—enough said! I was road ready and mountain bound!

Coincidently, I received a phone call from a classmate who had moved out to Breck ahead of me and was looking

---

[160] Proclaimers: "I'm Gonna Be (500 Miles)," from *Sunshine on Leith* (1988, Chrysalis); used in film *Benny and Joon* (1993) soundtrack by Rachel Portman (Milan, 1993).

for a roommate. So, I packed up a U-Haul with a bunk bed, and I said "Hasta la vista!"

I'm still not sure how many times I drove to Colorado and back over the next several years, but I enjoyed tracing the route along my mental topographic map as I lay in bed the night before I set out. Something intrigued me about seeing printed maps converge into landscapes and horizons. I suppose it was the visionary in me. Because, someone had to pen those maps, and if they did unfold into an accurate depiction of reality, then they were true. They were also worthy of trust, and of great use to the traveler who knew not where he traveled. And, if they *are* true, then the mapmaker must have known wherest he roamed. Really, is the Bible, or its author(s) any different? It is a map navigating the unknown. It gives direction to its reader while promising an eternal destination. And, as with any other map, it takes faith to believe and apply: "But without faith it is impossible to please Him, for he who comes to God must believe that He is, and that He is a rewarder of those who diligently seek Him" (Hebrews 11:6). So, why is trusting God to be unexpected?

❦ ❦ ❦

I spent the winter season doing just as I had hoped and originally planned. I worked for the resort at night and snowboarded *every* day. I even got to ride Loveland Pass a few moonlit nights! All I can say now is, "Wow, God is good!" But, God's gracious vision was not what was driving me. I was on a mission. I wanted what I wanted; and I was going to get it.

I rode hard, fast, and big. When the Breck snowboard park opened I held my own. My signature backside, semi-inverted spin over the tabletop or across the gap got me some recognition with a few locals. I helped out a friend at a local snowboard manufacturer with some product testing too. In return, I was allowed to design my own boards and graphics! What a dream! I was just starting to feel my wings open up…

And then, "CRACK!"

❦   ❦   ❦

With rumors of good snow, I shot over to Snowbird with a ski-bum from work for the weekend. We camped out in the parking lot and woke eager to tear it up—"Utah! Let's do it baby!" We left our Summit County passes on our jackets, just so they'd know where we came from! We were still getting loose. I don't think it was even the third run of the day when I nicked my shoulder on the ground spinning out in a little tumble. I've heard it only takes 9.6 lb of pressure to break your clavicle upon impact. Well, as I sat there feeling nauseated and trying to figure out what was wrong, my buddy flew by, so I shot up and chased him down. Only, my head didn't get that concept, and I nearly passed out before he could unstrap my board and walk me into the Ski Patrol hut. An hour later, we were at a doctor's office in Salt Lake getting X-rays. The Doc threw a sling over my shoulder and told me to "take two of these" and give it six to eight weeks. That was that. I was stopped dead in my tracks, and I didn't even get any of those Utah freshies!

Six weeks are a lot of minutes (60,480 to be exact); eight are even more! My broken dreams and crushed hopes sank further as I watched the water drip from the roof. Discouragement whispered depression's unkind and familiar voice. I had no place else to turn but to my spirituality. I delved deeper into astrology looking for my place and path into the future. I searched, and smudged, and offered up more incense. Reading, writing, and painting were not enough either. I had to symbolize this greater commitment to following my "spirit" with another permanent mark (tattoo) upon my flesh—two scorpions interlocking with my zodiac symbol. *Why was my dream not aligning with my life? I was doing everything I could; what more did the Great Spirit want from me?* My questions continued as I marked the days off the calendar…

My time was up! My prison doors flung open! I was free at last! I arrived at the medical clinic down-valley in Frisco at 1:00 p.m. The doctor gave me the "Okay!" So, I slid on my gear in the back of my truck and headed for the mountain. By 2:30 p.m. the snow was melting off my board as I rode up the lift. Spring season was raging, and I was back on my board! The sun was out, the birds were chirping, and the snow was melting. I had made it just in time!

And then, "CRACK!"

I think it was only my second run when I ollied off a small bump, and the shock of landing re-broke my clavicle. The break actually became worse as the bones shifted upon themselves. Today, I have a nice knobby protrusion on my left collarbone that makes wearing a backpack or seat belt a real joy! Understandably, a lot of snowboarders break collarbones, but two back-to-back was two too many for me. So, I had my roommate duct tape a Domino's pizza box over my sling and around my chest, and I fought back!

❧ ❧ ❧

Summer came and went, and I was ready for another season. I had a lot of ground to gain back, and focus was key. I could barely afford to live alone, but I couldn't afford the distractions. I had to push it hard, go big, and spin further! The season looked promising. I moved out of Breck and down to Silverthorne, closer to some friends, the snowboard manufacturer, and easy access to Copper, or "Compton" as we called it! My riding was coming together again, and I even got a few shots in a locally produced film. My spirits were soaring. We had been doing quite a bit of filming and shooting stills on the boards my friend was pressing. They had come a long way from some of the "explosion models" I rode the year before! They were actually sick boards, and I was super stoked to be riding one! My goal was to make it through the cold, hard of winter, so I could really kick it up once spring came. I had visions of touring in the summer out to Hood, Tahoe, and down to Bear to see what might shake loose. I had hoped to get some killer footage that might sign me a nice deal with a good company. I could feel my grade school dream getting closer. It was time!

February 19, 1996. I still remember the date! Perhaps, because it was exactly one year earlier, give or take a day, that I broke my collarbone. Regardless, it was a glorious afternoon in the snowboard park. It felt like spring. The energy was flowing, my board had a good pop, and the snow was fast. We shed a few layers, lined the runways with pine boughs, and rolled out the camcorder. I straightened my goggles as I approached the take-off… I wound up to spin that big backside air I loved to hold so long and float out so far… That was it.

Spring never came that year. Yes, the snow melted. And, summer never took me to Hood, or California. Somewhere in mid-rotation I knew I had gone too far. But, it was *too* late. I overshot the transition. On film, you could hear me swear before I even hit the ground. I stuck it clean; that wasn't the problem. But, my knee buckling upon impact with a flat landing wasn't good. I gracefully skidded out on my butt fifty yards downhill. Friends quickly gathered around and shared their words, but I already knew what I didn't want to. I just asked to be left alone; shock set in and I dozed off.

When I awoke, I managed to unstrap my board and hobble down out of the park while heads were turned. I wasn't sure about my insurance coverage and Ski Patrol policy, but I knew I couldn't afford an ambulance ride. I was two chairlifts up from the main lodge, so I had a little walk to get through. Fortunately, it was a sunny afternoon. A warm flat rock beckoned me to stop for a rest. I closed my eyes only to doze off again. Sometime later, a chill stirred me as the sun made its way down between the aspens. A Ski Patrol stopped and told me he'd keep an eye on me until I'd gotten off the mountain. I was tired and losing strength, and will, but subconsciously he motivated me to keep going. I finally made it to the bus stop. Now all I had to do was get to my truck and drive my clutch a half hour down valley to the clinic. And yes, it was my left knee.

I didn't go to the clinic. I decided to call-in to work and go straight home instead. I wanted to be alone and think things through for a while. I must have been preparing.

The following day I went to the clinic. I sat on the cold white paper as the doctor examined my knee. I knew what he knew by his expressions; he just couldn't voice it. So, he ordered some X-rays. Then he looked me in the eyes and broke it to me: "You've torn your ACL off the bone, son."

"But, what about snowboarding? Can I still snowboard?"

"No, son, you won't be doing any snowboarding."

"When? Ever?"

"I'm not sure, son."

Those words hurt more than any broken knee I'd ever had. He knew it; and the pain I was trying to hold in finally broke out in tears. My heart was wrenched. My dreams were shattered. My spirit was broken.[161]

Then the questions came: *Why? What about my dream? I was just starting to soar? Can this really be happening?* And, the battle of the mind began. Fortunately, or unfortunately, he prescribed me some Vicodin for my pain once the adrenaline wore off.

Life changed in one instant. One second—that's the power that life holds! The Bible has to speak into this

---

[161] Unknowingly, God was using these difficult dream-shattering circumstances to break my hardened will and independent spirit (see David's examples: Ps 34:18, 51:17).

somewhere… "Oh, how they are brought to desolation, *as in a moment!* They are utterly consumed with terrors" (Psalm 73:19, emphasis). Wait, that's a bit depressing, how about this: "*In a moment*, in the twinkling of an eye, at the last trumpet. For the trumpet will sound, and the dead will be raised incorruptible, and we shall be changed" (1 Corinthians 15:52, emphasis). Yes, that's more like it—an incorruptible body! Truly, there is always hope in Christ! For the believer's life is hidden in Christ with God, and one day soon we will be with Him in glory.[162] If only I knew that truth then! But, I didn't.

The Good Shepherd was not far away however. And, if you've ever seen that painting of Christ with the lamb over His shoulders[163] you'd understand what I mean. My mom had that painting in her hall a few years later when I learned about its significance. The shepherd would actually break the legs of the lamb that was prone to wander away. As it healed at the feet of the shepherd, the lamb learned to hear his voice and understand his ways. Though it was a painful act for both the lamb and shepherd, it was in genuine care and concern for the lamb's life and future. By now, I would think I'd have stopped running. But, I didn't know I was even in a race.[164]

I continued running room calls and stairs through the resort while I figured out where I would have surgery, only I hobbled; I did not run. Vail was known for their

---

[162] Col 3:3-4.

[163] Similar painting of the Good Shepherd: http://www.christcenteredmall.com/stores/art/weistling/the_lord_is_my_shepherd.htm.

[164] 1 Cor 9:24, 9:26; Heb 12:1.

outstanding knee surgeons. My dad's voice loomed in the background, however: "You can't afford to have any more broken knees!" In the end, I really only had one choice. I drove to Wisconsin and saw a knee specialist at the University Sports Medicine Hospital in Madison. My surgery was scheduled five weeks out. So, I slid my seat back, threw my Colorado tags in reverse, and pumped my clutch back to the mountains. I had pretty much mastered my peg leg! One thing I would have to admit is those stressful winter road trips made it awfully difficult to stay on board with my "quitting smoking." Drifted in behind a barn at an Iowa farmstead for the night in below zero temperatures and driving snow was never fun, no matter what the rating on your mummy bag was. I must have thrown out fifty packs of smokes over those two years. And, bought another fifty more!

I see God's grace in many of these events today, if not all. A key blessing was the great roommate I had acquired a few weeks before I got injured. So, when I returned to Colorado and told him I'd be leaving for good in a month, he offered to take over my lease. That was a relief. Not to mention, it was difficult for me to isolate with another person around. I did, however, continue my spiritual quest. As previously, I had nowhere else to turn but to my higher power. This time it was different. For the first time, I had come to the place of turning my back on snowboarding— my dream—and I made the conscious choice to pursue my spirituality with *all* my strength and will. I committed myself to the pursuit of becoming a shaman or a "medicine man,"[165] for a lack of better terms. I knew enough to know that a door was shut for me with snowboarding, and I couldn't keep trying to kick it down.[166]

Yes, you guessed it! I had to seal my commitment with another symbol. I realize that tattoos have different meanings to different people. But, in my mind and experience there was something very powerful about marking my body in such a permanent way that identified a belief I was pursuing with the entirety of my person. I suppose there's a connection here to Leviticus 19:28 where God commanded the Israelites *not* to cut or tattoo their bodies as did their pagan neighbors *in religious acts of worship.* Even so, as conscious as I was of balance, and reasons for particular placement of these symbols, there was only one place left to tie it all together.

It took a while to find an artist who would fulfill my request. But once I heard about that six shootin' cowgirl up in Carbondale, I knew I had my "man!" So, I shaved my head, measured, drew, and experimented with sizes and colors until I created the perfect piece. I designed a medicine wheel, more similar to a medicine shield, which encompassed my belief system. The wheel depicted where varying life forms and elements fit into the universal order. Interestingly, the empty circle (flesh colored) representing man was at the center. The overall design looked similar to a directional compass, or a target. And, with *man* at the center of my universe, I was right on target!

---

[165] See also chapter 8, pp. 134-36, and footnotes: 168-69, 171, 173 for greater definition.

[166] Acts 9:5, 26:14.

Coincidentally, the Greek defines the word for sin, *hamartia*, as "missing the mark." Well, I was spot on bullseye, only I had definitely missed the mark! But after all, I was my own God, so I had better be at the center of my universe.

❧   ❧   ❧

One last event took place in the Blue River Condos before I left Colorado. To my pleasant surprise, upon returning from Wisconsin, an intriguing visitor had moved in with my neighbor. And as it just so happened, she had to pass by my picture window and front door every time she came and went! As my spirit knew, and I learned, she also was on a spiritual quest. Inevitably, a friendship began that would ebb and flow over the terrain and years to come...

Colorado was difficult to leave behind. My heart was still in the mountains. But, I had come to pursue my dream, and I had pursued it with all my will. In some greater knowledge, I knew I would be back. For the mountains, for her, or for my own heart, I *knew* I would return.

8

COMING HOME

I HAD TO CHOOSE. The state of Nebraska offered some time to reflect. And in those days, Starbucks wasn't percolating along every interstate off-ramp. Turning the corner onto my street in my old neighborhood was not easy. Returning home was never my intention. Not that I felt I had failed, but in some deep sense, by coming home I was letting go of my childhood dream. And, maybe that's what I needed to do—surrender—surrender to the bigger picture of life, and where it was taking me. Maybe snowboarding really wasn't *life* after all? So, it was settled; I had to choose.

I had a lot of questions returning home, but one thing I had determined was to surrender myself completely to my spiritual calling. I considered it a calling even then. Although I didn't believe in a personal God, in the sense of God the Father, I did believe I was being pursued and called into that pursuit. By whom or what, I wasn't entirely sure; I'm not even certain I really cared. After all, I didn't believe in good and evil, or sin, and I was definitely ignorant of the spiritual battle waging.

A few years earlier I had received a set of Animal Medicine Cards (similar to Tarot cards). I was still waiting for the right time to pursue their guidance and give myself to their fate. Really, I think my heart was divided. I was fearful of their revelation; that is, if it would be congruent with what was already in my heart and manifesting through my pursuit. Because if it wasn't, the contradictions might disprove what I had known to be true, and my path of truth might not have been accurate (relativism[167]). But the time had come; it was now or never! I surrendered my will, and I made my choice.

I performed my ritual smudge and offered myself to the creator and his choosing of my Animal Spirit Guides (Shamanism).[168] I shuffled and spread out the fifty-plus cards randomly, face down on the floor of my bedroom. My Primary Animal Power would be my first draw, and my Subsequent Medicine Animals representing different powers[169] and directions would follow. Now, I had to choose.

---

[167] See Paul Copan's book on relativism and religious pluralism: *True for You but Not for Me* (Bethany House, 1998, 2009).

[168] Shamanism: the practice of communicating with the spiritual world as an intermediary with the natural/physical (for a full scope see: en.wikipedia.org/wiki/Shamanism). Concerning Animal Spirit Guides see: www.animalspirits.com/index1.html. For a practitioner of shamanism see Gregory Drambour's "Vortex Experiences" and Shamanism link at the bottom of page: http://www.sedona-spiritual-vacations.com/sedona/sedona-vortex-experiences.htm.

[169] Power as it relates to shamanism, see "The Web of Power and the Spirit World" at: www.wicca.com/celtic/wyldkat/shmnindex.htm. Note the term Wicca in the URL; Wicca is a neopagan form of modern witchcraft, see: www.religioustolerance.org/witchcra.htm.

It is still rather amazing to me that my Primary Card was the Eagle. Of course, I already believed this in my heart, and I had anticipated it being my first draw as I knelt before the cards in surrender to the Great Spirit. However, in the actuality of the Eagle card being drawn, I became fearful in a new way. Such an awesome experience only made my calling more concrete. I was not totally sure what would follow, or the cost it might demand, but I was definitely moved in a powerful and fearful way. I only shared that "sacred" information with one person—my treatment counselor from years earlier (whose continued friendship had evolved toward a spiritual mentor).

As I look back today, I know that God allowed that draw, and although I did not *yet* love Him, I believe He ultimately used it for good similarly to Romans 8:28: "[A]ll things work together for good to those who love God, to those who are the called according to His purpose." And perhaps, this "being called according to His purpose," was a holy and sovereign calling of His own accord, which overreached and superseded my own "calling." I know I could get into shaky theological ground here in several areas as I step out of "context"; however, I'm certain that God's ways are higher than man's and beyond his finding out,[170] especially concerning election. I'm also certain of Scripture's teaching on divination; it's an abomination to God! And, I'm aware that divination, with its numerable

---

[170] Isa 55:8-11; Rom 11:33; Job 9:10.

references in Scripture,[171] was a common practice in the Ancient Near East, and because so, God was amply familiar with counseling His people Israel concerning such practices. I don't believe God was or is fearful of man's sin (nor my honest search for my Creator); rather, His ground is solid, as are His ways, reasons, and footing. "He [God] is the rock; His ways are perfect" (Deuteronomy 32:4).[172] Ultimately, there were two callings at work: mine and God's. In that order! Or, not!

❧ ❧ ❧

I have been deliberate to leave these evil practices buried. Highlighting the purpose of these medicine cards, however, is beneficial. Surprisingly (or not), a quick search located them on the Web and offers valuable clarity. *Medicine Cards: The Discovery of Power Through the Ways of Animals;* "This divination system is based on the ancient teachings of Native America."[173] Specifically of note are the words *power* and *divination*. I was seeking knowledge and power through divination: the pagan practice of obtaining the unknown by spiritual means, primarily earthy (see footnotes 168-69), outside of the person and prescription of the biblical triune God. It might also be noted that a set

---

[171] The Hebrew word *qecem* is used interchangeably for divination and witchcraft: Lev 19:26, 20:6; Deut 18:10; 1 Sam 15:23; 2 Kings 9:22, 17:17, 21:6; 2 Chr 33:6; Jer 14:14; Acts 16:16.

[172] God/Christ is a rock: Deut 32:15, 32:18, 32:30; 1 Sam 2:2; 2 Sam 22:2, 22:32, 22:47, 23:3; Ps 18:2, 18:31, 18:46; Isa 17:10, 44:8; Hab 1:12; Matt 7:25, 16:18 (referencing Christ the Rock, not *Petros* the small stone as seen in: 1 Cor 10:4); 1 Cor 10:4. Jesus is a stone: 1 Pet 2:4-8; Ps 118:22; Isa 8:14.

[173] Opening page, paragraph one: http://www.medicinecards.com/.

of cards like these are likely available at any major bookstore; they aren't hidden away in some dark spooky place (as the Web reveals). Naturally, the occultist eats his or her breakfast cereal just like you or me… well, except for those balancing in a headstand, nude!

Today, the occult has infected every area of our postmodern culture. Yes, even the church. I am reminded of Walter Martin's address (dating back to 1955) concerning The New Age Cult in *The Kingdom of the Cults* (chapter 15), where he referenced his warning to the church concerning the rising growth of cults and the occult.[174] A more recent statistic: "Today, almost 60 million people throughout America and on foreign mission fields are involved in a cult organization, or are dabbling in New Age practice or occultic thinking."[175] That fact should open our eyes to the signs of the times. It's not a matter of where or when, but here and now! Actress Shirley MacLaine's[176] infamously shocking media attention has long since passed; one does not need to be a New Age guru to see the spiritual spins and twists thrown on nearly every big screen movie and magazine today. Spirituality, religion, and even Christianity can be and are big business. One must engage today's marketplace with increased knowledge and scrutiny: What is being sold, or pedaled? Who is being targeted? How are *we* marketing it? And greater yet, why?

---

[174] Walter Martin and Ravi Zacharias, ed., *The Kingdom of the Cults* (Bethany House: revised 2003), p. 405.

[175] Ibid., p. 405, from *Adherents.com*.

[176] Shirley MacLaine published *Out on a Limb* (1983), making her a predominant New Age advocate of the 80s.

Deeper Into the Abyss

Why? was still a difficult question I wrestled with as I laid down my crutches and grappled through physical therapy. Without my old dream driving me, my aspiration for rehabilitation faltered. With a wearied mind and no accountability, my discipline with my pain medication also grew weak. It was easier to live in that warm lucid place where life floated along in tranquility's song.

The only good memories enduring those days were shooting pool with a few friends and live music. It took a while for the *emo* scene to merge[177] with my punk-rock inundated brain. Jeremy Enigk's tireless voice finally began to hollow out its place, however melancholy I became. But, Sunny Day Real Estate was not the only sound around! Jawbreaker, Superchunk, Mineral, Boys Life, Directions In Music... Milwaukee's The Promise Ring, Chicago's Tortoise, D.C.'s Fugazi, non-Austinian Texas Is the Reason, Denver's Christie Front Drive, Seam's seamless "Autopilot," and Built to Spill's architectural melodies of mayhem sounded out across the country. But the list is borderless... sorry to all I can't mention here. Five bucks got you in to most shows, where your favorite bands stood inches away and "rocked your face off!" And then, there was Jawbox! Perhaps, one of the greatest shows ever played, anywhere—they actually played better at the Metro in Chicago, but the energy and sound in Green Bay wrecked

---

[177] Side note about Merge Records: McCaughan and Ballance of Superchunk (band) founded the independent label in 1989, which has produced reissues of Dinosaur Jr.

music history forever! Okay, okay, there were a few other shows that were *almost* as good!

My life was not terribly unlike "emo" music—always grasping for something it could never quite apprehend. My college education was no different. Unfortunately, in many respects, I attended college against my desire. I said unfortunately, because really, how blessed was I to have an opportunity to go to school with financial assistance? My father's offer had come to "use it or lose it" terms, however. So, against my belief in the necessity of higher education or hoofing with the herd through the career corral, I sought out the state's best environmental school. At least there, I thought I might bump into something of interest that I could relate to.

I thought wrong. The university was not up to par with my pursuits of nature and creation. If plant biology got any drier, our lab specimens would have shriveled up and croaked! Even my philosophy professor attempted to drown me in boredom with his lofty arrogance. The only course of value I took was an English Composition class, mostly because the professor had enough courage to stand up for her beliefs when I challenged them. And, she was actually willing to discourse with me on my writing, however misunderstood it was. The greatest discipline I received from her was to carry a pocket dictionary at all times—a writer's companion I would learn to cherish, not unlike the Christian's Bible. I kept an eye out for Webster[178]

---

[178] In respect to our postmodern age—the 1864/1884 edition of Webster's Dictionary references Scripture in its definitions!

in old bookstores, thrift shops, and coffeehouse libraries. Albeit, with the ease of my smart phone's dictionary App I've slacked off a bit over time; I suppose I need to tighten up the suspenders on my smarty-pants!

As it was, only one prescription could console my isolation... So, I searched out the local coffeehouse, lit up a smoke, and began to write. Of course, it didn't really matter what I wrote. As long as I was writing, that's what mattered. Only, this college coffeehouse was different from my writing dens of the past. It wouldn't be long before I turned twenty-one and those green glass bottles of ale stole my gaze. And, I suppose it only took one... because the gap between one and too many too often was not a chasm I ever had difficulties crossing. Isolation, depression, and strong drink, it sounds like the curse of writer's block!

But really, I was not okay. I was alone. I was lost in a system I didn't believe in. My dreams had been shattered. And, I didn't know where to turn next. I was hopeless. So, one too many nights fighting with my vacuum cleaner's extension cord wrapped around endless cubicles at the insurance company, and that was it. I'd had it! I yanked my plug, and I walked off the job muttering and kicking through the building. The next morning I went into the campus office and this time I "dis-enrolled" myself. I walked off the campus too. I never felt better!

I moved back home to my mom's with the plan of going to Alaska with my stepbrother in the summer. *Why is it always Alaska?* I think about that now when I hear about people on their quests. But, I just knew it was a long way away, and nobody would bother with me there. I knew there were a lot of trees, mountains, rivers, the ocean, and bears waiting to be discovered. Essentially, it was the farthest, most westerly, and wildest place on the planet I could drive to! Maybe I believed I would find what I was looking for? Maybe I was on a spiritual pilgrimage and just needed a destination? Regardless, I knew where I had to go and nothing was going to stop me.

So, when my stepbrother decided he couldn't go, my now girlfriend saddled up! In the meantime, I worked graveyard at an electronics plant, where I fell asleep soldering my rubber mat to the table. When the smoke caught my supervisor's attention I received a little pat on the back and was encouraged to "keep up the good work!" The real graveyard, however, was the bar we crashed mugs in after we got off work at seven a.m. What a way to wake up the day. And then we started all over again in the afternoon, drinking and playing cards in a friend's basement till just before shift change at eleven.

When spring rolled around, I had hoped my seasons would change too. I'd had enough of the dark smoky basement and the buzzing neon lights at work. I got hired at a large greenhouse and tree nursery. I was excited to work outdoors with the plants, and save money for the awaited Alaska trip in June. My first day on the job didn't go so hot, however; I suppose you have to show up for that. And no, I didn't have a fever. But yes, I did have a minor surgery and a hang…

Another party another night, it just so happened I was starting my coveted new job in the morning. Total idiocy, but I never said twenty-one was the golden age of wisdom!

The house owner and I got "out of control" in his basement smashing beer bottles when someone noticed blood pooling on the concrete floor. Apparently, the base of a bottle got inside my burgundy Vans between my bare foot and sole. It embedded into my heel from the violent jumping and roughhousing. Unbeknownst to me, blood was gushing out of my sneaker. Several partygoers hobbled me up the rickety wooden stairs dragging a trail of blood behind. They washed my foot in the bathtub and tried to wrap it in toilet paper and duct tape (a literal bloodbath). My girlfriend got a quick lesson in driving stick, and as I remember, she did a pretty great job. But despite her concerns, I wouldn't let her take me to the hospital. So, she took me home to my mom's house and put me to bed.

A close friend from Bible college a few years later related the incident this way:

> In all your abominations and acts of harlotry… when you were naked and bare, struggling in your blood. And when I [God] passed by you and saw you struggling in your own blood, I said to you in your blood, 'Live!' Yes, I said to you in your blood, 'Live!' (Ezekiel 16:22, 6)

The next morning was bright and sunny, a beautiful spring day for my first day on the job! Only, my mom received a phone call from my new boss inquiring my whereabouts. When she opened my bedroom door the intoxicating odor of alcohol, blood, and ammonia rushed out filling the hallway. It was 10:00 a.m. and I was still passed out in my "own blood" and urine. My mom could barely handle the mess and the stench. The blood on the carpet and sheets must have shot her back to events of four years earlier. And, when she saw the bloody cocoon of duct tape and black-crusted toilet paper insulating my throbbing foot, she became terrified and upset. A collision of concern and anger erupted. The wooden futon and cotton mattress were saturated with urine—everything had to go. I tried to make it to the shower, but I couldn't bare any weight on my foot. How could I work?

Of course, I could not work. And, I had to make up some lie about stepping off the curb onto some glass while getting the mail. When your (my) alcohol consumption is affecting your responsibilities and personal pursuits, you have a problem. Fortunately, the nursery wasn't too busy yet and my boss was a little aloof. I was a great employee once I got my alcohol straightened out.

Later that day, the doctor's scalpel probed deeper into my heel searching for embedded glass. He fished out some large brown pieces (unmistakably beer bottle). And, I knew that he'd been around long enough to know that my story didn't match up. But he was gracious, and so was God. I kept making it; I was still alive. No matter how hard I tried to drink myself to death, I never did die! Even a drunken overdose with cocaine, and being carried out of a bathroom over one's shoulder the previous New Year's Eve wasn't enough. God wouldn't let me die. Because in the end, that was what I was really looking for. I wanted a final release. I wanted out. I was tired. And I wanted it all to end.

Somehow, my prayer did get answered. I began to climb out of my black hole and shake off winter's heavy coat. The sun resurrected[179] and spring began to bloom. My seasons were changing. My new job caretaking living organisms in nature provoked a healthy response. My desire to be sober became greater than my desire to drink. I even quit smoking before we left on our trip for Alaska, which was amazing considering the miles of road that lay ahead. Really, I had an inner hatred for mixing these impurities into my spiritual quest; that conviction is what truly sobered me up both times. I couldn't live with myself. There was a purist in me that knew my spirituality wasn't absolutely authentic if I couldn't be sober. Of course, I now know that God's grace was at work drawing me to Himself and preparing me for a *great and final release!*

❦   ❦   ❦

Interestingly, as I've recently disclosed to a close friend concerning some of the battles I've struggled with over the past year, the temptation to be drunk has surfaced. Like I said, not to drink, but to *be* drunk—escape reality. As I mentioned in chapter 6 concerning suicidal thinking, and now drunkenness, my discipline "for obedience to the faith"[180] has been tested at a deeper level than ever before. These temptations to commit past sins and practices are new; they cut to the quick. I trust that God has allowed

---

[179] John 11:25—I am the resurrection. Acts 4:33—The apostles bore witness to the resurrection of the Lord Jesus.

[180] Rom 1:5, 16:26.

them in my life for several reasons as I press forward in my calling and yield myself to His work. And without exception, my adversary (Satan) stands in great resistance to *Phoenix Road*. Yes, the battle wages!

What I am really excited to share with you, however, is how God comforted me: "You never would have made it through this year if you'd have been drinking."[181] Why is that comforting? For three reasons mainly: (1) I had been obedient to His conviction to not drink; (2) Therefore, I was ready to respond to life's curve ball; and (3) He said, I *never* would have made it—that is true, I never would have. He *knows* me, my strengths, my weaknesses, and He knows what's inside my heart![182] Isn't that encouraging? He knows that "but by the grace of God,"[183] there go I. It was His grace that set me free from slavery to those addictions and sins, and it is His grace today that keeps me walking in that freedom. Why does Paul boast of God's grace so? I know why. By His grace I stand. Take comfort with me in this truth concerning the tireless battle with our flesh and the adversary of our souls:

> May the God of all grace, who called us to His eternal glory by Christ Jesus, after you have suffered a while, perfect, establish, strengthen, and settle you. (1 Peter 5:10)

---

[181] This may not have been His (God's) exact wording, but it gives you the gist.

[182] Luke 16:15.

[183] 2 Cor 1:12; 1 Cor 15:10.

Amen. God's grace is truly the only way out of the infinite abyss![184]

And, yes, I did go to Alaska...

THE WILD FRONTIER

Alaska was many things; one thing it never lacked, however, was adventure. My girlfriend and I packed up the Pathfinder and rolled out west on the old wagon trail. We followed some old familiar routes and visited a friend in Colorado. Then we headed north and wandered up toward the border. We crossed over into uncharted territory and began our ascent *Into the Great Wide Open.*[185]

My stepbrother did make it to Alaska, by the way. A few years later he mountain biked (no pun intended) with a buddy up from Montana! What an epic ride that must have been; worth waiting for, I'm sure!

But, I couldn't wait. There was a wild world waiting to be explored. New roads, new places, and new spaces begged my discovery. And, new faces! Hopefully, I would grow and evolve into the being I was destined to become. Whatever this trip was going to bring, and wherever it took me, I was ready. My life was wide open, and I wanted it all. My cards were on the table! *What could stop me now?*

---

[184] Infinite Abyss: "Good luck exploring your infinite abyss," (*Garden State* film, 2004). Ironically, Luke uses "abyss" (8:31, the deep) to describe the location a legion of demons did *not* want to go!

[185] In reference to Tom Petty's song "Learning to Fly"—similarly, I had believed that I would know why I was traveling *to God knows where* once I had arrived—off his album *Into the Great Wide Open* (1991, MCA).

Well, a few events did slow us down a bit. The first was a Mountie on a horse at Dawson City during a festival in the Land of Midnight Fun.[186] Apparently, the Royals frowned on too much fun; fining foreigners, citing unknown ordinances for public drinking. But, sin is sin, no matter what time or place, and it will always find you out.[187] That was the first time I ever got a sun tan at 11:00 p.m., though! Once we ferried across the Yukon River and made it through Tent City, we were on the Top of the World Highway! Skirting mountain ridges above tree line, the famed highway traverses clouds and sunrays illuming panoramas of unspeakable glory—like a stroll along celestial shores.

Eventually, we made it to Fairbanks and we had to head for the Arctic! One thing I remember about Alaska, there's a lot of it! Don't let the colored drawings fool you; there's a big country out there! We found that out somewhere beyond the Arctic Circle, well into our Dalton Highway experience. Two blown tires and a goose chase to the mechanic's house in the mud and rain, only to be greeted by his wife with a shotgun at the back door. We were out of luck! No more tread around these parts; we'd have to hitchhike with our spare. But, "We had come this far," so we gambled and caught the first ride heading north.

We arrived in Deadhorse at 1:00 a.m., where we were advised to pound on the door of the local mechanic's metal shop. So, I pounded! Sure enough, he stumbled out

---

[186] www.travelyukon.com/media/newsroom/yukon-feature-stories/ dawson-city-land-midnight-fun.

[187] Num 32:23.

pulling a ball cap over his head, and he was ready to work! He found us a *close* tread and size, and we were back on the road setting up our tent by 2:30 a.m. Travelers were few and far between. So just in case someone happened along, we piled up stones into an arrow pointing south in front of our tire. We never did make it to the Arctic Ocean. We tried to rest as we watched the sun's shadow graze the horizon on our tent wall and circle 'round again. What a thrill we got when the ground started to rumble! A herd of caribou came straight down the highway (a diked gravel road) as we sat in amazement a few feet by. With the warmth of morning an old overloaded Subaru putted up. And after we shared some camp stove beans, lassoed a few ropes, and made a few more rearrangements… we rolled and bumped back down Dalton's shaled spine.

Later that day, we got our rig straightened out and we were back on the road. "So what if our tires don't match and our tranny whines up the climbs!" I had a gut instinct when I took the guide book's advice: duct-tape, bailing wire, and gasoline. Life in Alaska had one motto: "You gotta do what you gotta do!" Things could have been worse. But, I got a scare as we made our way into a remote village, when my girlfriend crumpled over in abdominal pain. She cried violently as she rolled from side to side in the fetal position in the back of the truck. With the help of an Alaskan Indian woman, who diagnosed a severe urinary tract infection and gave us some medication, in a few days time we were spared from any worse fears. Living on the road was not always the carefree extravaganza it was chalked up to be. Today, with a few more miles under my belt, I thank God for His merciful hand that guided and sheltered us along the way.

❦   ❦   ❦

The Talkeetna Blue Grass Festival sung more blue notes than expected. My behavior shook myself, and my girl-friend. Maybe it was a protective instinct? Or, maybe it was fear? Either way, when a neighboring camper opened our front door and entered our truck to steal something while we were sitting on the tailgate, I came unglued. The next thing I knew a torn case of beer was flying up in the air, and they were pinned on the hood in a fury of shouting. And as clearly non-locals, onlookers' glaring eyes immedi-ately pinpointed us. I sat in the back of the truck shaking for hours, upset with addiction's reign over my neighbor and my own reaction. "I would have given it to them, if they would have just asked!" Disappointment droned out the festival's merriment. I was reminded of punching a hole in the wall as my mom and I argued months earlier. I might as well have been back in Wisconsin; the curse of my old habits had followed me all the way to the end of The Wild Frontier.

I couldn't run. I couldn't hide. I could not escape. There was nowhere left to go. There was no more *west* in the road! I had to face myself.

We had to stop. I needed to be still. I needed to settle into the vision for our trip. We set up camp outside of town along the Talkeetna River across from Denali National Park, home to Mt. McKinley. Several rivers joined at this unique juncture, giving Talkeetna its name: "Where the rivers join."[188] Alaskan Indians believed this site held great spiritual significance. My experience offered me the same conclusion. Granted, there was some danger to camping, as several campers were washed away in their sleeping bags with the rising tide of the river. Though they were spared by a jet boat, I'm sure they were terrified awaking to a white water ride! But as I said, Alaska was full of untamed adventure!

Sunrise was the best time to catch McKinley before the veil concealed his majesty. I sat cross-legged at the river's edge worshiping the creator and giving thanks for creation. I penned some offerings of poetry and sat still with my eyes closed meditating on my journey. The vision of my eagle had been appearing again, and when I opened my eyes the water had receded back a few feet. An amazing rock shaped like an eagle head lay at my feet. My calling was secure. The creator was speaking to me. I was still on my path. I was still "Learning to Fly" as I journeyed further *Into the Great Wide Open...*[189]

❧   ❧   ❧

A few days later, I had another bear encounter... Not like the brown bear charging through the open field, or the cub chasing me into the truck with a nice dive as he stood up and put his paws on the rear glass. Nor the daily wake-up

---

[188] Talkeetna is an Alaskan Indian word meaning "where the rivers join": www.talkeetnahistory.org/.

[189] Another reference to Tom Petty's iconic song "Learning to Fly"— depicting the struggles inherent to *flight without wings*—off his album *Into the Great Wide Open* (1991, MCA).

call of the local black bear sliding down a nearby poplar tree breaking off dead branches. But the "spirit of the bear" had captivated my awareness, and I knew the creator wanted to speak to me through the bear, or bring some element of the bear's spiritual power into my life. In my worship of animals, the bear (representing land and earth) was directly across from the eagle (representing winged and sky). I was open to this movement however intense it might be, despite the conflict that might result. After all, bears are wild animals with pointy teeth, and they're big! And, they're fast! But, I knew I needed to overcome my fear and welcome this unknown into my life. Besides, what was the worst thing that could happen; salmon were running upstream offering themselves daily.

I awoke early for a "spirit-walk." I crossed the train trestle over the river and ambled along the tracks through the dense forest. The vegetation was thick; the rainy season had begun. A slight mist dampened the earth. The forest was quiet and still. Actually, I started to have that eerie feeling like I knew there was something else around. A path into the woods beckoned me to explore. My natural instinct flashed red, but my spirit was calling me deeper into the forest. The light along the tracks grew dim behind me. And then, I heard a faint noise. I paused, waiting, listening... I stepped. I paused again... Nothing, no sound, no movement. Maybe I was imagining it. No, I knew I heard something. I *knew* there had to be a bear nearby; my spirit told me so. I took another half-step. Some green underbrush moved. I froze. A large black mass, like a Volkswagen Beetle, began to move out into the trail. I half-stepped backward trying not to make eye contact. I was awed in disbelief as if I'd just witnessed a miracle. Then I realized the severity of my situation.

I was forty feet from the world's largest bear, forty feet from the tracks, and another four hundred and forty from the bridge. Running didn't seem to be an option. So, I stood still, calmed myself, and tried to be at rest in the bear's space. Admittedly, the bear seemed to have an upper hand, or paw. But, I stood my ground. We had a stare-off, only I didn't stare; I did keep my head raised, though. An unknown period of time passed. And at some point, I felt I had transitioned into a peace agreement with her. So, when she finally dropped her head as to give me the "Okay," I gave her the nod! No, I didn't! I slowly backed myself out and down the path. I was awed and shaking as I hobbled the tracks back to the bridge. I took a few glances over my shoulder just to make sure. Perhaps I wasn't as selfless as a salmon!

❧   ❧   ❧

Before we departed, a letter postmarked in Hawaii arrived General Delivery from my neighbor in Colorado a few years earlier. (Just to clarify, before personal email devices, that meant she really wanted to communicate!) The timing of her letter in connection with this bear encounter penetrated my spirit. And, a friendship was born that set the distant horizon aglow with a warm question mark.

Meanwhile, the rain was beginning to drive us mad. The tarp overhead and the irrigation ditch I dug around the tent were not enough. One can only sleep in a soggy sleeping bag for so long. We were wet, worn out, and our romance was waning. Bussing tables at the roadhouse and tossing pizzas had earned us enough gas money to set out for the lower forty-eight. My spirit was content. I'd experienced what I'd needed to: my eagle rock, the bear, some sacred writing, I had crafted a new medicine wheel, and I had surrendered my drinking because I desired to. Coincidently, it was also here in the pouring rain that I witnessed a youth group enactment of the gospel. So, we wrung out our tent, packed up our Rubbermaids, and hitched up our farewell to The Rainy Frontier! I fired up the Pathfinder, and we set our eyes on sunnier skies…

COAST TO COAST

We shot down the ALCAN (Alaskan Highway) and dropped into B.C. Every border we crossed seemed like we were closer to civilization, and closer to home. We enjoyed the grandeur of Whistler and the greenery of Vancouver. And, we must have stopped in Seattle. But ultimately, our destination was Ashland, Oregon, and the California coast. We had an invitation from friends renting a house in Ashland to crash for a while and recharge in the energy field. Mt. Shasta's etheric crystal emanating nearby[190] was a vortex for vagabonds and gurus.

I think we were both disappointed with Ashland. Maybe we had "traveled" too far and seen too much, or

---

[190] New Age significance of Mt. Shasta: /www.mslpublishing.com/about-mt-shasta.htm; or spiritualharmonics.blogspot.com/2010/10/mt-shasta-etheric-om-crystal-activation.html.

maybe our spirits were trodden under reality? Or, maybe we were too sober? Spiritually speaking, I was skeptical of anything other-worldly happening there that wasn't anywhere else. Lithia Park and the Japanese Garden were a highlight, and the drive we took out to the swimming quarry in their old Volvo wagon with the dogs was nice. The simple things seemed to be all that remained—all that was pure. Even my friend's buddy crashing on his longboard skateboarding down a mountain was pure. A little bloody, and he tore up his new patchwork pants somersaulting down the asphalt, but it was real; I suppose I could say it was really pure! My Phoenix Motel detour, en route from Portland on my motorcycle a few years later, offered a refreshing float down the Rogue River—it was very pure. Meanwhile, our transient lifestyle was not, and our wanderlust had lost its luster.

We continued down to California, enjoying the warmth of the Pacific coast. Can anyone ever get enough of that stretch of road? We hit a detour at Santa Cruz. It's funny how that's as far as I got years earlier on my trip. There must have been an invisible roadblock standing in my life, like Balaam's angel.[191] As we sat on a blanket rubbing our toes in the golden sand, warming our bones, and starring at the sun's reflection off the waves, our tide moved in like an ocean gulf. Perhaps God was parting the "Red Sea?"[192] We looked into each other's eyes, shared some softly spoken words, and agreed. So, we stood up, shook

---

[191] Balaam encountered a roadblock on his donkey—the Angel of the LORD (Num 22:21-31).

[192] Ex 14:21-22.

the sand off our blanket, and drove home.

Home, yes, back to Wisconsin. I know, it's not even near "coast to coast," but hey! The transmission on the Pathfinder wouldn't have made it anyway! And I know for certain, our gas budget wouldn't have! Besides, we weren't in The Wild Frontier anymore; we couldn't live off Jiffy and wild raspberry sandwiches!

❧   ❧   ❧

I traveled farther and faster as the miles rolled by. My mind and spirit were racing. I had been released to my pursuit. I was going somewhere. I was ready for the next step, something deeper, something beyond me. My mind had met reality; the time was now. I was ready for my *final release*.

We stopped in Nevada to visit my stepbrother. Seeing a familiar face in our barren desert was needful. We sat in his van parked on the side of the road talking. I couldn't explain it really; and I wasn't even exactly sure what I meant, but I was certain I was about to "shatter all forms and boundaries of existence."[193] The road lay straight ahead.[194] I was ready for arrival. The Pathfinder was coming home.

---

[193] I uttered this phrase to my stepbrother in or near Elko, Nevada (circa 9/1/97). Worth noting is a similar phrase I found while researching a paper on cults for seminary in May, 2010: "Shatter all sense of limitation," from *The "I AM" Discourses*, vol. 3, #10 (Saint Germain Press, 1940), p. 122.

[194] Straight: Isa 40:4, 45:2; Luke 3:5; Heb 12:13. Similarly: narrow is the gate and difficult is the way which leads to life (Matt 7:14).

9

A GREAT FIRE

I SET THE ROCK ON HER TABLE. There was only one person I could share my spiritual journey with upon coming home. She was the only one who would understand. And, she might even have some insight to offer. When I explained about the eagle rock and the vision I had at "the joining of the rivers" under McKinley's shadow, she became electric. Part of me didn't want to boast, but *another man* inside begged to speak his voice. When I set the rock on the table she was struck with awe and certainty, as if something she knew or had been waiting for had finally appeared. With this knowledge a power and authority came over her—*another woman* I had not known. She affirmed my experiences and acknowledged the creator calling me through the eagle. She confirmed what I knew.

What she did next I did not know… but my ravenous spirit yearned as I opened myself wholly to the creator. I kneeled in the center of her living room as she circled around me with burning sage and a sacred eagle feather. She performed a Native American ritual offering me to the Great Spirit (I faintly recall her speaking in a native or foreign tongue). Fear and power came over me. My mind burned with clarity. I became one with my vision. I locked eyes with my eagle.

My relationship with my mother was not so sacred. The events of her divorce years earlier had consummated her faith in Jesus Christ. By now, she had become outspoken in her "religion." Her Christianity had continued to become a great contention between us. Over the next two months she increasingly represented a last remaining obstacle on my path toward a "transcendental release" or a "movement beyond my existence." Of course, it was not her directly, but the God whom she worshiped and who indwelt her by His Holy Spirit. Truly, He was my obstacle. The Bible's portrayal of Christ was accurate: the chief cornerstone, rejected and despised, a stumbling block and rock of offense.[195] I did not know it, but I was stumbling over Christ the Cornerstone.

❦   ❦   ❦

Upon returning home I had a very dramatic spiritual experience. While worshiping the Great Spirit on the hill (high place) I mentioned in chapter 6, I saw a vision of a "being of light" moving toward me on another dimensional plane. The crystal in my palm became an offense between this

---

[195] Cornerstone: Ps 118:22; Isa 28:16; Matt 21:42; Mark 12:10; Luke 20:17; Acts 4:11; 1 Pet 2:6-7. Stumbling Block: Isa 8:14, 57:14; Jer 6:21; Ezek 3:20; Rom 9:32-33; 1 Cor 1:23; 1 Pet 2:8.

being and me, and as I became aware of this it seemed to jump or spring out of my hand. This negative response was foreign. I had carried this crystal at all times, and it had always represented a "positive energy." But, this being was not interested in my rocks and my ephemeral fleshy notions. It had approached me; this being was interested in me.

Not long after, a comfortable warmth streamed through me. My nerves released and my spirit opened (I had entered into some form of a relational experience with this being). I abandoned myself freely as I disrobed[196] in an act of worship. I felt moved or invited to come down from the hill into the long dewy grass. A shift occurred as I entered into a trance-like enactment of a wild animal. Untamed raw power coursed through me, as if I was a tiger stalking its prey on all fours. I remember being so hot, as if I was burning up from an internal fire, and yet I could faintly see my breath in the autumn night air. When I came out of the trance and ascended the hill to gather my clothes, I was very chilled and disoriented. I was also grateful for my socks! My crystal was over ten feet away.

I hesitated to relate this incident, even vaguely, and several others that will follow; but again, I'm trusting God's discernment as He clarifies my journey. And, my concern is not so much with preserving my own reputation, as it is with allowing God to pave my road to redemption as

---

[196] Unclothing oneself is most commonly *naturistic*; however, Scripture does cite several examples of "nudity" and prophesying: 1 Sam 19:24; 2 Sam 6:14, 20-22; Isa 20:2-3; Mic 1:8. See the following "Christian Naturism" blog for related debate: http://thebiblicalnaturist.blogspot.com/.

it actually occurred. As we continue on this road, I want to point out a repeating signpost: CAUTIONARY, no doubt—take notice of the shift occurring from my pursuit, to me being pursued. Likewise, any *shifts* occurring in the spiritual realm must be highly regarded. Fortunately for believers, God has gifted us with spiritual discernment.[197] In summary, I was awed by this universal oneness I was experiencing with the Great Spirit in creation. I didn't fully comprehend whom I was worshiping or where it was leading, but I was moved and empowered in a forceful new way, and I wanted more.

On my walk home, however, I became a little anxious as I saw my shadow under a streetlight and felt totally separated from him (that person, me). I remember having a conversation with myself about him, and who he was and was not? By the time I made it home I felt unified in my body again. For some unknown reason, I woke my mom and told her about my powerful experience. I never shared my spirituality with her; I didn't agree with her Christianity, and I knew she didn't understand my beliefs. But, this night I felt I needed to share; maybe it was that *boastful man*, or maybe it was an unconsciously frightened youth? Or, maybe it was both? Perhaps God's sovereign hand moved me to share so my mother could pray more effectively. Regardless, her women's prayer group at church

---

[197] The Holy Spirit makes spiritual discernment available to the believer: 1 Cor 2:14; Heb 5:14; Phil 1:9; Prov 2:3. Note: the "believer" is a Christ-follower who has been regenerated by the Holy Spirit.

continued to intercede[198] for me. Not to mention, when I pulled into the driveway returning home from Alaska, she removed her "GPS" prayer pendant (an angel) from the bottom of my seat. I laughed at her foolishness, but she just smiled and said it was all the prayers of God's people that had brought me home safe. Safe or not, I was on a mission; she could believe what she wanted.

A few months later, after my conversion, she told me how she had become fearful that night in my presence for the first time. She confessed to physically experiencing some kind of spirit or spiritual movement (a "woosh") coming forth from me as I woke her and entered her room. It had been a little surreal explaining the vision to her, and I wasn't sure she understood it; she did know it was real and powerful. The next morning I sensed a greater release and independence. It was time to move out from under her roof so I could worship the creator freely and not be hindered by her Christianity. I felt empowered by an authority greater than myself. I had to obey my calling. And as I stated above, her Christ had become my stumbling block; and since God is the immovable, unchanging rock that He is—it was I who had to go!

My girlfriend and I were no longer together either. It was a difficult decision, but I knew I needed to let her go and fully embrace my spiritual path. I remembered reading how it was "better to have loved and let go, than never

---

[198] Intercession: 1 Sam 2:25; Isa 53:12; Rom 8:26-27, 8:34; Heb 7:25. See example with Abraham and Lot: Gen 18:23-33 (19:29).

to have loved at all,"[199] but it wasn't that easy. The heart never is! When you truly care for another's well-being and you've intimately shared your life with that person, how can "letting go" be simple? (The letting-go and loose-grip discipline became a long winding road for me, even as a believer.) Nevertheless, I let her go; and I believed it was an act of love to do so, not jeopardizing her will or destiny. Was I selfishly pursuing my calling? Maybe. Either way, my river ran straight ahead, and I couldn't take her down the next stretch. Although I made an attempt downstream, they were never her rapids to run.

I was on my own now. My road was all that lay ahead. Nothing and no one could stand between me and *my calling*. No one could alter my course. My direction was set. Destiny awaited my arrival! It was time to "shatter all forms and boundaries of existence."

ANGELS OF LIGHT

I bowed down to the earth as I crawled into the sweat lodge from the west. My mentor invited me to the "healing" ceremony held by a Native practicing group on sacred ground in the country. The fire-keeper brought seven glowing Grandfathers, or Elders (rocks), into the round dome representing Mother Earth's womb of healing (or rebirth). Seven more stones were added during each of the

---

[199] See article by John Buri, PhD, on Tennyson's quote: "Better to have loved and lost..." for a healthy perspective at: www.psychologytoday. com/blog/love-bytes/201101/tis-better-have-loved-and-lost-not-really.

"four doors," or rounds, throughout the ceremony[200] (see footnote for symbolization). Offerings, prayers, visions, chants, words of guidance, and songs sung in native tongues were shared amongst the circle. My willingness to attend was guided by my desire to experience the Great Spirit's power in a greater way. I considered it an honor and right to be included in the ceremony.

I yielded my spirit and my mind to the creator as the ceremony moved into its last door. I had yet to experience anything obviously supernatural in the previous doors. I sat cross-legged and erect before the twenty-eight glowing elders burning in the black sacred space. I sensed others' discomfort as the air sweltered and began to burn and choke our lungs of breath. I closed my eyes in meditation as the heat rose intensely. I ascended with it—higher above the ceiling, the lodge, the field and earth, higher into black space. A radiant light met me, not so much a "being" as I had previously encountered (coming on a horizontal plane), but a white light streaming over me like a cylindrical shower descending from heaven (vertically). My body regulated and my breathing relaxed. Clarity filled my mind as my spirit resonated with the vibrant rhythmic energy flooding over me. Some time passed as I rested in the light. At some point, I sensed a voice telling me to open my eyes; I was amazed to see worshipers' faces driven between their knees, their lips pressed to the earth drinking in any cool air remaining in the ground.

---

[200] Four doors symbolize the four directions, and seven stones symbolize completeness or complete direction, including: the four (N, S, E, W), plus Above, Below, Within.

Mother Earth slowly drew me back to the womb with her unbearable heat. The ceremony leader brought us to a close—we were complete.

The door opened. A rush of air filled my lungs like cool water. Dew glistened on the field grass surrounding the quaint earthy dome. Worshipers gathered around a fire as my eyes roamed the horizon and made their gaze heavenward. *Had anyone else seen it?* Stars radiated overhead, showering the Galaxy with light. I felt small, insignificant, and weak. *Who was out there?* Yet, I was awed and inspired by an overwhelming sense of destiny in the universe. *Why me?*

This experience in pursuit of "healing power" thrust me further out into the unknown world of spirits (supernatural beings, forces, energies) and spirituality. As I reflected on this encounter, I again was struck with awe and amazement that something or someone out there was initiating toward or upon me. After being empowered by this "light-force," another greater authority released itself in my life the following days. Anticipation and urgency clutched my mind, and my voice emboldened. Power was becoming my sustenance, often replacing food. The need for more power pressed me harder over the weeks ahead. Desperation and hunger drove me.

In regards to the sweat lodge practice, I've included this quote from *Christianity Today*: "The practice of the sweat lodge and its rituals are not restricted to merely medical [pursuit] of healing, but [are] in essence a way to contact and communicate with the spirit world through shamanism."[201] Interestingly, this quote is from The Band Council of Oujé-Bougoumou (largely Christian Native community) of Quebec regarding the dismantling of a Cree sweat lodge. The identifying word *shamanism* is key as I referenced in chapter 8. Ultimately, the sweat lodge ceremony is an open door to unknown spirits, mediums, and hosts. Of course, I cannot know or judge others' motivations, but my experience simply offers a documented encounter of a supernatural type. Again, my hope is that in relating my experience the footsteps of my spiritual path are illuminated. And although my steps may not be absolutely identifiable, and may generally be likened more accurately unto a process, I believe distinct guidelines and boundaries have and will result as my journey unfolds.

❦ ❦ ❦

In discerning the nature of the two "lights," the following possibilities might offer some clarity: (1) The lights were demonic spirits masquerading as *angels of light*, or (2) The lights were actual manifestations of the Christian God. As regarding angels of light, the Bible declares that: "Satan himself transforms himself into an angel of light" (2 Corinthians 11:14). Coincidentally, a New Age bookstore I frequented also included "Angels" and "Light" in its name. In reference to God manifesting as light, the Bible cites Christ as the "light of the world," the "light that illuminates the heavenly city," and the "light that shone down

---

[201] See article by Trevor Persaud: "Sweat Lodge Prayers: Native Christians Wrestle with Faith and Tradition" at: www.christianitytoday.com/ct/2011/april/sweatlodgeprayers.html.

from heaven" knocking Saul to the ground as he traveled to Damascus.[202] Paul also exhorts the believer to "put on the armor of light" in Romans (13:12). This list says nothing about the light emanating from God as seen by Moses, Isaiah, Ezekiel, John, the writer of Hebrews,[203] and others. In both of these encounters with a "light," I could make a case for Christ; however, based on motivation, context, and fruit produced, I am under the conviction that the "lights" I encountered were more likely demonic. Where as Saul's light produced immediate conversion, mine drew me further into darkness—that indicator alone sheds light on the matter!

BLACK-WINGED BIRD

I lined the interior with red corduroy. Finally, after twenty-four hours enslaved to a borrowed sewing machine, a masterful "medicine bag" slung out! Now my sacred objects for worship had a sacred hearth slung over my shoulder as I journeyed into the outdoors. My little apartment and wardrobe began to resemble those colors also—black and red. Red for the center of the earth (Mother Earth's womb), and all that was sacred. Red for indigenous peoples, and

---

[202] Christ is the light: John 8:12, 9:5, 12:36, 12:46; 1 Tim 6:16; 1 John 1:7. The Lamb lights New Jerusalem: Rev 21:23, 22:5; Isa 60:19-20. Saul's conversion by the Lord of light: Acts 9:3-5, 22:6, 26:13.

[203] Ex 33:22, 34:29-30, 34:35; Heb 1:3; Rev 1:16.

the soil of the Land Down Under.[204] And, red for life and blood.[205] And, black.

I entered my sacred space each morning by the north gate wearing my black pelted-fleece jacket and woolly black brimmed hat. The small woods west of town (The Oak Grove referenced in chapter 6) had become my sanctuary for worship. In my daily travels I had become aware of a group of crows traveling from tree to tree. I started to take notice of these illusory magicians after a few flying stunts and disappearing acts caught my eye. I quickly learned they were aware of my interest, as their seductive iridescent lure became more magical. When these black-winged messengers[206] began waiting outside my door in the morning, I had to ask.

I was forced to come down off my ladder while at work painting when a ferocious shift in the weather tore through the neighborhood. A black cloud circled and swooped, multiplying in the rushing wind; my boss's dog began to bark violently. She scurried home leaving the dog behind. The midnight host descended overhead and flocked a towering maple. My answer had come. I sat

---

[204] I had enrolled in a NOLS course in NW Australia—see National Outdoor Leadership School at: www.nols.edu/courses/locations/australia/. My primary interest was the spirituality of indigenous Aborigines; after my conversion I canceled the trip.

[205] Lev 17:11 states that "the life of the flesh is in the blood," which is an amazing and true statement proven by modern microbiology; however, that this blood is necessary for atonement for sin (a clear picture of the necessity of Christ's sacrifice) is of even greater reach and scope.

[206] Job 12:7—Ask… the birds of the air, and they will tell you; (cited in reference, not as a matter of truth).

silently under their tree as the storm darkened, offering my will and opening my spirit to nature's hurling winds. Once playful and friendly, the dog's hair now stood up in fear as she barked at my face and clawed at my arms and legs. I continued to sit silent; apparently, I had become an unknown threat-of-nature too.

A few days later, at the park's edge neighboring the woods, I watched a mature tree being uprooted from the earth by an enormous steel spaded extractor. After the massacre ceased and the machinery rolled out, I walked over to the gaping hole to pray and give an offering of tobacco (Native practice). At the edge of the oak grove before the grassy park I stopped in awe. A full-bodied crow lay dead; wings spread wide open with its breast facing the sky. It appeared lifelike, as if it had just dropped out of the sky. I knew the creator had accepted my offering of myself under the tree a few days earlier, and he was inviting me to walk in the spirit and power of his black messengers. I carefully plucked seven feathers from the wings and tail, and laid the bird to rest in the vacant grave with my offering and filled it with earth. I had become the tree the "murder of crows" had crowned.[207]

I returned home at once to create my new medicine wheel in honor of the black-winged bird. I pulled some sage from a bundle drying overhead to burn as a ritual cleanse before I asked the Great Spirit for guidance in creating the wheel. An album surfaced by Counting Crows

---

[207] "Murder/flock of crows": poetic, fifteenth century? Birds symbolizing wickedness: Ezek 31:12-14, 32:3-8; Dan 2:36-38, 4:11-16; Matt 13:4, 13:19, 13:32; Mark 4:4, 4:32; Luke 8:5, 13:19.

days earlier (go figure). "Rain King," a song I had not been previously enamored by now soothed my spirit with its morose melody and enchanting chorus about heaven, dying, a black-winged bird, and God.[208]

Of worth noting here is where Counting Crows got their name: "The band took its name from a divination rhyme about the crow, heard by Duritz [vocalist] in the film *Signs of Life*."[209] Obviously, I am not contributing my meditations or actions in any way to the band's music, or that the artists themselves are diviners, or motivated by demonic musings. However, the mentioning of a "divination rhyme" coupled with "Rain King's" lyrics stood out amongst my research today. Coincidentally, Wikipedia suggests the song's "title is a reference to Saul Bellow's *Henderson the Rain King*,"[210] which itself has spiritual underpinnings. Interpreted objectively through a biblical lens, I would have to say potential clearly exists for spiritual influence beyond or outside of Christ in Counting Crow's music.[211]

Moving beyond music, the truth is that blackbirds, crows, and ravens have been instrumental in divination

---

[208] "Rain King" by Counting Crows, off *August and Everything After* (1993, Geffen).

[209] Found at Wikipedia (http://en.wikipedia.org/wiki/Counting_Crows); cited from *Rolling Stone* article: "The Biggest New Band in America," June 30, 1994.

[210] See Wikipedia article "Rain King," accessed January 22, 2013: http://en.wikipedia.org/wiki/Rain_King_(Counting_Crows_song).

[211] Also see article quoting Duritz as having a dissociative disorder, which makes the world seem not real: BBC article "Talking Shop: Counting Crows" by Mark Savage (March 27, 2008) found at: http://news.bbc.co.uk/2/hi/entertainment/7315441.stm.

for centuries. The old European rhyme en-quote above only evidences this fact. These pagan practices of antiquity are not without significance; inherently diviners still peer through such windows today. If you recall my reference to blackbirds and Satan regarding Scriptural symbolism in chapter 4 (footnote 81), these identifying parallels can now be seen clearly as they manifested in my life. This symbolism is real. Satan is a factual being present in reality. "Yes," a spirit indeed; but, a being nonetheless.

※　※　※

My spiritual process continued en route toward greater authority and power. Obvious to any onlooker, one might have questioned the switch from the "light" (white power orientation) to worshiping a blackbird (potentially black magic). I, on the other hand, was blind to such logical analysis in the pursuit of power. My deception lay in the pursuit of "healing power." Again, logically speaking, I never would have worshiped Satan outright or pursued black magic. Healing power and light appeared healthy. Satan is an illusive artisan, however, and masquerades effortlessly. White power is no less evil than black.

Again, Satan is a pernicious tempter. And no one ever said the "fruit" didn't taste sweet! But just remember, those fig leaves really itched![212] Speaking of which, a childhood condition of burning itchy feet after showering (cleansing my body) had suddenly resurfaced; only now it had affected the palms of my hands too. I cannot positively

---

[212] Genesis account of Adam and Eve's fall in the garden of Eden: Gen 3:1-24 (6-7); note: my humor about discomfort is not in the text.

say this was a demonic outbreak (whether purely spiritual or natural/spiritual) in respect to Christ's nail-pierced hands and feet, but I can say I have not experienced this phenomenon since being saved. Of greater significance was the thread of concern it sewed in my conscience.

As the following weeks unraveled, there were several unsettling moments that I could not shake. My conscience was busy stringing these jewels together anticipating a great midnight ball. One particular instance was a psychological breakdown I had at a local coffee house as I sat writing. I was working on a book at the time. After all, when I was not in the woods, I was out about town, living a fairly average life as a fairly likeable guy—on the "down-low," of course. And, friends knew I was into "my thing," but overall my public life appeared relatively common, eccentric perhaps, but common among my peers.

In contrast, my private life was characterized by excessive isolation and introspection. The thought that haunted me as I sat in the local coffee house meditating was: *What if I have to live in this "mind-space" for eternity? What if I die and this "space-of-mind" is still the reality I must live in forever?* I broke down crying, shaken to my core by this foreign fear questioning my psyche. A friend I hadn't seen for sometime asked if I was okay. Clearly, I was not.

Truly, how could a kid who listened to creation's voice and followed birds across town be okay? Again, my intent in relaying these events is to show Satan's progressive overarching induction. Though I believed I was in control of my pursuit of healing power, it was actually Satan who was passionately pursuing me. The Bible accurately characterizes Lucifer's deceptive ploy: "the whole world lies [under the sway of] the wicked one" (1 John 5:19). And, if you've ever tangoed with Lucifer, you know just how alluring he is—an enchanting spirit of deception like none other. Eve's encounter in Genesis 3 clearly reveals his cunning expertise. And, Revelation reaffirms Satan, the Devil, as the one who "deceives the whole world."[213] I'd been duped! I was deceived. And more than that, I was not "okay."

I Have Come for My People

My mentor was not okay either. Her son had recently fallen backward off a cliff to his death. It was around this time that the spiritual battle surrounding my family and close relationships began to really unleash. Eternity's clock was ticking! Not by coincidence, my own father fell from a tree-stand while deer hunting within several days of my salvation. He was spared by God's grace as he fell backward to the ground arching over a large tree root. He was hospitalized for nearly a week, but suffered no major injuries. Satan was not only interested in me; nor does he merely desire you—he is wholeheartedly seeking[214] your friends and family with violent affection.

Consequently, the believer is commanded to: "Put on the whole armor of God, that you may be able to stand against the wiles of the devil" (Ephesians 6:10-18). "For

---

[213] Rev 12:9-11, 20:8, 20:10. Example of Eve's deceit: Gen 3:13.

[214] 1 Pet 5:8-9; Eph 6:11-12; John 8:44.

we do not wrestle against flesh and blood, but against principalities, against powers, against the rulers of the darkness of this age, against spiritual hosts of wickedness in the heavenly places." And, primary to the soldier's armor is his or her saving faith in Jesus Christ—his "helmet of salvation." Perhaps my fragile psyche was cracking under the continual hammering of Satan's chisel; or was it his needle and tweezers as he obsessed over my mind late into the night. Yet, the believer himself is not impervious to the Devil's "fiery arrows." Only, he or she has an effective shield in the heat of battle—his faith.

I must stop and ask, Do you? Do you have faith in a resurrected, eternal Being who is able to keep you? Have you asked Christ into your heart? Is Christ's Holy Spirit dwelling in you as you engage in the active duty of life?

The fact of the matter is we are in an actual battle! Being a twenty-first-century reader, one might be tempted to scoff at the imagery of the "soldier metaphor." But, when the apostle Paul penned his letter to the Ephesians, he was literally imprisoned in chains and being kept under guard by a Roman centurion.[215] The battle was real! It still is! Your and my personal experience is not what dictates this reality. The fact of the matter is I was in a spiritual battle. Did I know it? No. Would I have admittedly believed it? No. But, my conscience was beginning to question and compile single events and concerns that confronted me. I was not processing them logically, but their anxious prodding was becoming an increasingly incessant irritant.

---

[215] Paul's imprisonment: Eph 3:1, 4:1, 6:20; Acts 28:16.

This only fueled the urgency of my pursuit.

Ironically, it was my increasing authority that began to make me feel a little uncomfortable with myself. It had become unnatural; I had become "not me." Events and actions were occurring that I did not have control over any longer. The woods became "my" woods, and I watched it and protected it as a private possession. I was actually a great environmental conservationist, as I mentioned scouring the forest floor of man's refuse in chapter 6 (Creature Rather Than Creator). I had even constructed my own sacred sweat lodge, to which I invited my former girlfriend, and through which I believed the creator was calling her onto his path of healing and rebirth. Fortunately, after a single visit, she continued on her own path.

My altar held a greater control over me now too. It was no longer my altar; I had become enslaved to it. I now had to bow down in worship before it for hours before I felt released. In a very real sense, *I had become the altar!* [216] I was actively engaged in praying for various peoples and events as I moved objects, symbols, and cards around a directional wheel calling on different ruling authorities and spirits to empower me and move others. Interestingly, it was when I called on the Eagle to rush in on

---

[216] Even as the believer is the "temple of the Holy Spirit" (1 Cor 6:19), it should be no shock that Satan also desires to inhabit human beings.

the North[217] wind and moved my card into the Within position (center, complete), that another shift in authority occurred. Within a day or two as I stood washing the dishes, an audible voice spoke within me, and then I spoke out (or it spoke out) hearing *that man* for the first time. I trembled at the brazen dictatorial tone marching out my vocal chords. The command resonated through my spirit and body for days: "I have come for my people."

The Mystery of Life

My book was nearing completion; my riddle was nearly solved. My mind was breaking under the pressure and power driving me. *Who was I becoming? Where was I going? How long could this continue?*

I jumped out of the truck still rolling as it snubbed, grinding to a stop, and conked out in the grass. I tore up the hill (my high place) tripping and crawling out of my headlight's fading glow into the black canopy. Maddened, I hurled myself to my knees. "I have to know!" My fists assaulted the sky with cries and screams casting heavenward. Darkness weighed upon the earth. I wailed through the silence. "You must tell me!" I struck the sky,

---

[217] After years of Bible study, I am amazed at how often I have seen Satan *counterfeit* or attempt to mimic God's ways and order. In my directional worship the <u>North</u> represented the greatest power. In this Bible passage Lucifer is caught in treason, as he desires to reign from God's throne in the <u>North</u>: "For you have said in your heart: 'I will ascend into heaven, I will exalt my throne above the stars of God; I will also sit on the mount of the congregation on the farthest sides of the <u>north</u>'" (Isa 14:13).

breaking the air, smashing and crashing through the night. "My Maker!"[218] My spirit erupted, bursting and rupturing asphyxiated lungs. Heaven's sea of glass[219] shattered as waves rushed forth thrusting my voice skyward. My hill ascended the Mount. My Maker sat captivated. My cry wrung out sounding through eternity: "CREATOR! WHO ARE YOU?"

❦   ❦   ❦

I awoke the next morning still trembling under my red velvet comforter. I slid my bony legs into my dirty blue jeans and threw on my gnarled black fleece and cap. I took flight across town in my black truck and parked at the north gate. Stillness hung in the air. As I made my way across the park toward the wood, snowflakes began to fall and collect on my black furry shoulders. A quietness settled over the earth. My spirit plummeted in my soul as I entered the forest. Tears rolled down my cheeks as I dismantled the sweat lodge. My bones ached as I laid the timbers back upon the earth. I was leaving; no sign of my coming could be left behind.

I exited the woods through the south gate for one last walk through the oaks. The leaves were down; fall was passing too. I circled out to the edge of the grove where I could view the hill one last time. The plush field no longer welcomed me. The mount stood unapproachable. I

---

[218] The prophets reference the "LORD God of Israel" as man's Maker: Isa 17:7; Jer 51:19.

[219] A sea of glass is pictured before God's heavenly throne: Rev 4:6, 15:2.

remembered all the nights, the prayers, the light, the crow, the visions and the tiger. The previous night still echoed in my soul. I stayed in the grove and circled around toward the path heading back into the woods through the south gate. Suddenly, my spirit stopped me in my tracks.

A piece of loose-leaf notebook paper lay on top of the leaves twenty feet ahead before the path. *How did it get here?* Someone had been here since last night. *Who was it? What were they doing here? Why did they enter my grove?* …the diabolic voice drilled my brain burning with anger. But, I knew I had to pick it up, though I did not want to. I didn't want to even go near it. The paper appeared to glow or burn yellow-white with fire or heat energy.[220] Each step I took I became more enraged. As I approached closer I could see writing on it. The paper appeared timeless, faded, rain-soaked and worn, yet pristine and radiant? I *knew* this message was for me. Fear seized me as I stepped nearer? I crouched down slowly with the snowflakes to the loosely crinkled paper aloft the dried leaves. My hand began to burn as I extended my arm. Rage coursed through my blood. Hatred burned in my heart as I grasped the divine message.

Graphite reflected and shone forth brightly as I unfolded the silver-lined letter. To my horror and confusion, my divine message was a pencil rubbing of an embossed Bible cover. Not just any Bible, but the cover of a Good News

---

[220] I have now interpreted this phenomenon as God's *shekinah glory* (holy presence), or likened it to Moses' experience with the burning bush (Ex 3:2) and the Angel of the LORD. See "The Shekinah [Hb.—Sh'cheenah] Glory" at: www.bible-history.com/tabernacle/TAB4The_Shekinah_Glory.htm.

Bible with the symbol of an open book like bird wings at the bottom. I knew immediately that this was the exact gold Bible I had been given when I was "confirmed" in junior high. The same Bible I consciously discarded into the trash bag when I emptied my bottom desk drawer before leaving home for Colorado. *Who put this here? Who came into my woods? Who is watching me?* Someone had been here, someone who knew me. *Who are you? What do you want?*

❧ ❧ ❧

On the drive home I came to terms with some revelation about how my mother's god must have been trying to inform me that I was actually one with her in my worship and pursuit of the Great Spirit. This brought me comfort, as I knew I would be departing soon, and leaving her on peaceful terms was truly my desire. I placed the neatly folded paper on my altar when I arrived. My song continued to play as I sat on the couch silently. The afternoon sun filtered through a plant at a southern window warming the fiery-orange carpet. I settled into my sacred space. I picked up my notebook and began to pen my final chapter of *The Mystery of Life*. I knew what I had to say before I even wrote it (my inner *voice* was clear), but seeing my last written words paralyzed me for good. I couldn't stand. I couldn't move. I sat. I waited for my time.

I dazed in and out of consciousness, or some catatonic state, as I stared at my medicine wheels and sage hanging from the ceiling. The tall slender plant began to sway and move, taking on a seductive female form or voice. Perhaps it was the low light, or perhaps a spirit had embodied it? Coincidentally, however, as I just googled "House Plants," I found that this green and yellow variegated-leafed, pointy plant is commonly called Snake Plant (Mother-in-Law's Tongue). Ah, *Snake Plant!* Medusa must have bit me with her seductive serpentine locks!

The sun would set soon. *Where was I going? Who was coming for me? Was I really God?* Yes, it was true, I AM. I was one with the I AM being within me and in all things: I AM God. This "I AM" is not to be confused with Jehovah or Christ; the "angel of light" is the illusive being behind this uncanny counterfeit.[221]

As I starred through the room, a hazy mist[222] or smoke-type substance appeared swirling before me as a large vertigo spiral. It hovered in the center of the room spinning as I starred into it. As I gazed at it longer, it became more of a tunnel. Its pull beckoned my entrance. I sat still watching and contemplating. At the very conscious moment I determined (volition) to move toward it, stand up, or open myself to it, a *shift* occurred. Before I could even move, it sensed my will's surrender. The swirling, spiraling tunnel turned inside out and funneled toward me as a form of vortex. I continued to sit still; the spirit moved into me, through me, and over me. And then, it

---

[221] Jehovah reveals Himself to Moses as I AM (Ex 3:14); Jesus states that before Abraham was, "I AM" (John 8:58). Angel of light is another reference for Satan (2 Cor 11:14); remember that before Lucifer fell from heaven he was the *most highly exalted cherub*, no doubt a glorious "angel of light" (Isa 14:11-15; Ezek 28:12-19).

[222] Interestingly, the hand of the Lord blinds Elymas the sorcerer by a "dark mist" (Acts 13:11).

was gone? I sat paralyzed on the couch. *AM I God?* I wasn't sure I wanted this power anymore?

I Am God

Darkness fell. Paranoia set in. I waited. I knew it would not be long. Now that the "Mystery"[223] had been revealed, they would come. Everyone knew; I would be found out now. They all loomed; they watched feverishly awaiting my judgment. It was time.

Visions of torture and images of death overcame my mind. Hauntings of another world I had never seen invaded my spirit. Tortured bodies of mutilated flesh pressed in upon me. I couldn't see their faces. They called out for me. *Was I dying?* I sat still on the couch. I could not move. Black shadowed beings passed by in the dark outside. In a few hours it would be Halloween. *Why was this happening now? Why tonight? Where was I going? Who were these beings? Where were they taking me?*

I sat on the couch. A knock at the door horrified me. It knocked again, reverberating in my chest. I sat. Finally, I stood. I made my way to the door. I stood before the door. I put my hand on the knob. I breathed; I made the choice: *Whoever's there, whoever has come for me, I'm willing to go; I'm ready to depart. Wherever they take me… It's time.*

---

[223] Coincidentally, the Bible references the gospel of salvation as a *great mystery* kept secret since the world began, but now made manifest in Jesus Christ (Rom 16:25-26; 1 Cor 2:7; Eph 1:7-9, 3:2-4, 3:8-10, 6:19; Col 1:26-27, 2:2-3, 4:3; 1 Tim 3:9, 3:16).

I turned the brass[224] knob and slowly opened the door to the dark night. The grass, the tree, the night filled my sight, but no person, just the night? I stood in the doorway. I waited for something to pass through me. Nothing. Then a voice: "It's me, Mom."

I stepped out of the doorway onto the walk and saw my mom sitting on a stoop around the corner with her pillow in her arms (apparently, it took me a length of time to answer the door). Suddenly, I shifted and spoke boldly: "What are you doing here? You do not have permission to be here."

She replied firmly, "I'm here, and I'm not leaving," as she stepped up into my doorway.

I seemed powerless to force her to vacate. I was too weak; I was too tired. I sat back down on the edge of the couch where I had spent the afternoon. The hour was approximately 9:00 p.m., October thirtieth, 1997. She sat down adjacent to me, in the only chair. The length of the couch, a black trunk, and silence separated us.

❦   ❦   ❦

A voice reminded me of the letter I had found, and I spoke: "God gave me something for you."

She asked nervously, "What is it?" I said it was on my altar in my bedroom. The door lay open before us into the darkness; my altar was around the corner. I waited a while. I didn't want to get it. Another battle started to

---

[224] Brass or bronze symbolizes judgment in Scripture: Ex 27 (altar and utensils for the tabernacle, used for sacrifice and sin offerings), Deut 28:22-23; Num 21:9; John 3:14.

wage inside me as I contemplated standing up and going to my altar. I hadn't been in there all day. I didn't want to get the letter.

I turned the corner and reached for the folded paper. My hand clenched in anger as my arm burned with fire. Again, my spirit enraged. I calmed and breathed as I approached her. I gave her the message: "This is for you."

She unfolded it with uncertainty. Tears rolled down her cheeks as she stared at the pencil rubbing. "Where did you get this?" she asked.

"In the woods this morning."

She stood up and set it on the trunk in front of me. She said, "I think this is for *you*." She sat back down in her chair holding her pillow in her lap.

I got up and stood in front of her. I looked into her eyes, as if I was a child again, and I spoke. "Mom, do I need to be cautious?"

She looked at me directly and spoke sternly, "Yes son, you *need* to be cautious."

I returned to my cushion.

❦   ❦   ❦

At approximately 11:00 p.m. I became very anxious as visions moved upon me again. I couldn't sense her in the room anymore. The tortures started again. They increased in intensity. Bodies writhing in agony and grappling for life consumed my mind, penetrating my sight. Mangled figures pressed upon me. My mind started to hone in on one figure that I had seen repeatedly throughout the day. The disfigured body became more recognizable. I was caught up into the now trance-like vision; the torturous pain and agony started to pull and tear at my own body. Torment drove me to my knees. I collapsed on the carpet.

His body hung naked and hollow draped like a tent. Ribs and flesh torn open to the air. Blackness shrouded the sky and cloaked the earth. Blood stained His hair disguising the gnarled timber. He looked at me through his bludgeoned disfigured cheeks. I cried out in pain to stop the horror. *Stop torturing me! Stop! Stop killing me!*

My mom said something. All I heard was "Jesus," and "your heart." I remember pleading in anguish, "How?"

He wouldn't stop looking into my eyes. He was dying in front of my face. I was dying with Him.[225] My pain had become the source of His torture. My torment was killing Him in front of my eyes. I couldn't stop the suffering. He struggled for breath. His eyes penetrated my spirit; He saw through my soul. I was utterly undone.[226]

He was dying; He was giving up His spirit for me. He looked into my eyes. His eyes spoke into my heart. I spoke His name from my lips for the first time. I cried out in anguish and tears, wailing and seething in agony. Grief pressed my spirit; sorrow crushed my heart.[227] Hatred pierced my vengeful spirit. I gasped for air, sobbing and bellowing into the carpet. I hit the floor with my fists and kicked and screamed in repentance. *He died for me. Me. Who was I? Why me? It could not be. This could not be real.*

---

[225] Rom 6:4, 6:8; Col 3:3.

[226] Isa 6:5.

[227] The sacrifice God desires is a "broken spirit and a contrite heart": Ps 51:17, 34:18; Isa 57:15, 66:2.

This was not real. But, I saw His eyes look into me. He looked me in the eyes. He saw me. He knew me.

Peace stilled my shaking body. Mercy greeted my soul. Grace comforted my heart. My mom kneeled at my side and prayed over me as I rested. Visions of glory moved in calmly and lifted my shattered spirit. He was alive! Angelic beings hovered about an empty cross. A silver blue sky rose behind bright white clouds, and light emanated heavenward throughout eternity. His presence filled the vision—He was alive. He was dead. And now, He was alive! "I live forevermore."[228] His glory and ascension spoke His voice, "I am the way, the truth, and the life" (John 14:6). "He who believes in Me has everlasting life" (John 6:47).[229] My tongue confessed my faith for the first time.

Eternity's clock struck. My time had come! Heaven's angelic choir rejoiced[230] as the earth quaked: *"I shattered all forms and boundaries of existence!"* Hallelujah! I still rejoice in God's irony today; His ways truly are above and beyond man's finding out![231]

❧　❧　❧

On October thirty-first, 1997, at approximately 1:00 a.m.

---

[228] Rev 1:18—I am He who lives, and was dead, and behold, I am alive forevermore.

[229] Other promises for "He who believes in Me": John 5:24, 6:35, 6:47, 7:38, 11:25, 12:44, 14:12.

[230] Luke 15:10—There is joy in the presence of the angels of God over one sinner who repents.

[231] Job 9:10; Isa 55:8; Rom 11:33.

I died and rose in Christ.[232] I was born again[233] by grace through faith[234] as I believed and placed my trust in Jesus Christ of Nazareth as my personal Savior and Lord. I was nearly twenty-two years old. I was the brother to one sister, and the son to one mother and one father. I now was adopted into the family of God[235] by my heavenly Father and His Son, the Savior of my soul, through the might and eternal power of the only Holy and wise Spirit. Praise be to "He who is the blessed and only Potentate, the King of kings and Lord of lords, who alone has immortality, dwelling in unapproachable light... to whom be honor, glory, dominion, and everlasting power, both now and forever" (1 Timothy 6:15-16).[236] Hallelujah! Amen.

A CONSUMING FIRE

In concluding this chapter, I am speechless. Well, without many words! It must be said, however, that within a short period as I rest upon my knees, the assault came. An arsenal of demonic spirits, voices, images, and lies crashed upon my mind. My mom continued to pray, and

---

[232] The believer has died, been crucified, is buried with, and continues to reckon him/herself "dead in Christ," that he/she might also "walk in the newness of life" through Christ's resurrection (Rom 6:3-11).

[233] Born again: John 3:3, 3:7; 1 Pet 1:23. New creation: 2 Cor 5:17; Gal 6:15. New man: Eph 4:24; Col 3:10.

[234] Eph 2:8—For by grace you have been saved through faith, and that not of yourselves; it is the gift of God.

[235] Adoption into God's family: Rom 8:14-17; Gal 4:5-6; Eph 1:5.

[236] Taken primarily from 1 Tim 6:15-16, with additions from 1 Tim 1:17; Jude 1:25.

185

at some point in the early dawn she gutted my apartment, cramming every inch of her hatchback with my books, idols, rocks, animal cards, medicine wheels, herbs, artwork, music, *and* my writings. Essentially, all that was left of my life was in her car—my whole existence, only hours ago. And as the morning star[237] rose in the east, we left my world behind.

Later in the day, a couple from her church welcomed us at their farm west of town with several other church members. Their autumn "burn pile" fueled the greatest fire my eyes had ever seen. An inferno roared before me devouring everything that caught its flame. I fought through voices and tears, shuddering and struggling to surrender as I laid down my *old man* on the pyre of God's altar "once and for all."[238] Christ's flame consumed my spirit journal by journal, page by page... till all was gone, every word, and every letter. No rock, no wheel, no song, no vision; no man could have survived such a great fire.[239]

Stillness and clarity consumed my mind... *He alone is God. I am not God.* "For the LORD your God is a consuming fire, a jealous God" (Deuteronomy 4:24).[240] He

---

[237] Rev 22:16; 2 Pet 1:19.

[238] "But Christ came as High Priest of the good things to come, with the greater and more perfect tabernacle not made with hands, that is, not of this creation. Not with the blood of goats and calves, *but with His own blood He entered the Most Holy Place once for all,* having obtained eternal redemption" (Hebrews 9:11-12, emphasis). For further citation see: Heb 7:27, 9:28, 10:10, 10:12, 10:14; 1 Pet 3:18.

[239] Burning of magicians' books upon conversion: Acts 19:19. Jehu (King of Israel) destroyed the temple of Baal (pagan idolatrous god) and burned its sacred pillars: 2 Kings 10:21-28.

[240] Deut 4:24, 9:3; Heb 12:29; Ex 24:17.

alone consumes the hearts of men with heaven's eternal blaze. He is the flame. His Spirit is the fire.[241] Forever burning, He never ceases. He alone is holy. He alone is a holy consuming fire.

I stood alone as the coals smoldered; only ashes remained. I turned and stepped away, lifting my gaze westward over the plowed fields, beyond the wood silhouetted black against the horizon. The sky burned like brushfire. The sun's departure consumed every twig and thistle in the land. My search was over. My eyes drew back to a slit in the clouds; a white-winged bird floated through a blue sky[242] and a tear rolled down my cheek. He was there,[243] in my dying and in my rising, in my fire and in my ashes. In my mind and in my heart, He is here. *He is here.*

---

[241] God's Spirit as a tongue of fire: Acts 2:3-4; Isa 30:27.

[242] Of all my writing—being the most difficult thing to let go—a poem I wrote in high school surfaced as I stood facing away from the fire. "White Bird in a Blue Sky" emerged as a hopeful light (symbolic) on the horizon, which later gave flight to a self-published book of poetry (entitled *Arc the Sky*) contrasting the black-winged bird life.

[243] Jehovah Shammah—The LORD Is There (Ezek 48:35).

10

CALVARY ROAD

THE BATTLE DID NOT CEASE. I was not settled. Something within me still caused me to oscillate. My will had chosen Christ, but something in my spirit still retaliated on a gut level (no, not my "flesh"). My mom spoke with the head of prayer ministry at her church who had previous experience with demonic possession. It was agreed that I should be "delivered." We met the following day, with several others who were at the bonfire. The deliverance went peacefully, intense no doubt, but orderly and controlled.

We started by worshiping the Lord with several songs of praise, accompanied by a strumming guitar. Afterward, I was seated on the floor (I think I was on a white sheet). The woman performing the deliverance kneeled in front of me and explained what she was going to do, and asked if I had any questions. The others kneeled beside and around me. Then she looked me straight in the eyes and asked me several questions. I was aware of an inner struggle by the spirit[244] trying not to make direct eye contact with her, to no avail. The light had been turned on; there was no place to hide. The Lord seemed to be staring directly through her into my soul. The spirit finally had no choice but to submit and lock eyes; its obedience, however, was well disguised by its prideful revolt. She must have known she was looking at the spirit at this point, because she asked it its name. When the spirit presented itself as "Beast,"[245] she simply commanded it to come out by Jesus' authority.

Every pore in my skin and body opened up to let this Beast out. He came out charging like a steam train with

---

[244] This struggle represented the separating or *disintegration* taking place as the possessing spirit was being identified, isolated, and differentiated from "me," yet was still within me. This spirit/s was so familiar or natural to my nature/person, as though it were actually part of me as far as my experience or awareness could have determined, and yet once evicted, it was *not* "of me" obviously. In a practical, or functional sense, then, this spirit was inseparable from "me," though theoretically not "of me."

I find this same process in effect regarding the Spirit-filled, in-dwelt Christian as he/she becomes sanctified and transformed by the Holy Spirit—this seemingly "naturalness" of the supernatural/spiritual relationship. The Spirit inhabits the believer as a temple, yet the believer is not "One" with, or God, however. Though this inhabitation by the Holy Spirit does *not* correlate uniformly with *possession* and is characterized by the guidelines of mutuality in relationship, a correlation does exist necessarily.

Therefore—that this bond of unity/oneness appears inherent in such matters of being possessed or a state of possession, and can perhaps be seen in the acting individual's volitional commitment to or with said spirit whereby such agreement unifies not only the will, but the whole being, through an immediate exchange or a process of *integration*—I have identified this phenomenon as *Spiritual Integration*, or *Disintegration* as used above. Of greater assistance would be the defining of "possession."

[245] Interestingly, "beast" is used several times in Scripture to characterize demonic activity, Satan, or the Antichrist: Dan 4:16; Rev 11:7, chaps. 13–20.

a growlish roar that seemed to fill the vaulted sanctuary. I was momentarily paralyzed as I thrust back, balancing on my butt with my feet off the floor and my arms out wide. After an extended period of voicing itself, she commanded it to be silent and asked if there were any other spirits inside me. There were not. I'm not a demonologist, but I'm fairly certain Beast was more than one spirit, and that his name was a title of hierarchy for a group of spirits. When Beast came out of my house, I experienced a necessary relief and felt unusually "uncrowded" for the first time I could remember. I was physically exhausted, as if I had just maxed out the anaerobic threshold of every muscle in my body. But, the most amazing phenomenon was not the brute force of the deliverance; it was the peace of God.[246] The entire time I was being delivered I had an overwhelming sense of God's peace upon me. I was not afraid, nor was I anxious. Amazingly, or miraculously,[247] I was at rest. And I could be wrong, but I don't think anyone involved was fearful, that I know of anyway!

❦   ❦   ❦

I have been very honest in relating my experience. It is my sincere hope that you will not use it in an attempt to devise a demonology. I'm aware that the chronology of these events might present questions. I've had to wrestle

---

[246] God's peace is available to the believer in various forms via His Holy Spirit: Gal 5:22; Phil 4:7, 4:9; Col 3:15; Eph 2:14; Rom 14:17, 15:13, 16:20; 1 Cor 14:33; 1 Thes 5:23; 2 John 1:3; Isa 9:6, 52:7.

[247] Peace is a supernatural fruit of God's Spirit (Gal 5:22; 1 Thes 5:23; see also footnote 246).

with and seek God for that understanding as well. However, the order and occurrence of my experience is what it is. Ultimately, I would have to say God's ways are not man's ways.[248] As too is God's Word, not below or under, but above man, as is the Word who became flesh—who descended from above.[249] (I say this in respect to man's interpretations.) Discovery of God's ways and methods in the earth and spirit will be our joy and awe for eternity to come. I don't have all the answers; I have *some* insight, and not all of which have I or will I share here. Thank you for your understanding.

As I lay this matter to rest and continue on with my journey, I feel it is necessary to pause for a brief moment and acknowledge another topic of interest to many, no doubt. Yes, psychoanalysis. Without lengthy discourse and debate of diagnosis and disorders, I will simply say this: the very concept of *demonic possession* inherently has at its core the question of "sane versus insane." Concerning the demon possessed (obviously, I am presupposing that the state or condition can exist) one of two things are true: (A) One is insane, or (B) One's experiences actually are happening (sanity), however unreal they might appear to a detached observer. I suppose the line between the two can tend to become a little hazy, or even nonexistent in certain cases at definite times. Perhaps the terms *sane* and

---

[248] Rom 11:33; Job 9:10; Isa 55:8—"For My thoughts are not your thoughts nor are your ways My ways," says the LORD.

[249] Christ the Word <u>became flesh</u>: John 1:1-4, 1:14, 1:16-17; 1 John 5:7; Rev 19:13. Christ is <u>above</u>: He who comes from above is above all... (John 3:31, 8:23). Christ <u>descended</u>: Prov 30:4; John 3:13, 6:58, 6:62; Eph 4:10 (see also footnote 267).

insane should be defined and articulated more clearly; however, this is not my concern here.

My experience has been that He who created reality and brought all things into being—in whom all things consist and are upheld by the word of His power[250]—that this One is very well acquainted with man and the unseen realities[251] in which he lives, moves, and has his being;[252] primarily, the spirit[253] and the mind,[254] or psyche. As well, man's adversary, his accuser,[255] the head of all demonic influence,[256] being the author of all lies and confusion[257]— the master of deceit[258] and he who shrouds the eyes of the blind[259] can and does work efficiently trying to convince those held in captivity's clutch[260] that they are indeed

---

[250] Col 1:16-17; John 1:1-3; Heb 1:3; 1 Tim 6:13.

[251] 1 Tim 6:16—Whom [God] no man has seen or can see.

[252] Acts 17:28.

[253] John 4:24—God is Spirit. 2 Cor 3:17—The Lord is the Spirit.

[254] Rom 8:27, 12:2—Be transformed by the renewing of your mind. 1 Cor 2:16—"Who has known the mind of the LORD that he may instruct Him? But we have the mind of Christ." See also: Rom 7:25; 2 Thes 2:2; 1 Pet 1:13; Matt 22:37.

[255] 1 Pet 5:8—Adversary the Devil; Rev 12:10—Accuser of the brethren.

[256] Eph 6:11-12 (characterizes the hierarchy of demonic host under the Devil's influence).

[257] The Devil is the Father of lies (John 8:44). God is not the author of confusion (1 Cor 14:33; James 3:16).

[258] From Genesis to Revelation Satan is seen as the deceiver (Gen 3:1, 3:13; Rev 20:2-3, 20:7-8).

[259] 2 Cor 4:4.

[260] 2 Tim 2:26—And escape the snare of the devil, having been taken captive by him to do his will.

"insane" (which to some greater or lesser *unidentified* degree they just might be). However, none is so far gone, none is too far,[261] that He who shines into darkness,[262] He who opens prison doors, that He who proclaims liberty to captives,[263] cannot reach. No, for such did the Spirit of the LORD rest upon Christ,[264] for such did the Son of Man come![265] And still does, and will come today.

He alone is the Great Physician,[266] He alone has gone where, and sees what no man can see.[267] Only He can discern and diagnose[268] the spiritual conditions of spiritual beings, and only He holds the pen to prescribe[269] treatment for which He alone has authored: the author of eternal salvation—Jesus, the Author and Finisher of our

---

[261] Heb 7:25—He [Christ] is able to save to the uttermost.

[262] John 1:4-5—In Him [Christ] was life, the light of men, the light shines in the darkness. "I am the light of the world"—Jesus (John 8:12, 9:5).

[263] Spiritual liberty or freedom (2 Cor 3:17; John 8:32); Actual prison doors opened (Acts 5:19, 16:26). Also see: Eph 4:8-10 "led captivity captive," and 1 Pet 3:19 "preached to the spirits in prison."

[264] Isaiah prophesied concerning the Messiah (Isa 61:1-3), as seen fulfilled in Jesus (Luke 4:18-19).

[265] John 3:14-18—the Son of Man came to be lifted up [crucified] offering man eternal life.

[266] Matt 9:12; Mark 2:17; Luke 4:23, 5:31. Jesus as the Great Physician (John 5:1-15).

[267] Jesus from above, not of this world (John 8:23); Jesus descended from heaven (John 3:10-13); Matt 12:40—Jesus descended into hell [hades: Luke 16:19-31; 1 Pet 3:19; Eph 4:8-10]; Jesus ascended far above the heavens (Eph 4:8-10).

[268] Col 2:3—In whom (the Father and Christ) are hidden all the treasures of wisdom and knowledge.

[269] Isa 10:1—Woe to those who decree unrighteous decrees... which they [not God] have prescribed.

faith endured the cross and sat down at the right hand of the throne of God (Hebrews 5:9, 12:2). Of this truth, I am more than convinced; concerning alluded debate, however, I am not.

It is my hopeful prayer that God will guide you (and us) into all discernment. I'm also believing that as you reflect on your own journey, or another's close-by, God will mirror signposts or identifying parallels drawn from my path, giving you His wisdom and perspective. In this way, my road to redemption truly is a "living apologia," and *Phoenix Road* brings glory to The Only Glorious One who bore His life for my soul, and yours. Thank you for championing the course with me—we've made it through the crossroads! Now, let us adjust our mirrors, tilt our seats back a bit, and continue our journey down Calvary Road...

Living Water

It can be debated whether *a* church or *the* church speaks too much or too little about the Holy Spirit. One thing was certainly true in my life, however; I could not get enough! I needed every drop of His living water I could find. Bedrock, bone-dry, I was tapped out! Hydration became paramount to life. The Holy Spirit (God) filled my heart and life to overflowing "as the Scripture has said, out of his [believer's] heart will flow rivers [Grk., torrents] of living water" (John 7:38). Jesus' promised

Helper[270] became my lifeblood—my own personal Teacher, Guide, Counselor, and Comforter.[271] He must have known I would need the help!

❧　❧　❧

I realize that the term "born again" takes a bad rap, as in this bumper sticker: "Born OK the First Time." But beyond biblical, the term makes sense: as the believer's spirit is *regenerated* by the Holy Spirit. And beyond sensible, being born again was exactly what my spirit had been thirsting for. Again, Jesus' prescription was accurate:

> Unless one is born again, he cannot see the kingdom of God. That which is born of the flesh is flesh, and that which is born of the Spirit is spirit. Unless one is born of water [flesh/natural] and the Spirit [spiritual], he cannot enter the kingdom of God. (John 3:3-6)

Christ fulfilled my thirst. He quenched my dry bones. His Holy Spirit flooded my inner man—a regenerated man, a man born again not of the flesh but of the Spirit. My spiritual quest was over! My house had been renovated, swept clean, and a new tenant had moved in... There was and is no substitute. No power, no spirit (angel or demon), no experience can replace Christ! And really,

---

[270] Jesus promised to give the Holy Spirit (Helper: Grk.—*Paraclete*, or *Encourager*) upon His ascension: Luke 24:49; John 14:16, 14:26, 15:26, 16:7; Acts 1:2-8, 2:1-4, 2:33.

[271] The Holy Spirit teaches: Luke 12:12; John 14:26. Guides into all truth: John 16:13. Counsels according to God's will: Ps 73:24; Isa 11:12; John 16:13; Rom 8:26-27. Comforts: Acts 9:31.

how could there be? What or who can compete with an omni-personal-God? An infinite-holy-Being? A merciful-relentless-Lover? So, I was born again, and despite skeptics' notions, I guess I wasn't "born okay the first time!"

❧   ❧   ❧

My first evangelistic outreach was to my father in the hospital a day or two following my conversion. "I have to go to the farm!" I urgently persisted my mom that I had to go to the farm where I grew up hunting. I had been seeing visions of it all morning… and then the phone rang. My dad was being rushed to the hospital after falling out of a tree-stand onto his back while deer hunting! She was shocked at the news, and the Spirit's knowledge in me. I was affirmed in my seeing and "hearing God's voice."

The weeks and months ahead were much the same… I believe God desired to show me that He was the truly powerful, omniscient Being I desired. And no, He did not *have* to reveal Himself to me in profound experiences; He already had my heart. But, that is how He chose to confirm Himself to me, and of course He knew me best. As does He you. He knows every hair on your head and the thoughts of your heart.[272] He's got your name and address; I think He knows how to get a hold of you.

"Ring, Ring!" I think it's for you!

I had confessed my faith in Christ to one friend. I asked him if he would come to the hospital with me. I

---

[272] He numbered the hairs on your head (Matt 10:30; Luke 12:7); He knows your thoughts: (Jer 17:10; Matt 9:4; Luke 5:22; Rom 8:27; Heb 4:12).

stood before my dad in his wheelchair, and I looked into his eyes as I shared my "story" for the first time. Perhaps the news was a bit much, too raw, or too steeped with conviction, but not knowing the fate of his hospital stay, I had to tell him. My witness did not receive great applause, but I was encouraged by God's grace (and affirmed by His providence) the following morning when my friend phoned. He confessed his new faith he had experienced the previous night after returning home from the hospital. Apparently, my *story* was good news[273] to his ears, or at least to his heart. God was truly and uniquely good, daily proving Himself to be worthy of all my trust! And, now I had a brother to walk with along the Calvary Road.

❦ ❦ ❦

My journey into the heart of Rome captivated my "obedience to the faith."[274] God was busy plowing up my fallow ground and planting His Word of Truth[275] in my heart. I joined an adult "Sunday School"[276] class studying the book of Romans at a Methodist church down the street. And yes, I did make it to Italy a few blocks down the road!

In chapter 1, The Word of God[277] squared off with me

---

[273] The gospel is the "good news," as prophesied by Isaiah (Isa 52:7; Rom 10:15).

[274] Rom 1:5 and 16:26.

[275] John 17:17—Your word is truth; Ps 119:160.

[276] See Robert Raikes (eighteenth-century England) for the history of the "Sunday School" movement at: http://en.wikipedia.org/wiki/Robert_Raikes.

[277] Jesus is the Word of God: Rev 19:13; John 1:1, 1:4.

straight out of the gate. Paul's pen had judged me accurately two millennia prior! I was without excuse,

> God had revealed Himself through His creation, but I did not glorify Him; I worshiped and served the creature *rather than* the Creator, whereby God gave me up to my futile thinking and vile passions. (Romans 1:18-26, emphasis)

I could not get enough of Romans into my heart: I read it, studied it, memorized it, and prayed it… I spent months encountering the Word of God as I sojourned on Romans Road. God's Word was and is living and active.[278] Every step I took God confronted my heart with His living presence.

The pastor teaching the Romans class was not from "Christian America." His reliance on the gospel's power and its necessity for life was exactly what I needed. He saw beyond my past and through my strengths, simply honoring me as a brother needing God's grace. He extended his hand to me when many did not, and I still believe God brought him to my neighborhood just for me! And to this day, every time I read about the spiritual battle in Ephesians chapter 6, I still remember him demonstrating how we can "put on" the soldier's armor in prayer, equipping ourselves for the day ahead. Above all, it was his Christlike character that validated his walk, and set an example.

My first ministry experience was also at the Methodist church on the corner. I assisted with the youth group.

---

[278] The word of God is living and active (Heb 4:12, NASB); Christ's word is spirit and life (John 6:63).

Actually, as is often the case, I think I was probably ministered to more than they were (once I got over myself and my preferences). I lent a hand wherever it was needed… most often at the 6:00 a.m. prayer breakfast or pulling an all-nighter! As a result, God paired me with another older brother who poured over the Scriptures with me on Tuesday nights after dinner. And now that I think about it, there were two other families who were instrumental in discipling me. Wow, that was a lot of dinners! That must have been what He meant: "Everyone who thirsts, come to the waters; and you who have no money, come, buy and eat" (Isaiah 55:1)!

Well, God did know I needed a healthy diet of His Word.[279] But truly, He was using these godly men and families to soften my calloused heart, confront my misconceptions, and heal my brokenness. For the first time in years I began to believe in marriage again! Today, as I teach discipleship, I am indebted to the many hours of counsel and prayer unselfish men poured into my life. And their wives' selflessness, as the nights waxed long! At the end of the day, this truly is the "heroic" call of ministry—*making disciples* (The Great Commission: Matthew 28:19, 20).

CORNERSTONE

If I were to say everything was smooth sailing after

---

[279] Hebrews 5:14 references the "word of righteousness," stating that the mature eat solid food (not bottle-fed milk), and by reason of use (chewing and assimilating nutrients) they can discern both good and evil.

surrendering my tempestuous life to Christ, I would be perhaps, to quote James, "double-minded."[280] It wasn't the first month of nightly torment and sleepless battles, or my first six months bearing under condemnation's weight. Nor was it my departure from certain circles of friends and social practices, difficulties with family or employers, or my loss of all my possessions and creative works. But, what challenged and confronted me most often was the "Christianese subculture" prevalent in most all the churches I explored. And, there were many! Realistically, I attended nearly every potential candidate in a fifty-mile radius, as I worshiped three or more times throughout the week. Those walls (the church) were the hardest to climb.

Fortunately, Christ is the cornerstone of the church.[281] And, His headship[282] is worthy of all submission, obedience, love of His people, and denial of self-rights and preferences. However, all this talk about waves and the sea has reminded me of being an "Unwed Sailor."[283] In July of 1998 I was blessed to attend my first Cornerstone music festival in Illinois. It was a relief to hear sounds coming from guitars that I enjoyed! To let down the guard and be at home with some fellow believers was a breath of air…

[280] James references the double-minded man as one who oscillates between faith and doubt, "like a wave of the sea driven and tossed by the wind" (James 1:6-8).

[281] Christ was prophesied to be and was directly referenced as the "cornerstone": Ps 118:22; Isa 28:16; Zec 10:4; Matt 21:42; Mark 12:10; Luke 20:17; Acts 4:11; 1 Pet 2:6-7.

[282] Christ is the head of man, His body the church, and all principalities: 1 Cor 11:3; Eph 1:22, 4:15, 5:23; Col 1:18, 2:10, 2:19.

[283] Musician Johnathon Ford formed Unwed Sailor as an instrumental project in 1998.

Despite the humidity and the sour gases that seeped up from the old cow fields, not to mention the "Johnny on the Spots!" The community and music shared (in most circles) was water in a dry cup. David Bazan and Damien Jurado overflowed with grace *and* rock! As I peer through a poster on my wall today,[284] I smile remembering the faces crowded under a lit-up red and white-striped big top tent.

❧ ❧ ❧

Back home, God had begun a great work in our community. Two brothers and I began a "house of prayer" hosting a Bible study and worship in our apartment. God drew many people to Himself during that period (1998–99), and fused many lasting friendships through nightly fellowship and camaraderie. Even the PD got a taste of grace, entering on more than one late night to bust the party, only to find worshiping hearts, coffee and pancakes, and heated games of Scrabble! Friends' of Jesus[285] came and went from all around the country… True community is treasure indeed—often sought but rarely found!

"You have to meet this guy I know! He's traveling home from a castle in Austria…" The local barista was adamant that her friend and I must meet. A few weeks later while sitting in with two band mates at her birthday party and rocking out a Tortoise cover, she got her wish! I suppose

---

[284] "Pedro The Lion," 2002, by Jason Munn as seen in: *The Small Stakes—Music Posters* (Chronicle Books, 2010), p. 14.

[285] The fellowship was titled: Arise—Friends' of Jesus (1998-99); although the study was eventually dissolved after some difficult leadership challenges, the community laid the groundwork for several lasting friendships and marriages!

the invasion of H. Chinaski's[286] music that electrified the
Valley the following year was shocking, but the flint of
brotherhood that sparked our hearts and minds was divine.
For, "As iron sharpens iron, so a man sharpens the coun-
tenance of his friend" (Proverbs 27:17). And, more than
late night coffee fixes, or amplified rock mixes, it was
"fellowship of the Spirit" (Philippians 2:1) that ignited
our souls.

Above all, it was my brother's yielded spirit and avail-
ability that God used to speak into my life: like that castle
(Schloss Heroldeck)[287] he had just returned home from,
coupled with an abandoned paperback I found while driving down *The Calvary Road*.[288] Those were two signs God
knew I couldn't miss! And, when I "arbitrarily" attended
a pastors' conference (hosted by Calvary Chapel) and was
exposed to the simple exposition of God's Word, I knew
that God was calling me into a time of study. Why? Very
simply, my knowledge of the Bible was insufficient to
fulfill His call to share and defend my faith. Beyond that,
I had been asking how He was going to equip me, and
where? And, when a family from church invited me over
for dinner at the end of summer and surprised me with
my first semester's tuition, I thought, *Hmm? Maybe You
(God) really do want me to go to Bible college!*

---

[286] See Double Plus Good (DPG) Records at: http://doubleplusgo
odrecords.com/C3/bands/hchinaski/index.htm.

[287] At the time Schloss Heroldeck was Calvary Chapel Bible College's European campus: http://castle.cccm.com.

[288] Roy Hession, *The Calvary Road* (Fort Washington, PA: CLC
Publications, 1990 [London, 1950]). Ironically, a required text at Calvary's Bible college.

Baptizo

Mid summer a friend invited me to a church retreat (of the same movement) in central Wisconsin. He was going to help out with some worship, so I tagged along to see what God was up to. I enjoyed being out in creation, but even more I enjoyed worshiping the Creator! Sleeping in the back of my truck while stargazing in an open field was glorious. Undoubtedly, however, the baptism at the neighboring lake was of greater glory!

In those fire-filled "experiential" days of my infant walk, I knew with great expectancy that whenever I attended an event God had a divine purpose in meeting with me there (Jehovah Shammah, chapter 1). Like the time He led me to stop at a "random" midweek church service in my dirty work clothes, and the Holy Spirit moved in such a powerful way during worship that the preacher never got to preach—the congregation was too busy repenting and praising God on their faces, myself included! To my surprise the church had never experienced such a movement of God, and they inquired of me (a foreigner) if I had somehow been responsible for it. Of course, I hadn't. I was just another attendee invited by God! And yes, He met me too, anointing me with His Spirit and endowing me with another spiritual gift.[289] I was blessed indeed as I got back into my truck and continued driving home in my dirty jeans and muddy boots, praising and worshiping God all the way!

---

[289] God released the gift of "tongues" (1 Cor 12:10) in me that night as my worship exceeded my natural faculties!

Perhaps I should pause for a moment and expound on my "experiential" comment above. God definitely desires to be present and known in every moment and act of our life and experience; there is no doubt about that. What I was referring to, however, was my manner in which I sought God in the early days after coming out of the occult. If you remember, I was heavily entrenched in seeking the "next experience" for my power and life source. So, naturally, some of that seeking gravitated over into my worship of Jehovah God. In retrospect, I was often waiting and looking for the next movement of God in my life. If my senses weren't "sensing," then I wasn't relating with Him. This experience-driven worship, however, forfeits to know and honor God solely for who He is. Yes, God desired and still desires to make Himself known to me in supernatural ways, but first and foremost, He simply deserves worship for being God, despite what He does or does not do, or how my nerve endings respond!

❧ ❧ ❧

Baptizo: to be immersed or submerged (see footnote 291). My baptism was a gift from my heavenly Father. I had neither intention nor any idea a baptism was going to occur over the weekend. But, my Father did. And, when the baptism was announced to take place at a nearby lake,[290] God stirred in my heart that it was my time. This was the opportunity, this was the place, this was the day! And truly, this was the reason He brought me to the retreat, so

---

[290] To the best of my knowledge, the baptism took place at a lake near Menominee, WI.

205

I could fulfill Scripture's command to be baptized. And, of course, He knew what He'd planned… A local rural lake in Wisconsin's outdoors was perfect—it was my Jordan River. Not to mention the like-minded believers gathered in a large circle in the lake, praising and worshiping God with an acoustic guitar. So, with each baptism I cheered and celebrated as I prayed and waited upon God's hand.

When I noticed a large hawk or eagle soaring and circling high above the lake, I approached the pastors in the center. They laid hands on me in prayer and words of prophecy, giving praise to God. His Spirit was anointing us in a powerful way, as if to be saying: "My son, with you I am well pleased." And then, the cool clear liquid flooded in over my face. The sun illuminated my eyes as I looked up at the heavens. When my face emerged I saw the bird still circling in the blue sky above. The sound of worshipers singing in glorious song to God filled my ears. The smiles of the men at my side, water dripping from one's beard, brought joy to my heart as I thrust my hands skyward: "Hallelujah!" The *old man* had died in Christ; the *new man* had risen indeed![291]

Paul's words reverberated in my heart, taking on more flesh:

---

[291] Baptism *symbolizes* the believer's death with Christ and his resurrection with and in Christ (Rom 6:3-11). It is commanded by Scripture (Matt 28:19) as an adult (or mature) act of obedience declaring externally Christ's work in the believer's inner heart/man/woman. Baptism (Grk., *baptizo*) references the method of *immersing or submerging* the believer fully underwater as if to be drowned, and then resurrected upon emerging. The act in no way "saves" the believer. Christ also fulfilled the act (Matt 3:13-17), exemplifying obedience to the Father.

I have been crucified with Christ; it is no longer I who live, but Christ lives in me; and the life which I now live in the flesh I live by faith in the Son of God, who loved me and gave Himself for me. (Galatians 2:20)

My Father was good; He knew me and proved Himself to me yet again. His divine purpose and plan in working all things together for my good[292] continued to blow my mind! And, if I must say so, I was not divining or worshiping the eagle; however, this was one symbol God had redeemed and continued to, and still continues to use today.

❧   ❧   ❧

Calvary Road was a whole new world to be explored in a whole new man! Sounds like quite the holistic experience, doesn't it? God did, definitely, meet me around every bend, twist, and turn, and even a few long straight-aways I thought would never end. His Word was true; the more I knew His truth the more I was set free.[293] My faith was growing too.[294] Knowing Him[295] was life's greatest discovery. Each day was new,[296] a new road to be traveled and

---

[292] Rom 8:28; it is key to remember who this verse is directed toward—those who *love* God.

[293] John 8:32.

[294] Rom 10:17—faith comes by hearing, and hearing by the word of God.

[295] Phil 3:7-14 (10).

[296] "Behold, I [God] make all things new" (Rev 21:5).

explored as I walked with Him step-by-step.[297]

As things looked on the horizon, I was about to be heading west again. I suppose it was only right. And, perhaps, it was only His miracle that I had returned home and hung around for two years. But, it was time. I was born again, baptized, and Bible college was calling… California was a stone's skip away. I could hear the palms waving in the coastal breeze, silhouetted against the salty orange sky. The Word of God was waiting for me.

---

[297] The believer is instructed to "walk in": the newness of life, the Spirit, love, Him (Christ), wisdom, the light, the truth, His (God's) commandments, and good works (cited respectively: Rom 6:4; Gal 5:16, 5:25; Eph 5:2; Col 2:6, 4:5; 1 John 1:7; 2 John 1:4, 1:6; 3 John 1:3, 4; Eph 2:10).

11

PLANES, TRAINS, AND BICYCLES

IN THE "SUMMER OF '99"[298] I rolled out of Wisconsin in my little two-wheel drive pick-up truck with an aluminum topper, some hand-stitched drapes, and a plywood shelf for a bed. What else did a twenty-three-year-old guy need? I downsized apartment life to a backpack full of clothes, a wooden crate of essential books, a guitar, and a bicycle on the roof. Bunk beds and dormitory life were going to be an adjustment—six guys in a six-by-six box "working out their salvation in fear and trembling!"[299] Yes, things were about to change, but until then, I was "On the Road Again!"[300]

Before I drift off into the west and let the sun set on my

---

[298] I couldn't resist playing off Ryan Adam's hit "Summer of '69," from his album *Reckless*, 1984.

[299] Phil 2:12, see footnote 339 for further reference.

[300] While I was on a roll, I thought I'd throw in a little Willie: "On the Road Again," by Willie Nelson from the film *Honeysuckle Rose*, 1980.

skateboarding career for good, I just remembered one last stunt that I pulled off before my departure… The local skatepark was a long time in coming. Having grown up without a park in our town and being harassed by the cops at every bank parking lot, post office ledge, and the notorious city parking ramp, our own skatepark did not evolve without sweat and tears. So, when the city finally decided to ante up and build a park, they built it adjacent to the new police headquarters, not to miss a beat! Within a few months, however, there was talk that the park might get shut down if *we* couldn't keep our trash in the proper receptacles and out of the neighbors' yards.

Well, as young grommits[301] snaked and thrashed the park, hurling pop cans and Doritos bags to the wind, I was moved to take action atop the large ramp in the center of the park. A confused downtrodden kid lit up when I handed him my skateboard "for keeps" before ascending the ramp. I heaved an overflowing trashcan above my head toward the sky; the park came to a standstill. As a reputable worker at the local skate shop, I employed my authority to speak on behalf of the skateboard community exhorting them to keep the park clean and to treat it with respect and privilege—a privilege that many who came before did not have. And, while I had their attention, I exalted God as the Creator of heaven and earth and shared His creative words of life to a lost and dying generation. I was then moved to give them an immediate action point when I dumped out the trash; cans and plastic bottles

---

[301] Grommit defined sufficiently enough at: www.urbandictionary.com/define.php?term=grommit (3.).

crashed on the asphalt below, sprawling across the park. Before I could descend to clean it up, kids came running with fear and fire, ready to pick up *their* park! I can't be certain, but I believe God met a few of those kids that day and gave them something to think about... for the "Summer of '99" anyway!

❧ ❧ ❧

So, as I said, I rolled out of Wisconsin and headed west. This time I jumped on I-90 and shot across Minnesota, gave a wink to the Ol' Presidents at Rushmore, clipped Wyoming's sideburns heading north, and rolled into that Big Blue Sky again. I took her north to Missoula, where I met a friend for breakfast at a diner, and kept on climbing. Somewhere in the high country of Idaho's Panhandle I caught an epic ride... Evergreens surfed a winding range amongst dense hovering clouds, while fresh rain sparkled and steamed as the sun broke through on the road ahead. *So, this is Idaho!* I had to throw 'er in neutral and let her coast a while with both windows down, inhaling the green breeze. Chills raced and charged my nerves, sparking at the tip of every electrified hair. My lungs drank deep; the air was cool spring water bubbling up in the sunlight. The Creator was bigger and broader than ever; I was overwhelmed with the reality of being created to worship this awesome Being.

God is Spirit, and those who worship Him must worship in spirit and truth. Now is, when the true worshipers will worship the Father in spirit and truth;

for the Father is seeking such to worship Him. (John 4:24, 23)

Under the conviction that God truly did desire my worship, and not the reiterations of worship artists' rehearsals, I pulled off the road, snipped the wires on my tape deck with my Leatherman, and made a direct deposit into the proper wayside receptacle. I rolled back onto the road with a lighter load, worshiping the God of All Creation[302] from a pure heart and overflowing Spirit. The freedom to worship Him alone, as the eternal and Supreme Being, was liberating and life breathing. "Now the Lord is the Spirit: and where the Spirit of the Lord is, there is liberty" (2 Corinthians 3:17). Besides, I didn't resonate with everything vibrating through Nashville's cords anyway, and now I had a perfect slot in my dash for my Bible and journal!

❦   ❦   ❦

"There it is again! Whew! What is that reek odor? Is that *my* truck?" Somewhere near Spokane I decided to pull her over and check her out. "Yep! She's a stinkin'! Those ain't rotten potatoes either; EGGS, rotten cooped-up ol' constipated hen!" I managed to coast her down to Seattle and into California before the alternator fried and hard-boiled my battery. I tried to pop in on a friend in Seattle, but no luck. Another in Tacoma, but he had vacated

---

[302] Col 1:15-17 references Christ as the Creator and God over all creation; Psalm 19 reveals God's glorious handiwork in the heavens and earth.

a day before. I was too late; I-90 must have called his name![303] So, I rolled downstream and enjoyed the coast! I'm not sure if I hit Portland or not. I felt God sliding me through the Northwest quickly—too many temptations knocking at my door! Besides, the truck was wearying, and I just wanted to get her down the road. California finally came, and she pooped out on me rolling into a garage in Redding. I crawled into the back and caught some Zs. In the morning the mechanic woke me, and I was back on the road by noon. She set me back a few "hunge" but it could have been worse. All in all, she was a good little truck and got me where I needed to go... "Down the Road Again!"

CALIFORNIA HOT SPRINGS

My first stop as I arrived in Murrieta Hot Springs, California, was a local taco shop. "Mmm, that salsa is muy bueno!" Actually, I got a bit excited there, "Slow down Conquistador!"

Back up the coast, I sailed into Orange County and docked with a fellow Wisconian in Huntington Beach. He had blown in ahead of me ridin' the coast down from Seattle looking to land a gig as a pilot. Somehow, aeronautics seemed to fly second to surfing pier-breaks, flip-flops, and bikinis! We crashed in his garage-converted-bedroom,

---

[303] The Singing Mechanic (artist Vincent Voss): track "East Coast/West Coast" off his album *It Wouldn't Be What It Is*, 2001.

showered with East European housemates, and scrambled eggs with his quirky elderly homeowners. Our fellowship enjoyed great hilarity and lively conversation!

❧   ❧   ❧

Arriving after hours, I slept in my truck down the road from the front gate of the school (that was before track homes and strip malls propagated in the desert). Mid-morning I leapt out of my sleeping bag dripping in sweat, sun broiled and well done! I made my way onto school grounds and into the check-in line, where I received my first disciplinary exhortation (from a fellow student) for breaking school dress code. To my ignorance, my old tank-top was inappropriate attire. And, I began to learn quickly who was who, and how I was supposed to act and *do* Christianity. Of course, my edges were a bit hairy, or unshaven, or rough! But, was I really a "mystic?"

Well, all I can say was that after two weeks of that escapade, I was certain I had made a mistake. I stripped my bed, packed my bags, loaded my truck, and donated my books to the nearest "proper receptacle." And *then*, I prayed! And then, God squared up with me. "You can leave if you want to, son, but I am here" (Jehovah Sham-mah—The Lord Is There). He affirmed that He hadn't made a mistake in calling me "there." Apparently, I needed something this institution had. So, by His grace, I broke. I reclaimed my books and my bed, made a few adjustments to my schedule, and I committed to "knowing Him, in this place." And, I did know Him; He met me through His Word in new ways, tearing off old layers, sanding edges, molding corners… And yes, of course, there was heavy demolition too!

The majority of my first year at Bible college can be referred to as laying foundation. And, I suppose my Servanthood Class was just where God wanted me—construction. But, we were not really constructing anything, yet. We were demoing an old bathhouse (the school grounds are a renovation of an old hot springs resort) in preparation for constructing a new building. I jackhammered, sledge-hammered, picked, and wheel-barrowed in the desert sun all fall. Just as semester was winding up, we got the forms set and the rebar laid. A new foundation was ready to be poured at last!

When God wasn't breaking me at work, I was on my knees in the chapel broken in His Spirit: "The sacrifices of God are a broken spirit, A broken and a contrite heart— These, O God, You will not despise" (Psalm 51:17). This was true discipleship, by the Word of God! As David wrote elsewhere, "The LORD is near to those who have a broken heart, and saves such as have a contrite spirit" (Psalm 34:18). God was transforming my inner man; He was teaching me what it actually meant when He said: "God resists the proud, but gives grace to the humble" (1 Peter 5:5). So, He humbled me; "Christ, the Cornerstone of His church, knew how He desired to build me up into His spiritual house (His holy priest) to offer up sacrifices acceptable to Him."[304] In the end, He knew what He was

---

[304] 1 Pet 2:4-9.

up to, though many others, faculty and myself included, were not so certain. But, God was drawing the map, and He knew every bend and bridge in "the road less traveled."[305]

It was an intense semester no doubt: Back in Wisconsin, two close brothers had abandoned our band of bachelors, while an exemplary Christian family lost their mother in a tragic auto accident. At school, a lone student I had befriended took his life the very morning I happened to be in the pulpit praying for the student body while giving a "Devotion." (This student's memory was also an encouraging factor in my name change a year or so later.) Indeed, lives shifted and worlds were born in those four short months. It is often beyond comprehension how much God can allow or do with "how little" sometimes,[306] isn't it? But, that wasn't all... Thanksgiving break took me to Sin City for an outreach on the strip. And if I must say so, I had never been frisked and had my license run by the police after preaching on a corner before! Meanwhile, while raising money to smuggle Bibles into China over Christmas break, a team pioneering a trip to Indonesia voiced its need for another male leader. Hence, upon a Friday afternoon's notice, I was now going to Indonesia! *Where exactly was Bali, Indonesia, anyway?* As I said, God knew what He was up to!

---

[305] From "The Road Not Taken," by Robert Frost, *Mountain Interval*, 1916.

[306] Jesus' miracles often multiplied what was a lacking amount into a sufficient and exceeding quantity: Matt 14:19 (5,000 fed); Matt 15:36 (4,000 fed); John 2:9 (transformed water into wine).

Indonesian Peanut Satay

I flew home to Wisconsin for Christmas to ring in a New Year's Eve (2000) wedding, only to return and hit the ground walking through California's southern landscape a week later. I had another week to kill before our team flew out for "Indo," so I thought I'd walk to campus. Roughly, it's a five-day walk from Ontario, California, to Murrieta Hot Springs, and actually it would be appropriate to say hike, being that I had well over seventy-five pounds on my back. I knew the trip overseas was going to test our team; I used the walk as a prayer and fasting meditation. Apparently, dropping off the grid like that for a few days can get some people a little anxious, especially a caring mom. But, I was ready, and by His strong hand of encouragement, I knew He (God) was definitely ready. Besides, the way I saw it, I was created for this hour,[307] and really, I was only just about to step off the grid, or the radar, for that matter.

We landed in Denpasar, Bali, a day later. A young native pastor picked us up at the airport in a small compact van. Our entire team crammed in vertically, horizontally, and any and every which way—we sardined ourselves and all of our *too-much* gear in just far enough to throw the sliding door shut! I can see the locals' faces now: "The Americans have arrived!" Did I mention it was humid? Hot, wet, and stinky! Was it us, or the air? I'm not sure; both, but definitely us! Our loose plans and many unknowns were

---

[307] John 12:27—But for this purpose I came to this hour (see also footnote 308).

quickly discovered en route to our base church as we sped and stopped through the smoggy, motor scooter-swarmed streets. When the pastor piped up amongst the awestruck eyes and pointing fingers and asked, "Who will be preaching?" the laughter stopped, and all eyes fell to me. "Good, you will be preaching then." And, that was that, my first official Introduction to Preaching 101, not to mention the hurdle over the language blockade! But, the entire team was thrust into new and challenging opportunities daily. God had set our itinerary; we were just along for the ride…

The local pastor and his associate guided our team from church to church and orphanage, where we performed skits, sung songs, and provided activities and games for the kids. In the churches he introduced us, our team leader gave an opening testimony, and we usually played a few worship songs. And then, I preached. That was the general order of our days, times two, morning and evening, and sometimes lunch too! We lived on the go, and if we had a spare moment we stopped into various house churches or village Bible studies to encourage the believers, and I shared the Word. Truthfully, I had never preached or taught that much before ever, especially in two weeks time. Most of my studying was done bumping along the road in a back corner of the van, pressed up against the glass observing the foreign people and landscape in prayer, while other team members passed out from exhaustion.

But, the more pressed I became,[308] the more His Spirit filled me to overflowing![309] For the most part, I just sought God for His timely word to His people, and I learned quickly that He, not I, always had one!

In Bali, Hindu women scurried the streets in colorful sarongs balancing temple offerings on their heads. Little children bathed in any moving water they could find. Dense jungle thronged the mountains. Rice farmers bent over in wide-brimmed pointy hats wading through water-filled terraces. Coffee plantations flourished. Village trails snaked along rivers through the jungle; bananas and rambutans (a *hairy* red skin surrounds a clear fruit with a brown-skinned nut) hung in hand's reach. Passion fruit, mangoes, and durians (a large green-yellow spiked gourd with creamy *odorous* fruit) filled the markets. Avocado puree with or without chocolate was a treat found on most corners in a plastic bag with a colorful bendy-straw. Spicy chicken-fried rice wrapped in banana leaf, Indonesian peanut satay, or frog-leg soup were local favorites bubbling, broiling, or sizzling over coconut-husk fires along every curbside kiosk, or two-wheeled cart. Bali was lively: colors, smells, and smiles populated the dense green jewel, burying lifetimes of treasured memories in the traveler's heart.

---

[308] An interesting note here concerning "pressed": it was in the Garden of Gethsemane (literally oil press) that Christ bore His soul before the Father (Luke 22:42-44), preparing Him for His crucifixion—the "hour for which He was sent" (John 12:27).

[309] John 7:38—He who believes in Me [Jesus], as the Scripture has said, out of his heart shall flow rivers of living water [lit. torrents, floods].

❧   ❧   ❧

Not all islands were so colorful. Two others and I had just reunited with our team in Mataram, Lombok, from a stint in Sumbawa to visit a group of believers, when the January 2000 Christian persecution (following Ramadan, Muslim holy month) erupted in Jakarta and spilled over. Fire and violence fueled hatred amongst rioting Muslims as they burned churches, killed pastors, and destroyed Christian businesses and property in Mataram. Fortunately and not so fortunately, our native pastor flew off island with a team member sick with malaria. The rest of the team fled in the van, dashing through the club-fisted mob-ruled neighborhoods, racing the clock in hope of pushing our way onto the submerging ferry. By faith,[310] we made it! Peaceable Bali never felt so much like home! Many of the friends and believers we had met off-island now filled the churches on Bali. No one knew more the refuge that Christ Himself was (and is): "The God of my strength, in whom I will trust; my shield... my stronghold and *my refuge... You save me from violence*" (2 Samuel 22:3, emphasis).

God did amazing acts on our trip (continuing the N.T. record of Acts),[311] as He extended Himself to His people, loving them through our yielded hearts. My highlight was a hike and stream crossing into a village, where we

---

[310] Hebrews 11 details the "Hall of Faith," referencing many biblical heroes of faith who have lived faithfully and victoriously for the LORD *by faith.*

[311] Acts 2:42-47.

showed the *Jesus* film[312] with a generator, and I was able to expound God's truth to animistic natives while the chief listened receptively for the first time. God's hand of mercy and loving concern for His people are what truly brought Christ's witness to bear upon the Indonesians' hearts. To partner in this privilege was beyond any words any of us could share back in the States at our home churches. We went to serve faithfully, but the True and Faithful One[313] had served us! None returned the same man, woman, or student—Terima Kasih Yesus (Thank You, Jesus)!

AUSTRIAN ALPS

I landed in California long enough to crash out at my buddy's crash-pad in Orange County and spread my wings again at LAX. I arrived in München, Germany, where I caught a train to Spittal, Austria, and was finally escorted to The Schloss (castle) just outside of Millstatt. I was ready to seek God again through the study of His Word and prayer. The Bible college's European campus perched on the northern shore of Millstätter See (Lake Millstatt) in the Central Eastern Alps seemed to be as great as place as any! Even my accommodations in the renovated Nazi dungeon,

---

[312] The *Jesus* film was released by Campus Crusade for Christ in 1979; in 1981 The JESUS Film Project was organized for distribution resulting in over 6 billion viewings worldwide; more info at: http://jesusfilm.org/.

[313] Christ referenced as Faithful and True: Rev 3:14, 19:11.

or the "Villa" as it were,[314] exceeded my expectations!

Each morning woke me to a glorious hike in the pristine old-growth evergreens to wander trails and scale rocks and cliffs to perch and pray. The deer nosed about the undergrowth, while a loon or two called from the lake below. The head of my Servanthood Class (grounds maintenance) invited several students and me to go paragliding with a local friend of his. Imagine the silent thrill of gliding on the wind, sweeping and arcing the Alps above green rolling hills dotted with white woolen sheep. It's been a decade, and I can still feel the butterflies in my stomach as we "ran like a bull," caught the wind, and launched off the mountainside—sailing the sky, gliding the morning thermals! We sailed the sea too! Only, our "experienced" fellow sailor (student) got us into a bit more breeze than expected, and we were welcomed back to moor in the harbor by a bearded mouthful of German—all for the glory of God, I suppose!

❧ ❧ ❧

A jaunt down to Roma… actually, what am I talking about, it was no jaunt. Eight students traversing the mountains in a snowstorm for what I remember being an eleven-hour journey into the heart of Italy. But, our Slovenian student driver was a Meister; he guided us effortlessly, and even picked the liveliest border pubs to stop off for potty

---

[314] Side note concerning the phrase "as it were": see the informative and humorous article "As It Were" (2006-09-27) posted by Brad Pasanek on his blog The Mind is a Metaphor at: http://mind.textdriven.com/archive/10/as-it-were.

breaks! In Rome, we ministered alongside a local church plant. Ironically, the pastor (an American) had felt called to Romania, but God brought him to Rome and filled his church with Romanian immigrants. His vision for our team was to focus on reaching out to the universities and colleges.

We learned and saw a lot, no doubt! God revealed Himself in many ways, stripping back the illusion of travel and European city life. One thing was certain, Rome had been there a long time, and based on my teammate's brief exchange of words with the Pope at St. Peter's Basilica, I don't think too much has changed. But, we shared God's heart with as many people as we could and pulled the rug on several pickpockets and Roma (gypsies) stealing ignorant passersbys' money. Above all, it was the religious idolatry[315] that cut my heart in Rome. No presence of "grace and truth,"[316] no Jesus to be found in the midst of the pomp and parade of sacred rite, only a man, or men in splendid apparel[317]—not much has changed since the days of St. Francis[318] and Martin Luther.[319] God have mercy on the Bishop of Rome!

---

[315] A good example would be the bronze statue of Peter in St. Peter's Basilica, with its worn foot from the tears and touch of pilgrims flocking to pay homage and receive blessing; view at: www.saintpeters basilica.org/Statues/StPeter/StPeter.htm.

[316] John 1:14-17—Jesus came in the fullness of grace and truth.

[317] These references give an overview of God's impression of such pomp; however, they must also be viewed within their contexts: 1 Pet 3:3-4; 1 Tim 2:9; James 2:1-3.

[318] Franco Zeffirelli's provocative film captures St. Francis of Assisi's life and the Roman papacy in: *Brother Sun, Sister Moon* (1972).

[319] *Luther* (2003, film).

Upon returning to the castle in Austria, I realized my passport had disappeared. The following night I had a dream in which it reappeared again, but until then, I thought it best to jump a train to Vienna and shoot for the embassy. So, the following sunrise, a fellow adventurer and I did just that, and to everyone's amazement, we arrived back the same night with a new passport in hand and pocketbook of stories to top! My passport did arrive in the mail from Rome randomly a week or two later. The semester was winding down, and it was time to leave the mountaintop and descend into the valley again. Most of all, I would miss ascending the Prayer Tower (six-story round tower) into the "cloud of unknowing"[320] for the daily unveiling of God's glory. Before I made my descent home, I received two "words from the Lord," both open to speculation and controversy—both of which, I suppose, were not unfamiliar ground to me. So, I was ready for another "practicum!" As we used to joke, "You're either a *Goer* or a *Stayer*; which one do you want to be?" After all, what was all that head knowledge for if it didn't find its way to my feet? I mean, heart! No, really, I mean feet!

"Endo" to Indo

Before I made the trek down from the mountain, I was raking leaves on the hillside listening to an O.T. Bible

---

[320] *The Cloud of Unknowing* is an anonymous fourteenth-century Christian mysticism work on contemplative prayer (Thomas à Kempis' *The Imitation of Christ* is a similar work, pre or post dating).

Survey when another "colorful prophet"[321] confronted
my heart and prayer life: Hosea, a prophet of God, being
sent to a woman with child. And so, I prayed, and prayed,
returned to California, harbored with a brother in Bakersfield for a month, studied a cassette series on *Growing in
the Grace of God*,[322] and I prayed.

Then, I made my move. I rustled up an old rusty motorcycle from a lawnmower repairman out in Shafter. After
evicting the mice from the seat, getting some fire to the
gas, and using a roll of strategically stuck duct tape I pretty
much had her running. Pretty much, other than a daily
fuse change on the highway in 110-degree heat.

So, I saddled up "Ol' Grace Faithful" and headed out
across the desert for the heartland. I made it to my first
watering hole; a quick pit stop to visit some family friends;
consequently, they put me to work under the Vegas sun!
An old roommate in Wisconsin was getting married a few
weeks down the road, so I couldn't stray too far. Only, I
thought I'd stop in the mountains and check in on a girl.
Yes, the one from Colorado, years back. My heart was
still wondering, or, was it wandering? After about a week
camped out by the river kicking around Telluride, there
she was, just as the Lord had foretold. And yes, she was
"with child…"

In the meantime, I made it back to Wisconsin with Ol'

---

[321] My memory has often recalled Chuck Smith's (teacher of the
Bible Survey) reference to "God's prophets being colorful people";
however, due to the great expanse of Bible exposition and long oration
of *Chuck's Tracks*, the said citation has lapsed my mind!

[322] Teaching series by Bob Hoekstra, founder of Living In Christ
Ministries at: www.livinginchrist.org/index.php.

Grace lassoed in the back of a '72 El Camino; her lungs choked out at ten thousand feet. Back in the flatland she ran pretty smooth, for a while, not a very long while, but long enough before I had to put her down. My buddy got married, my mom packed up her life for California, and I wrestled a few old friends out of the woodwork to help me move her and venture back over to Indonesia. Because, along with God's word from Hosea before departing Austria, I had received a handwritten letter from a pastor in Indonesia requesting my return to minister in the mountain village. Apparently, God was doing a great work amongst the villagers, and He believed I could be of assistance.

So, I prayed, and prayed, and navigated the U-Haul through the snow-packed Rockies and descended into "the promise land" north of San Diego. And I prayed as I departed to Colorado once again for a short visit before our three-man team would venture out for Indo, leaving LAX in the dust, or smog! ("California can't see the sun rise, / Smoke doesn't climb like it lingers."[323] That line from a Midwestern indie-pop band always comes to mind; I couldn't resist!) So, I prayed, and we took flight arriving in Bali a day later, just in time for Christmas and New Year's Eve 2001.

❦   ❦   ❦

By now I'd be asking who was funding all these faith adventures. Actually, I probably wouldn't be, but many

---

[323] Line from the song "Between Pacific Coasts," off The Promise Ring's album *30° Everywhere* (Jade Tree, 1996).

often did ask. And, of course, the answer ultimately was God, and my college education fund, private persons, home churches, the sale of personal possessions, and whatever other means God put in my life on any given day in answer to prayer. The Methodist church I attended briefly in Wisconsin funded a great portion of the missionary work in Indonesia. Our most recent trip to Israel (forthcoming) was aided by a substantial family gift. Several other testimonies of provision will be worthy of mentioning (to the glory of God) as we continue our travels down *Phoenix Road*.

❧   ❧   ❧

Plans changed in Indonesia. Imagine that! As it turned out, the village had widely come to Christ, and as a result a neighboring Muslim group burned it and ran the villagers out. We made the journey in with a local guide, just to see it firsthand and find some closure. I can still see the torched hut we had gathered in a year earlier for worship and teaching. But, God was still near, and that was life in Indonesia.

Our native pastor didn't waste any time creating a three-month itinerary for us. I preached and taught while the other guys shared testimonies and played worship (one was newly saved, the other recently rededicated). When we weren't busy we helped out with the crew building the church next door, although we mostly just messed around and got in the way! The laughs and camaraderie all played their part, even in winning over the heart of an off-island Muslim construction worker. And actually, the Indonesians' building methods weren't the only thing that challenged my western mind; their simple faith and reliance upon God were stunning. Yes, I was *stunned* on more than one occasion!

We traveled throughout Bali and headed west to Java, where we were handed over to another local family pastor, the father. Or, more rightly, the "God Father!" His low Indo-American accent came out like an old Italian gangster, and whatever he said was obeyed, no questions asked! I learned that firsthand, when after finishing dinner the first or second night, he turned and looked at me and said, "You preach now." And, in my westerly logic, I thought to myself, *Is that a question?* But, when we went downstairs to the adjacent church building where people were gathering, I realized he understood perfectly well what he said. And, to my surprise, "I preached now!" That was how most of our ministry on Java occurred. We were also blessed to spend a week at a local Bible college, where I taught several classes daily, and we helped the students break their week-long fast with the largest twenty-plus-pound clusters of red grapes we had ever seen. They cost us a fortune in rupiahs, but we blessed them with the fruit of their Heavenly Father's True Vine[324] that night as we loved[325] them and showered them with His grace.

---

[324] John 15:1, 15:5, 15:8—I [Jesus] am the true vine... he who abides in Me, and I in him, bears much fruit... so you will be My disciples.

[325] John 13:35—By this all will know that you are My [Jesus'] disciples, if you have love for one another.

Escape to Oz

Back in Bali, our visas were up, so as planned, we shot over to Australia—a long awaited tour for me. After several anticipated years of prayer I had made it at last! In departing Indonesia, however, I had a lot on my mind. We were scheduled to return for another three months after Oz, and I had received an invitation to pastor. My heart was torn. I truly loved the people, but I just wasn't sure it was the right time to give myself to it.

The border police in Darwin didn't exactly welcome us home! After an assault of accusations and a thorough search of our bags, and persons, we had made it back to The West. It was refreshing, as it always is, to get a breath of familiarity. We got the lay of the land[326] as we circled the island continent by bus, train, and plane. We must have fit the vagabond part well by the time we hit Sydney, not that the officers in Darwin were warranted in assuming we were smuggling drugs through Australia's back door. Either way, we were blessed with the bagged lunches a local church group gave us while taking shade in the park: Vegemite sandwiches!

By the time we rounded the corner to Melbourne, the team was beginning to shift and take new direction. God called one of the brothers down to Tasmania to join up with Youth With A Mission. It had become clear he needed to step out and venture on his own path. The

---

[326] While studying through Joshua while traveling, God gave me a similar vision of "surveying the land" as seen in Joshua 18:1-9 (3 men and 7 parts/cities).

younger brother traveled with me to Perth, which had become a point of interest in connection with Indonesia as a possible base of operations for equipping and releasing natives. En train route west, I'd never seen such other-worldly landscape before. Glowing green foliage canopied loose and wide high above the radiating red earth, while kangaroos bounced amongst the sun's playful setting rays. The first time I saw a roo in the distance I thought I was seeing a mirage, or hallucinating, but on double-take it was as my eyes had seen, "a hop, hop…" Our midnight journey through the southern Outback on a neon-lit train car was surreal… I might as well have been on the moon, or a galactic moonlit train!

My younger brother, however, was also looking paler, or greener, by the day. He had not been well since Indo. I couldn't risk taking him back for another round of bad water, diarrhea, and infection. His immune system was shutting down; I needed to get him home. So, we enjoyed a last ferry ride on the Swan River, and caught a bird's-eye view from the lookout tower in Kings Park. Then we hopped a plane over to Sydney and back to LA. In California, we regrouped at my mom's, and he boarded a bus to Wisconsin. Suddenly, I was back in the States again, and asking, *What now, Lord?*

❦ ❦ ❦

In my interim, a pastor invited me to share a testimony at the Bible college, which helped me refocus and get my bearings. Inevitably, the Rocky Mountains began to call my name again. Or was it a woman rooted deep in my heart? Or perhaps, I was stretched somewhere between California and Wisconsin, and Colorado had become the closest thing to home. Soon after, a close brother I had met in Austria was taking a road trip, and he thought he'd swing by San Diego and pick me up. Yes, he was a *Goer!* He dropped me off in the mountains in early May in sixteen inches of wet snow! I think my barometric clock was coming unwound, with all the climates and landscapes I had crossed in the past months. I stayed a week or two and hitched a ride down valley, where I caught a bus to Minneapolis to visit my sister, and then on to Wisconsin to visit my dad and retrieve my clutter from his garage.

My El Camino had not sold, and I thought I would have a better chance selling it in California, which I did. But secretly, of course, part of me longed to hit el camino (the road) and roll the windows down for a while, crank up a little Bruce on the American highway, and sleep on a country road under the stars. I longed to hear the miles of corn rustle in crescendo singing night's song, to feel the cool damp breeze condense on my brow. To be a youth again, to be alive, to be free. To drift out beyond dream's shore, beyond the magical lanterns hovering and flickering in the tall cascading field grass... beyond the swaying reeds, beyond time's watercourse meandering westward in search of eternity's tide-less sea. To be somewhere on a Midwestern road—somewhere, or anywhere, on a road closer to home. Indonesia could do that to you.

When it sold, I bought a black low-rider cruiser and saddled it up with some weathered leather bags. I headed north on circuit again. I called upon my brother in

Bakersfield. I galloped up to Boise to raise swords with a
squire from Schloss Heroldeck who had gallantly cava-
liered from the east coast to pursue acts of highest chivalry
(a beloved princess). I leapt over to Portland and rounded
up another warlord of the King. Having reached all my
posts, I laced up I-5 all the way back to Bako, and down
to Oceanside. We honored our holy *koinonia* (fellowship)
as we shared testimonies of God's grace, sharpened swords
of valor, prayed fervently, and spurred one another on to
greater works for our Lord His Sovereign Majesty![327]

Detour En Route to Éire

It was decided then. I would go to Ireland. So, I sold
my motorcycle and traded my saddlebags in for panniers.
I bought a bicycle, loaded it down, and began training
in the southern California hills. I especially enjoyed a
route through the orange groves inland from Oceanside
over Sleeping Indian. The couple from Boise was fit to
be married and set sail for Éire to shepherd a flock. The
only problem was, which flock? And, which green field
exactly? Hence, it was decided, I, the apt pursuer of the
Great Shepherd[328] and all things in motion, would go for
the team! So, I went. As *Goers* do, I *go-ed*...

---

[327] Cited respectively: 2 Cor 12:9 (My grace is sufficient for you);
Prov 27:17 (as iron sharpens iron...); 1 Chr 12:1-8 (David's mighty
men of valor); James 5:16 (the fervent prayer of a righteous man avails
much); Heb 3:13 (exhort one another daily).

[328] Great Shepherd: Heb 13:20. Chief Shepherd: 1 Pet 5:4. Good
Shepherd: John 10:11, 10:14. Shepherd: Ps 23, 80:1; Eze 34:23; Zech
13:7; Matt 2:6, 26:31; 1 Pet 2:25; Rev 7:17.

I stripped down my two-pedaled steed, boxed it up, and flew to Wisconsin for a visit before I caught my final leg out of Chicago. Coincidentally, I was just in time to catch a stepbrother dashing to the courthouse, ring in hand. I was informed at the dinner party, coincidentally, that my stepsister would be in Dublin for a marathon when I arrived. And, coincidentally, I might even have a place to crash a night or two. How like my heavenly Father to pave the road ahead!

How has God paved your road? Do you see any bricks being laid around the bend? "Oh, don't worry[329] about that." *Detours* are part of the adventure!

My detour to Wisconsin presented me with a somewhat unexpected life change. I suppose that's what detours are. There I stood, back in my hometown. The Lord's footsteps had preceded my arrival.[330] It was at this time that the Lord moved me to pursue my change of name (He gave me the opportunity to do so; He didn't command it). I often refer to such an opportunity as a "window of opportunity," in the sense that God has opened it, I should pursue it, and it may never open again. Though a name change had been on my mind for a few years, and my heavenly Father had already been referring to me by it for some time, I had not anticipated returning home to make the change.

---

[329] *Worry* as seen in: anxious, anxiety, and care (Phil 4:6; Luke 12:29; Jer 17:8; Prov 12:25; 1 Pet 5:7).

[330] Isa 45:2—"I will go before you and make the crooked places straight; I will break in pieces the gates of bronze and cut the bars of iron." Interestingly, this verse is from the passage God spoke to me confirming my name change.

However, while detoured in Wisconsin studying through Isaiah, God spoke to me personally through Isaiah 45 concerning changing my name: "I have even called thee by thy name: I have surnamed thee, though thou hast not known me" (45:4, KJV).

I believed God was opening this "window" to me as a symbol of my being adopted into His family. My relationship with my heavenly Father has always been one in which faith *and* obedience are blessed. So, I pursued the necessary legal documentation and had a court appearance scheduled for my return three months later (February, 2002), which I attended alone and read the passage from Isaiah 45:1-6 before sworn oath.

It was an intense process to walk through. How could it not be? It most definitely affected my family, friends, and relationships. How could it not? The purpose, however, was to obey what my Father had already done in His Spirit and to align my outward identity with His inward work and voice. In this sense, it was another type of baptism (death and resurrection), or a further symbol of His grafting me (a wild branch) into His Son, the root.[331] The change also symbolized the guarantee of His purchased possession, waiting in promise for His final redemption.[332] Truly, after everything my former life had characterized, a *new name* was only in suit with a *new character*. Coincidentally, Revelation teaches that the believer will receive

---

[331] Rom 11:16-18; prior note: Christ uses baptism in a *typological* sense in Luke 12:50 ("I have a baptism to be baptized with") in reference to His coming death.

[332] Eph 1:14; 2 Cor 1:22, 5:5.

a new name in heaven, and that the Lord has a new name as well.[333]

Likewise, the apostle Paul, once known as Saul, referred to himself as the "chief of sinners,"[334] and I'm certain no one understands better the transformation from sinner to saint than Paul; or, perhaps John Newton the ex-slave ship captain, and author of the hymn "Amazing Grace" (1779). I suppose John Bunyan's spiritual autobiography is also of note: *Grace Abounding to the Chief of Sinners* (1666). It appears that every "chief sinner" has had his or her encounter with Christ's immeasurable treasure of grace.[335] Certainly, none would disagree that God's grace is truly amazing, and that beyond awe and wonder, it is sufficient[336] for life and godliness.[337]

So, as my first man had died, and my second became the first,[338] so the new man rose in Christ by "the gift of God's grace" (meaning of Jon). Of course, this entire transformational work of faith was to the glory of the only

---

[333] Believers who overcome shall receive a white stone with a *new name* (Rev 2:17). Christ will bear a *new name* (Rev 3:12); and Rev 19:16—this name, though already published, will be *new* in the sense of its final or complete inauguration in the earth.

[334] 1 Tim 1:15.

[335] Christ's measure of grace: Luke 6:38; John 3:34; Eph 4:7, 4:13. Christ's riches: Rom 9:23, 11:33; Eph 1:7, 1:18, 2:7, 3:8, 3:16; Phi 4:19; Col 1:27, 2:2; 1 Tim 6:17; Heb 11:26. Christ's gift: John 4:10; Acts 2:38; Rom 5:16-18, 6:23; 1 Cor 1:7; 2 Cor 9:15; Eph 2:8, 4:7; 1 Tim 4:14; 2 Tim 1:6; Heb 6:4; James 1:17; 1 Pet 4:10.

[336] 2 Cor 9:8 is a life verse of mine—And God is able to make all grace abound toward you, that you, *always having all sufficiency in all things*, may have an abundance for every good work (emphasis).

[337] 2 Pet 1:3.

[338] Mark 9:35.

begotten Son, who gave Himself in exchange for me. My works did not accomplish it; only, my faith and obedience continued the work already begun (another "reckoning" perhaps, or a "working out" my salvation [deliverance]).[339] God's gift of grace was and is the spiritual substance necessary for the transformational life of faith in Jesus Christ. Of this, I, Jon, am fully convinced! So, for the record, there you have it—my new name.

❦ ❦ ❦

Ironically, I didn't know how Irish Jon Kelly was until I landed in Dublin and realized I was now the prideful owner of many a pub or local shoppe and had bicycled my way to international stardom (John "Sean" Kelly, 1956–). But by the time I departed Ireland, I had gotten the point; God had confirmed my new name on and around every corner! Even my bicycle (Sirrus model) affirmed the passage God had spoke to me from Isaiah forty-five concerning his prophecy to "Cyrus." Not to mention the sticker I still have on my bicycle today—an Irish crest from county Offaly with a phoenix rising out of the flames.[340] Well, I'm sure you didn't buy this book to read about me! So, I better get on with what God did in Éire.

And, "What did God do in Éire, exactly?" That's simple. He did exactly what He did when you were in Éire. Or, when your neighbor was in Éire. God did what He always

---

[339] Reckon yourselves dead to sin, alive to God (Rom 6:11); work out your salvation (Phil 2:12); see pp. 85-86 and footnotes 122, 232.

[340] County Offaly (Éire) Crest: www.abitofhome.ca/page/C1/PROD/4010923.

does in Éire—He reigned. I mean, He rained! Actually, He did both, but you thought I was going to say, "He blessed the Blarney Stone," didn't you!

IRELAND: THE EMERALD OF HIS ISLES

The plane descended into a mass of clouds and gray as the island approached. My thoughts raced as businessmen straightened their sport coats and women closed their books and gathered their purses... The storm spit us out into green fields and civilization a few feet before the wheels plunged and sprayed on the runway. We taxied, and I prayed... *My first solo mission...* Did I mention this was a faith exercise,[341] and my funds were wanting?

In a few hours there would be no daylight. I had to assemble my bike, gear-up for the rain, navigate my way into Dublin, and find a hostel for the night. POW! My tube exploded in the baggage terminal as I struggled with my frame-pump. *Another valve stem!* Yes, this was going to be an adventure!

I hung around Dublin to cheer my stepsister on for her marathon and crashed on the floor of her four star hotel behind the couch. I even received an invitation to an event party, which happened to serve up my favorite dish—grilled salmon! Then, I hosteled near Trinity College, catching culture and coffee in Phoenix Perk (local coffee house). I cycled out to Phoenix Park to spend time in prayer and meditate on God's Word as I got my compass

---

[341] 1 Tim 4:7-8—Exercise yourself toward godliness. For bodily exercise profits a little, but godliness is profitable for all things.

set and adjusted my antennas. Conveniently, the park had its own Phoenix Café for park-goers and passersby on bicycles needing to pop in for a scone and tea!

Living on the road was rough, with its unexpected entrées and hidden sanctuaries of shelter... My heavenly Father never fell short; He sees every sparrow that falls to the ground (Matthew 10:29-31). That reminds me of my little robin friends who flew by my side along the overgrown vines and stone hedgerows—I thoroughly enjoyed their company! I would venture back this very moment to bicycle with those ruddy-breasted flyers!

❧ ❧ ❧

I knocked on the caretaker's door around back. It was raining and well past dark. I was a dirty stinky mess, soaked in sweat under my rubbers, and covered in grit and grime from tire spray off the cobbles. As I said, life on the road was rough, or bumpy anyway, getting pushed off the narrow motorways by speeding side mirrors and herds of sheep. My first potential contact was a Bible school director south of Dublin. My friend had visited his ministry several times on mission trips in the past. So, I introduced myself as so-and-so stranger in the dark, from so-and-so place across the Atlantic with so-and-so purpose, connected with so-and-so, "Do you remember him?"

Well, he didn't, but that didn't stop his wife from inviting me in for tea. And before I knew it, I had my own bunk bed in the school and was on my way over to meet the local youth pastor, a missionary from California, who was hosting an alternative Halloween gathering that night (October 31, 2001). As it turned out, we had traveled similar paths and made some familiar acquaintances amongst churches and circles of peers. I served alongside him ministering to his youth for a week, as I took in what the Lord was doing, and prayed for wisdom and direction.

As I mentioned earlier my budget was tight, so I was extremely blessed when I met a security guard for Trinity's library, who got me a free entrance pass to see the Book of Kells,[342] something I had passed up earlier for lack of funds (or lack of faith). Jehovah Jireh had become much more than a name: The Lord provided (Genesis 22:14)!

But, don't take my word for it:

> Therefore I say to you, do not worry about your life, what you will eat or what you will drink; nor about your body, what you will put on. Is not life more than food and the body more than clothing? Look at the birds of the air, for they neither sow nor reap nor gather into barns; yet your heavenly Father feeds them. Are you not of more value than they? (Matthew 6:25-26)

So, spread your wings, take faith and fly! Why not?[343] Why wouldn't you, or I, trust the caring hand of a loving Father?

---

[342] The *Book of Kells* (c AD 800) contains the four gospels in Latin, ornate illuminations and calligraphy created by Celtic monks.

[343] The petition, "Why Not?" had been instrumental in prodding my faith. 2 Cor 1:20 also spurred my confidence to trust my heavenly Father—All the promises of God in Him [Christ] are Yes, and in Him Amen.

Of course, there are too many feeble reasons, but, "Why not?" Why not believe in the *value* He has placed upon you, and upon me? Why not step out and follow Him? Why not go where He leads? Why not take faith? He's there—Jehovah Shammah! Let us go to Him. Be a *Goer!*

❧   ❧   ❧

Now, where was that bicicletta taking me?[344] Oh yes, along the coast of southern Ireland! It was a glorious journey: the landscapes, friendly country folks, eclectic hostels, raw coastlines, and the fish and chips doused in malt vinegar and sea salt! I cycled my way to Waterford and down to Cork, where I met with a missionary pastor of a local church plant. I had lunch with his family after a Sunday service, and they welcomed me to stay for a while. I enjoyed the warmth of their family and country cottage; I even took their golden retriever for a few walks in the morning after throwing a brick of peat on the fire. It didn't take me long to know that this missionary family and church was the reason I was in Ireland. This was the county, field, and flock God had His eye on.

So, when I was informed of a trip the pastor would be taking back to the U.S. (they were from California), and he asked me to interim as the pastor and watch over the church, it didn't surprise me. Coincidentally, the couple

---

[344] Here's a few bike culture hot spots for your *fixie*: the next time you're touring through Fort Collins, Colorado stop by the Bean Cycle (http://thebeancycle.com/); www.bikekulture.com/ is a great site for vintage posters; and Winnipeg Cycle Chick's blog on La Bicicletta in Toronto (shop) is all things *bicicletta*: http://winnipegcyclechick. com/?p=1399.

from Boise would be in California at the same time, so a meeting was conveniently arranged between them at a pastors' conference. And to make a long story very short, several months later, the knight and his princess laid foot on the Emerald Isle to pastor their flock…

And, what of me? Well, before the pastor needed me in Cork, I had over a month to continue my tour west and north. Dingle was outrageous! The pass crossing the center of the peninsula was STEEP! *Yowzas!* I thought I might tip backward over my panniers and roll back down! I pedaled out to Tralee, and up to Tarbert, where I boarded a ferry to skip over to Shannon. Another pastor in Galway had invited me to visit and see what the Lord was doing. I had some great fellowship and attended a service, but it only confirmed that Cork was the field and treasure[345] I was searching for. So, I visited Ballynahinch Castle and kept heading north. My goal was to cycle around the coast of Ireland, taking a couple detours and train rides inland as time permitted. My next stop was St. Patrick's monument in Westport. I continued north, and my wits became a little taxed; I should say heavily taxed.

The weather was ramping up for winter, and the cold rains and rough roads were not my sunny California orange groves! I got lost late one evening as darkness shrouded the land, only to have a door shut in my face at a lone bungalow. I was hitting my wall. *Cliff* would be more accurate! Thoughts of hurling myself off a cliff, or doubts as to whether I would make it to a town, or

---

[345] Matt 13:44—The kingdom of heaven is like treasure hidden in a field…

anywhere that night were very real. And obviously, God knew I was coming unglued. Besides, I think I was down to a $150 or less. The next day, as it would be, I took a pretty intense crash in the rain when I hit some gravel at the run-out of a long hill coming into a village where tourists flocked the street near a historic cemetery. Everything seemed okay, until the following day somewhere outside Sligo. I came to a halt. My bike broke.

I know, bicycles don't just break. But, my rear drop had bent all the way back, launching my derailleur into outer space. So, why didn't I replace the hanger, or have a blacksmith re-weld the steel frame? Well, I am embarrassed to say, it was aluminum, and the hanger was part of my frame, not bolted on. Hence, my "wall" had truly come. I crashed straight into it, midday—no rain, no speeding car, no sheep, no tourist, no hill, no pothole, and no, no cliff. My bicicletta was no more! No bike shop or craftsman could repair its electric blue sparkle, or its swift downhill descent cutting through the autumn breeze. Some things, like choosing *steel* for touring, you have to learn by experience, by life on the road...

Do you have any of those stories? I bet you do! Let's get pedaling... we'll catch up down the road!

Early the next morning I hopped a train to Dublin to have an "authorized" dealer see if my bicycle could be repaired. They laughed and handed me my front fork back. They were doubtful about a warranty, but I kept my receipts anyway. They junked my frame and gave me a cardboard box in return. I packed up my wheels, components, and panniers to ship back to California by ground (or boat!). My Russian bunkmate from the hostel helped me tote my box across town. I wasn't left with much! A pair of jeans and a few T-shirts. Coincidentally, my friend in the States emailed to check in and inquired about my funds; God had provided again! So, I bought a daypack and a pair of "runners," as my Russian companion called them. Apparently, I was going to need them.

Las Ramblas en Barcelona

Meanwhile, I still had two weeks to burn before I needed to return to "The People's Republic of Cork." The hostel I was staying in was next to the bus station in north Dublin. I had recently received an email from some missionaries I knew in Spain, and as I was walking past the bus station I noticed a map in an alley highlighting bus routes all the way to Paris. I inquired about the fares, and to my surprise they were affordable. And, I'd have my own reclining bed! So, the next morning I departed my quarrelsome friends clanging in "their" kitchen,[346] and I set sail for England, by bus! …on a ferry to England, road to London, tunnel to France, and by road to Paris! Wow! The Arc de Triomphe! I had made it!

"Jon, Jon?" "Jon, is that you?" Of all the hostels I could have picked in Paris, two travelers I had shared the gospel with in Dublin six weeks earlier bumped into me in a

---

[346] Several Italian travelers contended with me daily concerning Italy's heritage, St. Peter's papal authority, and Catholic right. The fruit of their spirits was nothing familiar to love, only *clanging* pots and pans (see 1 Cor 13:1), not to mention it was a "community" kitchen!

corner market down the street. They were staying at my hostel, or I suppose I was staying at theirs! But most definitely, we both were staying at God's! I guess He "reigned" in France too! We shared dinner that night, and I was able to expound upon more of Jesus' grace and truth.[347] No doubt, God was still aware of my travels; now He was just leading me step by step in my new runners!

I boarded a train to Lyon within a day or two. Somewhere near the Spanish border, and a few *cafés con leche* later, I had finally set my pack down long enough to recoup. My immune system fought long and hard weathering those Irish roads, but had surrendered at last to my billowing sinuses! As we neared Madrid, terracotta landscapes radiated through my window. The soil and air were dry. I drank in the sun's penetrating rays. I hadn't enjoyed such warmth since leaving California months ago. My body smiled as I soaked up the rest. God was giving me a breather, and preparing me for the days ahead.

Finally, I had made it to Seville where I was welcomed by two missionary couples. Their hospitality was refreshing! They even showed me the Plaza de España as seen in *Star Wars:* Episode II (film, 2002). One particular afternoon, after venturing out by foot to the city center, I wandered into a quiet local park to rest my feet before returning to their flat. A sun-drenched bench in a far end of the park beckoned me. Not long after I sat down, I watched two men navigate the length of the park. As they drew closer, and closer, I realized their sights were

---

[347] John 1:14-17—Jesus came in the fullness of grace and truth.

set on me. A quick observation of the park told me I was trapped. So, I waited and prayed as they cornered in…

After some preliminary shouting and obscene gestures, a few slaps in the face, and looting my pockets, the confrontation continued to heighten showing no signs of me exiting peacefully. (The less aggressive of the two had his hand behind his back as if to be holding a weapon; at this point it was a bit of a psychological game determining if he was holding a knife, a gun, or nothing. I had come to the conclusion that if it was a knife he or his buddy would have had it out already, so it had to be a gun, or a bluff?) By now, the language confusion, which I initially leveraged to my advantage, was waning. Time was ticking; I continued to wait…

Suddenly, my spirit stood alert, quickened with urgency. Next, I stood up in the power of the Holy Spirit and dropped my head as I charged straight at them. I bulldozed my way through their tackles; but one man clung to my courier bag, whipping me around and round, nearly tearing its last threads off my shoulder. I dodged, scrambled, and rolled in the dirt, darting and circling through a loose grove of trees. At the faintest glimpse that the Spaniards were tiring, I surged a final sprint toward an adjacent fence. I hurled myself ten feet over the chain-link and never looked back. I had escaped!

Fortunately, I didn't get raped by, or stoned with any

of the large rocks the aggressor threatened me with.[348] I was only beaten and bruised a bit, and lost a little pocket cash. It was an intense hands-on encounter of learning to listen to my Father under critical pressure, and to act when He gave the command! I was also encouraged to witness the transformed work of His Spirit in me, as I did not retaliate in some raged fit of violence, as I would have years earlier, whether to my destruction or not. Apparently, my *runners* were now officially broken-in! But, it was only my warm-up!

I traveled up the coast to Barcelona to see some of Gaudi's architecture and Picasso's works. Soon after, I began to feel like I had a target on the back of my head! A drug addict attached himself to me walking up the Las Ramblas in mid-daylight. He slipped a syringe out of his coat sleeve and began to reason with me, threatening to stab my gut if I didn't give him my money. I didn't have much money, and I didn't know if he really had HIV or he was lying, but I kept my cool and just walked with him. I didn't feel like screaming was the right protocol; He was English, so I shared the gospel with him. Really, I was just buying time and waiting for the Lord's direction. And then it came, "Run!" I broke free and ran, and ran, and ran… until my *runners* were in flames! I don't think

---

[348] Of note here is that God had spoken a personal promise into my life—"I will not violate you."—while doing some healing within me shortly after I was saved. He used this situation to prove Himself to me again. I don't relate this as a general promise to all in every circumstance; this was a personal promise to me concerning specific abusive contexts.

I stopped looking over my shoulder till I made it back to Cork!

When the "Spanish Boxer" stepped in for me at the bus stop waiting to depart Barcelona, and zipped up the hood over a thug's head whose gang had circled around me, I knew for sure that God's angelic host was watching over me! I couldn't escape España fast enough! My runners were still smokin' under my seat as the bus rolled back into Paris.

❧ ❧ ❧

I befriended a student from Japan at the Eiffel Tower and clothed him in a sweater. Peculiar to me, he toted a little insignificant knapsack, no jacket, and a camera. He was lost. I had learned enough my first time traveling through Paris to give him a basic tour, and see a few new sights along the way. Cathédrale Notre-Dame's imagery helped me translate the gospel message and share Christ's love with him.

My trip back through London to Dublin was quick and less eventful. I made it to Cork just in time for Christmas and pastored through January (2002) until my visa expired in February. It was interesting to watch the "Celtic Tiger" adjust its diet as the currency switched to the Euro. As I counted the church offering, different thoughts came to mind. *Was I watching biblical prophecy unfold before my eyes?* As I held the coin in my hand depicting a woman riding a beast, I wondered, *Were my fingers unfolding the pages of Revelation 17?*

Back stateside, things were coming together as my

friends met the pastor, and he decided it was time to bring his family back to California. God had found their flock! As if the Great Shepherd could ever misplace His sheep! Not even one goes astray without His sight.[349] Cork's little fellowship above the old sewing machine shop was home to some wonderful believers. A few years ago, when Alisa and I were living in Anacortes, Washington, we were encouraged to meet up with a couple visiting Seattle. Now, Alisa keeps in touch with her through email, as they both are in the "new" motherhood stage. The journey continues!

❦   ❦   ❦

Aer Lingus touched down on the runway at O'Hare, and I was home. Mission accomplished! A generous Christian family took me in while I wrapped up my name change with the State of Wisconsin. A few weeks later, my dad dropped me off back in Chicago, and I boarded a train to California. It was good to be heading west, stuck on a train for several days. It gave me time to actually "land," and get it out of gear. Familiar landscapes rolled by as the days grew warmer. My journal filled up with memories. The Pacific breeze soothed my cheeks as I disembarked in Los Angeles. I caught the Coaster down south, and my mom picked me up at the train station. A few weeks later my boat came in from Ireland; my bike box had arrived! I wrote the company and they *did* warranty my bike! They upgraded my frame by one year and one model, plus they threw in a carbon fiber fork! I kept my old shiny blue fork

---

[349] Matt 18:11-14.

as a souvenir of victory... I guess God had "blessed the Blarney Stone" after all!

There was only one thing left for me to do. So, I saddled my new mount, clicked in, and pedaled out to Sleeping Indian through my orange grove, praising God for all His marvelous works He had performed on *Phoenix Road*: "Great and marvelous are Your works, Lord God Almighty! Just and true are Your ways, O King of the saints!"[350] "For He has done marvelous things; His right hand and His holy arm have gained Him the victory" (Psalm 98:1). Amen.[351]

---

[350] Rev 15:3.

[351] Amen: so be it, so it is, or may it be fulfilled (as a response of agreement by the hearer of God's Word, and in doing so, making it his or her own); "It was a custom, which passed over from the synagogues to the Christian assemblies, that when he who had read or discoursed, had offered up solemn prayer to God, the others responded *Amen*, and thus made the substance of what was uttered their own." "The word 'amen'... was transliterated directly from the Hebrew into the Greek of the New Testament, then into Latin and into English and many other languages, so that it is practically a universal word. It has been called the best known word in human speech. The word is directly related... to the Hebrew word for 'believe' (amam), or faithful. Thus, it came to mean 'sure' or 'truly,' an expression of absolute trust and confidence. —HMM" From: Blue Letter Bible lexicon at: http://www.blueletterbible.org/lang/lexicon/lexicon.cfm?Strongs=G281&t=NKJV (accessed April 14, 2013).

HIGH DESERT YEARS

THE SLEEPING INDIAN GREW RESTLESS. I suppose it was bound to happen, and probably even right that he would do so. And natural of a certainty, for "it is not good that man should be alone…"

Well, as the story goes, "the LORD God caused a deep sleep to fall on Adam, and he slept" while the Lord fashioned his rib into a woman, "and He brought her to the man" (Genesis 2:18-22). Indeed, the Indian had grown restless… In his much coming and going, in his knapsack life, in his loss of warriors and tribesmen to breeding life, moon after moon he grew restless.

The starry desert nights began to wane as he curled up lone asleep in his fleece beneath the heat of "Ol' Grace's" exhaust pipe. Where was his "bone of my bone, and flesh of my flesh?" Where was his "woman, whom was taken out of man" (2:23)? And so, Sleeping Indian stirred restless, chilled in the early morning dawn. The light of sun had not broken the tree before he journeyed to a mountain far away, beyond the warm springs and long flowing river. Sleeping Indian walked half-asleep to a high mountain plain. His journey was without map or compass; faith led his heart to a mountain life far above the sea, far above the low hot place. These are the High Desert Years...

12

COLORADO STILL CALLING

YES, IT'S TRUE, SHE WAS. Or, it was. Or, I was? My journey back to Colorado was sometimes questioned as a "going back to Egypt?" I did not believe so. Perhaps it was my less familiar route traveling from the west coast back toward the east. Or, maybe it was the unexplored range of Rockies tucked along the backside, in the southwest corner of the state. Or, maybe my new man had more backbone to believe that God was truly able to move mountains,[352] and turn the hearts of girls and boys, like that of a king's.[353] One might reply, "Or, maybe it was old roots and undying infatuation?" And another, "It could have been faith. It could have been hope. And, it could have been love."[354] But, in the end, as faith's race nears exhaustion, one can

---

[352] Matt 17:20, 21:21.

[353] Prov 21:1—The king's heart is in the hand of the LORD, like rivers of water; He turns it wherever He wishes.

[354] 1 Cor 13:13—Faith, hope, and love; but the greatest of these is love.

see God waving His beloved around every bend and corner, cheering her on toward the finish line…

❧ ❧ ❧

It was time to face the cards. Shooting past San Diego, I returned with my friend to Boise as he and his "glorious crown" finalized their countdown to Ireland. These were exciting days, no doubt! Like children in the grass awaiting the Fourth of July, faith ignited our hearts and launched us out… *Would our boom reverberate in their chests? Would our sparks shower the sky? Would they clap and cheer for more? Or, would we be a dud? Where would we land once we came back down?*

Myriad questions circled our minds and loomed in our hearts. We clung to God's Word and lifted our eyes unto Him from whence comes our help.[355] And, as we escaped from the city to pray atop an overlooking hill, God gifted my brother with a passage bearing prophetic insight for me from 2 Kings concerning an "upper room with a bed, table, chair, and lamp," prepared for the prophet Elijah by a notable woman (4:10). So, I loaded up my bike and backpack into their, now my, or God's Pathfinder[356] as we waved each other on, and I descended southward, off the grid, to Colorado's back door.

"Knock, knock?" Slam!

---

[355] Ps 121:1-2.

[356] This gift of generosity was actually the fulfillment of a promise of God to me from a few years earlier when I had gifted a vehicle to someone "by faith." This is the testimony of God's people living out Acts 2:44-45.

Just kidding! Well, almost! I arrived in Telluride unbeknownst, as was my usual rhythm in such faith pursuits.
Which, by the way, has its pros and cons! But one thing it
does very consistently, it puts the cards on the table, face
up—make no mistake about it! So, I was committed to
see what the Lord might finally do, once and for all, with
this Rocky Mountain girl, and this "love" in my heart. I
came to face the music. Dance with the piper! Sing with
the fat lady? But, you know what, I didn't dance, I didn't
sing, and I didn't even get to hear any music. Which might
really be a shame, concerning the thousands of people
who flock into Telluride's acoustic box canyon for music
festivals yearly. But, I suppose that's beside the point.

So, what did happen? She gave me "the hug" and said
something to the effect of, "I love you, but I can't do it."
It, meaning: commit to me, to Christ, or to a future. So,
she walked out to leave for a holiday, and that was it! I
never saw her face, or back again. The years, the letters,
the prayers, the powerful movements of God through His
creation (like the bear in her kitchen, or the hummingbird
in her living room), the mutual desire for abandonment
to spirituality, and the hearts' exchanges of promises…
No. That was *it!*

Of course, my heart could not accept "it" that simply.
But somehow, in my spirit, I knew that this was truly time
to "let go." Why, or how? Well, those were two totally
different animals I wasn't even ready to face! But, as I
stood down the road at the corner store thinking, *Now
what, Lord?* I flipped open the classifieds, and the first ad in
the upper left corner under Rentals read: "One Bedroom

Upper Room." And, despite its uncertain location in a nearby town down-valley, I knew "it" was where God was leading me. Which also meant that God knew how the events were going to unfold before I had even arrived, before He even put the prophetic word into my brother's heart in Boise. And, yes, long before that!

In some spiritual way I had been liberated. My heart, however, kept on the lookout, watching, waiting for something, someone who would never come. My heart mourned a loss, and grieved as if someone had passed away. And, I suppose, that was the process that I needed to go through, the *how* of beginning to "let go." My heart had to let go. And, by God's grace it could, and did. And, my mind followed. Isn't it comforting to know that God's grace is always sufficient, at all times, and in all places[357]— even in the innermost depths of our hearts?

You know me well enough by now, right? So, you know that I'm about to turn the tables and ask if you have any cards that you need to lay down? So, do you? Is there anything tugging at your heart that you know you need to surrender to the Lord? You can trust Him; He cares for you,[358] and He is worthy of your trust. "Yes, I know, even with your heart." Remember, He sacrificed His only Son's life for you. So, as Francois Fénelon (1651–1715) rightly said, "Let Go" (published 1973), and many have since added, "Let God!" And in the end, it begins with a choice. You can choose to "let go," you can choose to "let

---

[357] One of my life verses: 2 Cor 9:8 (see also footnote 336).

[358] 1 Pet 5:5—Casting all your care upon Him, for He cares for you.

God!" God has equipped us with the power and freedom to choose! And, if you're anything like me, you're going to have to square up to that choice, go head to head, and stare it in the eyes: "There's no way around this one, son!"

❧   ❧   ❧

Interestingly, the woman God did wake me out of sleep with years later also had a similar engagement of heart in Telluride. Well, perhaps I should say, the woman God drew to my side, the "comparable helper" (Genesis 2:18); because, I was not truly fast asleep, I was secretly peeping through one eye. Nevertheless, she did catch me off guard. But, this isn't her story! And, there's plenty more to mine (and lines between lines), so let's keep on truckin' down *Phoenix Road.*

TRUE GRIT

Could anything good come out of Montrose?[359] Sure, I had no doubt whatsoever that this was where God's prophetic word had put my feet down: the *upper room* apartment fit Isaiah's description to the "T," the owner was a woman and a Christian, she even prayed with me while finalizing the rental contract, and lowered my rent and waved my deposit as a result (which was extremely gracious and needed). But still, *Why Montrose? Where was Montrose, anyway? How did Montrose fit into the picture?* I still recall some friends passing through from Portland

---

[359] John 1:46—Can anything good come out of Nazareth?

that year; they were baffled, "What are you doing here?"
And, "Why Montrose?"

Well, I wasn't sure. And, hopefully time would tell. But
until then, I was broke, back in the "real world," and
I needed a job. A few weeks passed before I got hired
on with a big construction outfit building a high-dollar
ranch on Wilson Mesa outside of Telluride. My commute
through Ridgway, home to John Wayne's *True Grit* (film,
1969), took me over Dallas Divide around the backside
(south) of the San Juan Mountains, to follow the San
Miguel River east climbing elevation into the San Miguels.
All said and done, it was an hour and a half commute
after picking up my three hombres, who couldn't keep the
greatest of conversation and crashed out daily on the drive
home—keeping one eye on the road was the toughest job!
But just like all men, we were trying to make ends meet
and bring home the money with sweat on our brow and
grit in our teeth. I got promoted not long after, and in a
few short months I found myself being borrowed-out to a
local woodworking shop to keep up with the production
of the ranch's custom barn-wood doors.

That's when I met the Big Dog! Of course, as all "big
dogs" are, he was big, and boss. No, not necessarily Hugo
Boss, more Carhartt than finely German tailored. I suppose he saved that for his precision Martin Woodworking
Machinery. My current boss bought out my contract with
a local hiring agency and set me free. In my mind, I felt
like the slave Christ purchased[360] off the auction block. I

---

[360] Eph 1:14 (Christ's "purchased possession" is His body of believers); 1 Cor 6:19-20 (you are not your own, you were bought at a price).

was a free agent at last! In reality, he turned me over to Big Dog, who gave me the opportunity to work inside a nice warm shop all winter and learn the trade of a master craftsman. And truly, I was blessed. *What did I know about woodwork and bright blue German machinery?* Not much, and I suppose that was apparent. But, Big Dog was gracious and lined me out daily, teaching me the ropes, or the grains, have you. Now that I think of it, "teachability" and humility was my greatest door to success. Working with wood was therapeutic, and it fit well into the context of life on the Western Slope. Besides, wasn't Christ a carpenter? I know, McDowell rightly stated that Jesus was *More Than a Carpenter* (1977) in his classic apologia.[361] Working with my hands also gave my mind time to think. Time to ask some questions. Time to reflect on the past several years of coming and going. Time to recalibrate and stand in the present. And, time to pray about where the future was leading me.

When I wasn't up in the high-country working, I retreated back home to the "banana belt," as my old Italian coworker used to joke. Secretly, he was hinting at how much he'd like to come down off the mountain and play a few rounds of golf early in the spring. Montrose rests in the Uncompahgre River Valley running north to Grand Mesa and south to the San Juan Mountains. As such, it is often referred to as the Gateway to the San Juans, however, don't tell anyone in Ridgway I said that!

The banana belt offered something else beyond moderate

---

[361] Apologia—speaking in defense; see Paul's apologia in Acts 26:2 where he "answers for himself."

temps and fertile agriculture. The valley provided great routes to pedal on my bicicletta! And, as is true in most of Colorado, one need not go far before going up or going down! So, I really had to leg-up my horses to keep 'em trotting up the climbs. My first ride out to the Black Canyon National Park east of Montrose caught me a few spurs in the butt. My little steed ran out of water after the second cattle guard and I had to turn 'er back; I was out of gas! But soon enough, I was climbing all the local passes and racing down the descents: Cimarron, Dallas, Keystone, Red Mountain, Molas, and Coal Bank. In the morning for breakfast, after work racing the sunset, and all day Saturday—I cycled them all, and back!

Oh yeah, I almost forgot a classic, the Colorado National Monument just west of Grand Junction (as seen in *American Flyers*, 1985). You don't want to miss that one; just keep an eye out for Ranger Rick's speed trap on your descent! And, DO NOT cross the yellow to pass!

❦ ❦ ❦

It was at a local Bible teaching church that I really became part of a community. In our individualistic western culture where "I can do it," self-determination often forfeits true community. Even in small towns, or "mountain communities," where one would think community is essential, and the norm, it is not. Unlike our western Do-It-Yourself attitude, Christians are called to be in community. Beyond that, we are *created for community*. Hear these words of Paul spoken to his Roman brothers and sisters: "We, being many, are one body in Christ, and individually members of one another" (Romans 12:5). *Members of one another!* When is the last time you saw that tagline on your community knitting group flier? Too often, we go it alone, or we look in the wrong places for community. But, as Paul revealed, Christ's body of believers is formed of many diverse persons, each with unique personalities and essential qualities for the whole.[362] While Christ remains the head,[363] His body is entirely holistic. *Every* member is necessary! I need you locally; we need you globally!

So, if you're craving a healthy others-centered community—one that you can give yourself to, and be supported by—understand that God has created you for community. Allow me to challenge you to find a true Christ-like body, take on Christ's skin, and do your part today!

Getting back to the local church, it was there that God opened doors for ministry (service).[364] And very simply stated, *service to people* should be expected within an others-centered community, Shouldn't it? I was blessed with several opportunities to invest in the lives of youth. The small town offered ample instances for unexpected accountability, unplanned admonishments, and spontaneous outreach among peers. Basically, I was an older brother, doing my part!

It was also there, in community, that God planted His first seed of faith concerning a future trip to Phoenix,

---

[362] Rom 12:4; 1 Cor 12:4-7, 18-20, 25-27.

[363] Col 1:18; Eph 5:23.

[364] Ministry simply means "service," from *diakonia* in Greek.

Crete,[365] as we studied through Acts chapter twenty-seven. It wasn't much later that I started receiving various emails from people ministering in Greece (a Greek woman my mother knew in her church had obviously spread the word around the globe about my prayerful interest). Ironically, a couple from church who invited me over for dinner had a picture of Greece in their kitchen, which apparently was a duplicate. I left that night with the same picture in hand for my wall, only slightly wrinkled! It would be seven years, however, before the vision grew wings and we (the dream included my future bride) flew to the Caldera in Santorini. To my naivety, however, this was the exact location of the picture on my wall all those years, but had gone unrealized until returning home to view it with Grecian eyes. As I starred at the picture eating breakfast one morning, it finally hit me as I exclaimed: "We were right there; I stood right in that spot!" Of all the places on the planet, "I've been right there!" Another Jehovah Shammah—The LORD Is There—experience no doubt! Yes, the vision and grace of God are triumphant indeed!

❧   ❧   ❧

Triumphant! Can I throw it in "idle" a moment and tell you about how God blessed me with a Triumph motorcycle last year? No, I won't get too sidetracked! Maybe a bit kick-started, though!

I was jobless. We had recently returned to Montrose and I happened to see a used motorcycle for sale. So,

---

[365] Acts 27:12—Phoenix Harbor, southwestern Crete, Greece.

one glorious afternoon I invited my gracious wife to go for a drive and I just happen to wander north of town… Remember, I was jobless and we were broke; don't try this one at home, boys! "Do you want to hear it run?" asked the salesman as my wife's eyes met mine. "Yes, I'd love to hear it turn over!" *Growl! Growl! Growl!* Of course, next he asked me if I wanted to ride it. But, I denied testosterone's call to throttle back into the wind; I said, "No, I'm fine," as I looked back at my wife. So, we got into the car, and as I reversed out of the parking lot I noticed a familiar face at an adjacent business—a delivery terminal. And having managed a delivery route before, I pulled forward and asked him if the company was hiring. Long story short, we reversed back out of the parking lot past the sparkling green motorcycle that day, only now I had a job! Praise God! He knows all our desires and what makes us tick! And, *Growl!*

Oh yeah, you wanted to know about the motorcycle, I almost forgot! It sold; or so I thought. But, a year later as I pulled into the terminal after work, there was the "Growler" again! And, I almost couldn't believe my eyes, the way its green and silver tank sparkled in the sun… *How could this be; what was it doing back in my life?* Well, now I had a little money saved, so my gracious wife agreed to offer a low price for it, and it was mine—Emerald Tiger now resides in my garage! But more often, I suppose you can hear him *Growling* down Main Street near my office. And to top it off, in true Jehovah Jireh[366] manner, I just

---

[366] Gen 22:13-14—God provided for Abraham's sacrifice in perfect timing: The-LORD-Will-Provide (Jehovah Jireh).

happened to be teaching a men's Bible study through 2 Corinthians chapter 2 that very week: "Thanks be to God who always leads us in *triumph* in Christ" (2:14, emphasis). Yes, triumphant indeed!

❦ ❦ ❦

We had better get back on track… we've got seven years of roads to travel down, so you can't keep kick-starting me like that. Yes, like to our Israeli tour guide, or the Gateway to the San Juan Islands, or our Garden Island paradise in Kauai. Or, the 2,500 Athenian Marathon Anniversary. He was a great guide by the way! And we did return to Nazareth for that heavenly lotion (chapter 1). And yes, we did finish the race running into the Olympic Stadium beneath the Acropolis. But, I've got a mission to accomplish here; don't distract me! And if I'm navigating correctly, I think I can get us there in a few more clicks… I know for sure I can burn up the next several years real quick, racing around the track! As I used to say to Ol' Big Dog when he commented on my Monk-ish[367] attention to detail, "I do everything slow, except win!" So, here's to you, Big Dog! Who's the Top Dog on the track now?

FIGHTING FERRARI

I pulled into the gravel driveway unannounced. I had forgotten my shampoo at a couple's house from church

---

[367] Apparently, some of my perfectionism reminded my boss of *Monk* (a TV sitcom); not owning a TV myself, however, I was relatively ignorant of Monk's behaviors!

the summer I "free-grazed," as Big Dog liked to chuckle. Ironically, I had rented a house from the couple earlier that year, before I moved out into my truck to save money. She came out to greet me and took notice of my bicycle on the roof rack. She asked if I knew how to swim. "Swim? Of course, I could swim. But, swim, like for real? No, the closest thing was a few laps in gym class." Then she mentioned she did a sprint triathlon the previous year, the race was coming up again, and that I should do it. I asked if she was going to be doing it again, and she said, "No, I don't have the time, but you should do it…"

So, that was that, I came for shampoo and I left with, "I *should* do a triathlon!" I suppose, as with most of my stories, there's a bit more to it; as my wife would say, "You always have a reason." And, I suppose, the magazine I accidentally acquired from the bike shop in California before I went to Ireland, was no different.

A triathlon magazine somehow made its way into a heap of free publications I had gathered off a table of literature. I breezed through it noticing the pictures of determined athletes and their lean fit bodies as they gave it their all swimming through open water swells, biking through scorching lava fields, and crawling across the finish lines of brutal marathons. I didn't think much of it at the time, other than they were in a whole other race—not mine! My race was the "race of faith."[368] I tossed the magazine aside and forgot about it. But, as those seeds do, somewhere in

---

[368] Paul the apostle often exhorted believers to run their "race of faith" with perseverance to receive the prize: Acts 20:24; 1 Cor 9:24; 2 Tim 4:7; Heb 12:1.

the back of my mind, or heart, a little sprout had begun to germinate. And the thought went something like this, *God had promised me He would heal me entirely, not just my spiritual, mental, emotional person, but even my physical man, after all the broken bones and broken dreams of my past life.* So, when I heard her telling me I *should* do a triathlon, something reverberated deep in my soul, as if to be God saying, "Jon, here's an opportunity for Me to prove to you that I *have* healed you, even physically, 'Why Not,' do it and find out?" And so, that was really that; that was my reason! I never did find that old magazine in my trunk, though.

I started teaching myself to swim the next day. And I really went for it, all the way down to the Speedos! A coworker had graciously offered me a rent-free cottage to stay in for the fall in Ouray while I continued to save money. The Ouray Hot Springs pool had convenient outdoor lap lanes, so I ran down nightly from my little cottage and trained in the pool. Ouray sits at 7,770 feet above sea level, so my training was right on target for peak performance! I pre-raced the course a week or so prior to race day; my coach clocked me in and said, "If you hit that time, we'll be lookin' real good." Of course, as coaches do, *God* knew the course and field best. So, I just trusted Him and raced my race!

My mom came out for her first visit to Montrose and cheered me on! The film *Seabiscuit* (2003) opened the same summer, and I took great encouragement from the wheezy limping colt and underdog alcoholic jockey. I think my mom was as surprised as I was; however, when

I streaked across the finish line in my Speedos to the podium, winning first place in my Age Group. Wow! What a rush! I was hooked, and just as my coach had prophesied, "I'd be sittin' real good," if I could just keep 'er on track. My "faith" moved mountains that day as I "raced my race!" And it just so happened that just up the road at Telluride's Skyline Ranch,[369] Hollywood star Fighting Ferrari (Seabiscuit) was grazing in the paddock. I'm not totally certain, however, that the Biscuit would classify as "free-grazer" status!

I followed the Colorado downstream to Arizona for another late season race. Another Age Group win sealed the deal; I was sold! "Spinning to win" in a wide new world became my new race of faith! In Arizona I met a brother racing for Athlete's In Action, a nonprofit Christian organization, which was just launching out into triathlon. My passion to do all things for the Lord[370] made an affiliation with AIA a great fit and provided opportunities to share my faith and encourage other racers. Hopefully, toward their *race of faith!*

Returning from Arizona, Colorado was growing cold, and Ouray's box canyon had grown dark. With no permanent shelter to dwell in, and no prized companion to take home after my victories, I set my sights on California. Catalina Island to be exact! A warm late-late season race centered in the Mediterranean-esque Avalon Bay was

---

[369] See related article: "Cinema's Seabiscuit Retires to Telluride's Skyline Ranch to Enjoy the Good Life," by John Fugatt in *Guidebook America* (www.guidebookamerica.com/news/seabiscuit/index.htm).

[370] 1 Cor 10:31; Col 3:17, 3:23.

God-breathed! A spectacular premonition of my glorious Greece, perhaps! After the race, however, as I harbored in Bakersfield, I was confronted by my Coach. He advised me that I "should" consider returning to Bible college and "finish my race." I should also add that "school" was not on my radar, nor my race calendar! Nevertheless, I heeded my Coach's advice: I put my cargo trailer up for sale, sold my possessions, and set sail for Murrieta Hot Springs once again. I knew the routine well by now, so I chose to live off campus, flying low profile under the radar. Interestingly, God was still there (Jehovah Shammah), and He was still calling me.

Well, after a semester (Spring 2004) of joblessness, living by faith off of church food bank donations, and rent supplements by a gracious brother in San Diego, I began to ask the Lord what He had in mind for summer. I happened to be studying through the book of Jeremiah when several passages referencing God's restoration of the "towns of the western foothills" captured my attention. And further stating that "deeds would be signed, sealed, and witnessed," and that the "voice of bride and bridegroom" would be heard once more in the land![371]

Several days later I received a mysterious letter from my grandma with magazine clippings from Ouray, Colorado. A few days after that, Big Dog emailed me and asked if I'd be interested in returning to work in June. So, to my stubborn refusal, I pulled the anchor and let 'er drift back to Colorado, from whence I came. Which, considering I

---

[371] Jer 32:44, 33:11, 33:13-14 (all NIV).

only had one semester left to complete my two-year degree (going on 4 years now), the plan didn't make much sense to me. But, I heard the wind blow, and soon enough the seas began to stir… I took courage, confronted by Christ's word: "So is everyone who is born of the Spirit."[372] Yet, headstrong, I wrestled with my Captain[373] through the night[374] as I churned and circled, stuck in the current, until finally surrendering my oars to the sea…

REVIVAL OF THE HEART

I washed up on the shore of the Western Slope at the foot of my old house in Montrose. Amazingly enough, God had heard my disgruntled prayer (if you can call it that): "I will not start over again." But, as He handed me the keys to my old house, and I drove back to my former job down the same mountain road, He whispered in my ear, "You're not starting over; you're picking up where you left off!" I could handle that, I guess! So, I hopped back on my trusty two-wheeled steed and spun off into the western foothills. My horses were chompin' at the bit; all of that running in the California hills over the winter must have paid off. One ride up to the Black Canyon opened

---

[372] John 3:8—The wind blows where it wishes, and you hear the sound of it, but cannot tell where it comes from and where it goes. So is everyone who is born of the Spirit.

[373] Heb 2:10—Having brought many sons to glory, Jesus is the captain of salvation.

[374] Jacob wrestled with a Man (perhaps the Angel of the LORD) through the night, until the Man finally dislocated his hip and blessed him (Gen 32:24-29).

up my spirit and my lungs; I gave a loud "Woop!" out to the snow-covered panorama cradling the green valley. Springtime in the mountains! My heart told me it was great to be home! The San Juans can do that to you; make any man a gunslinger, a real cowboy at heart!

God opened the doors of a different church to me when I arrived. Their youth and college ministry was more suited to my gifts and personality. I was invited to tag along as a mentor on a trip back to Illinois. Yes, how'd you guess? Cornerstone music festival! It was great to come full circle and see God's bigger picture; I even bumped into a few friends from the Midwest. I assisted the youth pastor throughout the year as his family adjusted to "baby life." The last time we caught up over pizza was traveling through Portland a few years ago. It is always encouraging to connect with old friends and join in with what God is doing in their lives. We even got to grab a coffee together down by Burnside Bridge. It's changed a bit since those high school days I "ripped" it with my buddy!

❧   ❧   ❧

The holidays brought me back to California several times that year to visit my mom. After stumbling into a former schoolmate from a Systematic Theology class, I suppose I had other motives as well. She lassoed me with her eyes, and our hearts entwined quickly. Before long we were traveling down fate's road to wedlock. The road threw some twists and turns at our engagement, however, and when we finally hit a wall, I can only believe God unlocked our hearts and futures with His keys of sovereignty.

Have you ever experienced heartbreak? Let me rephrase that, have you ever had that gut-wrenching, tearing, twisting, churning, helpless feeling deep in your soul, deeper than you even knew you had a soul? I've experienced that lovely slice of life a few times, perhaps a few times too many. But, if you're willing to keep seeking your First Love, and keep opening your heart to His breath, I know He will work even this for your greater good according to His good pleasure.[375]

God is there (Ezekiel 48:35), even in the depths of our hearts' most difficult journeys.[376] We must draw deep from the Spirit's well of love. He is our First Love, "and we love Him because He first loved us" (1 John 4:19). If, in all our vulnerability, we abandon ourselves to Him naked and raw, He has the power to heal and mold our hearts into the whole man or woman He longs, and we truly long to be. Our First Love is a transforming Lover! God authored our divine romance; He wrote the novel! He is writing on your fleshy heart right now.[377] God *is* love,[378] and He *is* loving you right now. Open your heart... Hear

---

[375] Rev 2:4 (first Love); Rom 8:28 (all things work together for good...); Phil 2:13; Eph 1:5, 1:9 (according to His good pleasure); 2 Thes 1:11 (that God would fulfill all the good pleasure of his goodness).

[376] Rom 8:35-39 (nothing can separate us from the love of Christ); Heb 4:12 (the word of God is a discerner of the thoughts and intents of the heart); Eph 3:16-21 (His love surpasses knowledge and thought); Ps 73:26 (my flesh and heart fail, but God is the strength of my heart and my portion forever).

[377] 2 Cor 3:3—You are an epistle of Christ... written by the Spirit of the living God, not on tablets of stone but on tablets of flesh, of the heart.

[378] 1 John 4:8, 4:16; not to be confused with the popular and misinterpreted statement: "Love is God."

Him speak to your soul… Sense His relentless jealousy… His delight in you… You are His portion… God is love.[379]

❧ ❧ ❧

So, what was a guy to do? Yep, I kept on racing! I dug in deep and kept my "race of faith" rolling down *Phoenix Road.* Interestingly, my road did take me to Phoenix. Sowing deep into my First Love blossomed into a season of newness of life.[380] A new job revived my mind. A new ministry opportunity revived my spirit. A new bicycle revived my faith (2 years in praying). A new level of racing revived my body. And eventually as God would have it, a new love in my life revived my heart. To my ignorance, I had shut the door of my heart airtight like a sealed jar! But as I said, all these things worked together for my good and His good pleasure, as God opened my heart and breathed new life into my soul.

As Jesus rightly declared, "I am the door. If anyone enters by Me, he will be saved… I have come that they may have life, and that they may have it more abundantly" (John 10:9-10). My First Love opened the door of my heart to His abundant life. He is still breathing new life and opening the door of my heart wider today! Abundant

---

[379] Cited respectively: Heb 3:7-8 (Today, if you will hear His voice, do not harden your heart); Rev 2:27 (he [/she] who has an ear, hear what the Spirit says to the church); Ex 34:14 (for the LORD whose name is Jealous, is a jealous God); Ps 18:19 (He delivered me because He delighted in me); Ps 149:4 (the LORD takes delight in His people—NIV); Deut 32:9 (for the LORD's portion is His people); Zech 2:12 (the LORD will inherit Judah as his portion—ESV); 1 John 4:8 (God is love; see also footnote 378).

[380] Rom 6:4, 7:6—Newness of life/of the Spirit.

life is beyond anything any earthly heart can pluck up out of the dirt. Have you opened the door of your heart to the "light of the world?"[381] Is new and vigorous life beginning to sprout in your life? Or, like me, do you need revival of the heart?

IRONMAN

The Phoenix Half Ironman[382] in October 2005 was a test. I missed my goal by three minutes. But after five hours of racing in mid eighties temps, having had trained in the forties, I was content. And, more than content, I sensed God's "good pleasure" when I came across the finish line celebrating my spiritual birthday (the following day was 10/31) and rejoicing in a race well run! My sights were set on Ironman, that mysterious creature lurking and taking form somewhere out in the distant mist.

In the meantime, I rose to the call to lead a college group at church through the book of Romans. And, as it would be, while faithfully and quietly searching the Scriptures and expounding upon God's truth… there she was (Jehovah Shammah). Up from the ashes she grew, fragrant and full of beauty she arose. "Like a lily among thorns, so is my love among the daughters" (Song of Songs 2:2). The Lord woke me at last, opening my heart and wooing my spirit after His virtuous daughter, adorned in splendor

---

[381] John 8:12—I [Christ] am the light of the world, he who follows me shall have the light of life.

[382] The Soma Triathlon—Half Ironman Distance, Tempe, AZ (October 30, 2005): 13th Age Group 25–29, 5:03:01.

and fine purple linen (Proverbs 31:10, 22).

For a moment she fled over the mountains back to Boulder, but I skipped over the Rockies following swiftly after. I surrendered my community, friendships, and livelihood to pursue her captive embrace. Our stories were too similar, our families, our pasts, our pilgrimages to Montrose, only our heavenly Father could have orchestrated such hearts to cross paths. But mostly, it was our unity and oneness in God's presence that assured my heart with peace and abundant grace that God Most High was glorified in this unity of hearts. So, it was only fitting that we returned to the San Juans to ascend the Bridge of Heaven and seal our commitment with a promise ring. Our covenant would also be sealed in the San Juans, but I'm not ready to share that yet! Almost, but not yet, there's still racing to be done!

I raced the Boulder Half Ironman[383] in August 2006. I woke early before work to log miles on my bike, and after digging trenches and picking boulders all day, I ran to the pool, swam, and ran back home for a workout. Everything was building for Ironman. On Sunday mornings Alisa and I attended a twelve-week premarital class, but I still snuck in a ride in the afternoon. Actually, you can't really sneak a five-hour bike ride in. You just have to knock it out! Mondays were my day off, from training, not work. At work I still broke my back, picking trenches for irrigation and hoisting boulders out of the earth. The only encouragement I had, which was oftentimes more torturous, was watching CU's track and field athletes train on the track

---

[383] 5430 Triathlon—Half Ironman Distance, Boulder, CO (August 13, 2006): 25th Age Group 30–34, 5:05:59.

we were working around. Yes, there were days I wanted to lay down my shovel and leave them in the smoke. I probably would have put in some good splits too, with all that pent-up energy!

And then, as usual, there it went. I don't think I raced a single race in four seasons without some minor injury to overcome by faith. This time, "it" was the 'ol shoulder blade muscle (rhomboid, I believe). Bad! But, my race was scheduled, and I had all my training in, so we packed it up for Nevada, and I saw an Active Release Technique (ART) specialist at the race expo and did what I could. I trusted my Coach, and I prayed.

I raced the Silverman Ironman Triathlon[384] on my physical birthday in November 2006. The race boasted the "Toughest Ironman Distance Course in North America!" And, as far as I knew, it was! And just in case your ears are itching, and you're beginning to contemplate racing your own Ironman, a race consists of a 2.4 mile swim, 112 mile bike, and 26.2 mile run. So, with a 3-plus-foot chop on Lake Mead, strong winds, 9,700 feet of elevation gain on the bike, and an additional 2,000 feet on the run, it was a long day! But, the toughest part of the day came 8 minutes into my race when I hit my wall in the swim. I'm not sure if it was the overwhelming reality of the day and years of preparing, my injury, or the waves, but I almost bonked before I even began. I must have had an anxiety attack or something? *But God* met me as I floated on my back, taking deep breaths and rearranging

---

[384] Silverman Triathlon—Ironman Distance, Henderson, NV (November 12, 2006): 8th Age Group 30–34, 12:50:54.

my goggles; He calmed my nerves and encouraged my mind with His Spirit. And, Alisa was never too far away to cheer me on! I never had a single issue the rest of the day (other than my left pectoral muscle swelling up like a breast from punching through the waves with my torn shoulder)! Starting a race at dawn and finishing in the dark is a long day—12 hours, 50 minutes, and 54 seconds to be exact. I would add that thirteen hours is a long time to be doing anything, especially self-propelling one's body across the sea and earth!

In the end, racing triathlon was not about the races, the discipline and meticulous lifestyle, the shoebox of Age Group medals, nor even the banana-peach Carb Boom energy gels! It wasn't about placing 3rd in Age Group at the Rim Rock Run (37k with 2,000 feet elevation gain and loss) in celebration of my thirtieth birthday, nor the triumphal agony of my boastful bunions! It wasn't the days of training on back roads and open water without a soul to be seen, without a soul to cheer one on. No; it wasn't even the emotional breakdowns; or hitting the wall on a training run bending the gravel corner near the cattails when the autumn wind rushed through my soul, with only the voice of God left to carry me. No; and I suppose it wasn't even the mantras He whispered over my shoulder as I crouched over my bars, "It's just you, and Me, and the road. It's just you, and Me, and the wind, son." Or, descending a steep mountain run: "I've got you! Lean into Me! Trust Me; I'll hold you. Let it out!" No; because triathlon was all those things, and many more, and many beyond words, beyond knowledge. And with Jesus Christ as one's coach, how could it not be?

But in the end, it was something deeper still. It was His word. The promise of His word to my heart, *"I will heal you Jon."* And, as a faithful Coach, He kept His word. At every turn, around every bend, and through every stroke, He proved Himself to be greater in me[385] than my broken and defeated body, than my wearied and tired soul, than my condemning[386] and doubtful heart. He proved to be victorious, always sufficient, ever present, and reigning King immortal over all flesh, earth, and sea! Christ is the conqueror! Christ is the champion, the victor, the true *Ironman!* Christ is the what, the how, and the why! Christ is the here, the there, and the everywhere! Christ is the cause, the reason, and the purpose! Christ is the author, the finisher, and the winner of life's eternal *race of faith!* In the end, it was simple. In the end, it was Christ.

---

[385] 1 John 4:4—You are of God, little children, and have overcome them [false prophets, spirit of the Antichrist], because He [Christ] who is in you is greater than he who is in the world.

[386] Rom 8:1—There is therefore now no condemnation to those who are in Christ Jesus. 1 John 3:20-21—For if our heart condemns us, God is greater than our heart, and knows all things. [Note: the context for both of these verses is in reference to the believer.]

13

A NEW GENERATION

I'VE BEEN HOLDING THIS BACK three days now!
Like a cork that cannot be held underwater... Like the
pen of a ready writer, my heart is overflowing with a
good theme (Psalm 45:1)! I could not be more blessed or
bubbling in greater elation to share my excitement with
you today. Nor could a transition into the final chapter
of *Phoenix Road* be more perfect... For today is truly the
day of *A New Generation!*

❧ ❧ ❧

"Old Prince Nymph" was a keeper! Since returning back
to the San Juans, and having hung up my Ironman adventures, my roots have furrowed out toward the riverbank
once again. Alisa grew up with her brothers fishing on
the river too. In the Midwest as a young angler, I never
saw a rainbow trout of any size. But late last fall, after
returning from our trip to the Middle East, I slipped
into the Uncompahgre just south of town in a commonly

fished stretch of water. Throughout the summer months this water saw a lot of traffic, but all the fishermen had gone home for the season. If truth be told, I hadn't really planned on catching anything either. I was just relaxing and settling back into rural mountain America, enjoying one of autumn's last days on the river.

A calm cool breeze wisped through my line as I cast my fly across stream. Beyond a sunken timber, a dark flowing hole pooled deep and black in the shadow of several large gray boulders. Dried golden field grass, burgundy dogwoods, and burnt ocher willow fronds swayed along the bank. I unwrapped a brittle stick of clove chewing gum[387] with my fingerless wool gloves. The first few chews warmed the gum in my mouth as sweet spicy sap excited my palette. It was good to be on the river; it was a trip beyond imagination, but it was good to be home. *I never fish this hole; what am I doing fishing this hole?* But today, it just felt right. It just seemed to be one of those days when God was catching me out of my routine, calling me upstream with different eyes, around another bend into His company.

So, I fished on. I cast another nymph across stream and floated it through the deep hole. *There it is; I can't fish it any better than that.* (Where all things come together: the water and wind, the line and fly, the feel of the rod flexing in the hand, and the fisherman's intuition.) *Either no one's home, or no one's hungry...*

The black water rolled and the surface bubbled gold like

---

[387] Nostalgia Chewing Gums and retro candy can be found at: http://www.oldtimecandy.com/black-jack-beemans-clove-gum.htm.

beer. I thought it was a brown by his weight and the way he went down south. Either way, he was big, and I only hoped I'd get to see him up close before losing him. It really was quite magical, the way he turned and rose, as if to be reading my mind. He broke the surface, showing me his unique rust-colored stripe, and looked me in the eye. Perhaps he knew it was his day, perhaps I faintly believed it was mine. When I got him close enough to land with my net, I was amazed at his glorious wonder. And for a fleeting moment, I thought I just might keep him. I knew for sure, however, that I must let him return to his deep black water. Then, as I reached out to cradle him in my net, I heard a voice whisper in the breeze, "This one's a keeper, Jon." So, to my own astonishment, as I looked him in the eye, and laid him on the grassy bank in my wooden net, he did not return to his deep black water. Ol' Prince Nymph was a keeper; he returned home with me.

Today, I can still see through his eye, on my old brick office wall, as if to say, "Remember… remember the autumn day I bid you to come upstream, where I waited for you in the deep black water, where I broke the golden surface and we met eyes for the first time… Remember, remember, Jon?"

❧   ❧   ❧

Well, I know there's really no comparison, but, three days ago, I caught a real "keeper!" She weighed in at double the weight and one inch shy of my trophy last fall. After thirty-eight weeks hooked to her lifeline, she broke her water and emerged from her deep black womb into the sunlight for the first time—my wife gave birth to our first child, and daughter! My nose burns, and my eyes tear up as I recount the surreal miracle we have just witnessed, and in some magical way have even performed! Hallelujah! Every good and perfect gift is from above, and does truly come down from our Father of lights, in whom there is no variation or shadow of turning (James 1:17). Praise be to God, the only wise[388] and Holy Creative One,[389] in whom there is no spot or blemish.[390] For as Solomon adored his beloved, so you too my dearest child "are all fair, my love, and there is no spot in you" (Song of Songs 4:7).

Hence, today is the day of *A New Generation* indeed! Not merely in the mind and heart of a ready writer, or the hopeful expectation of a visionary's clouded dream. Today a new generation is born! Today a new generation lives!

THREEFOLD CORD

Husbands, love your wives, just as Christ also loved the church and gave Himself for her, that He might sanctify and cleanse her with the washing of water by the word, that He might present her to Himself

---

[388] 1 Tim 1:17 (referencing God); Jude 1:25 (referencing Christ).

[389] Isa 41:20, 40:28 (I am the LORD, your Holy One, The Creator of Israel, your King); Isa 45:12, 45:18; Mal 2:10 (all have one father, all have been created by one God); Eph 3:9; Col 1:16; John 1:3; Heb 1:2-3; Col 3:10 (Christ the Creator);1 Pet 4:19; Gen 1:1, 2:4, 5:1-2; Rev 4:11.

[390] 1 Pet 1:19—You were redeemed with the precious blood of Christ, as of a lamb without blemish and without spot.

a glorious church, not having spot or wrinkle or any such thing, but that she should be holy and without blemish. (Ephesians 5:25-27)

Alisa and I were joined together as "joint heirs of the grace of life"[391] in May of 2007. As I noted earlier, we returned from the Front Range to seal our vows and celebrate our marriage union in the San Juan Mountains of our meeting. As I reflect on signing our marriage license, I can't help but recall God's promise concerning "deeds which would be witnessed and signed in the towns of the western foothills."[392] Soon we will be returning to the courthouse to sign our daughter's birth certificate. Undeniably, God's ways are not man's, nor are they woman's.[393] They are His alone:

Who has directed the Spirit of the LORD, or as His counselor has taught Him? With whom did He take counsel, and who instructed Him, and taught Him in the path of justice? Who taught Him knowledge, and showed Him the way of understanding? (Isaiah 40:13-14)

---

[391] 1 Pet 3:7—A husband is to honor his wife, as being heirs together of the grace of life.

[392] Jer 32:44, 33:11, 33:13-14 (all NIV).

[393] Isa 55:8.

He alone speaks that which is not as though it was...[394] He alone has called the seas to a halt[395] and cast the moon into night lighting the dark.[396] He alone created man and took woman from his side.[397] He alone crosses the stars of lovers with the tides and seasons in rapture's eternal kiss. He alone fertilizes the egg with sperm, igniting glorious wonder and awe far above and beyond man's microscopic, telescopic, epistemological eye.[398] He alone is "I AM WHO I AM."[399] He alone is God.[400]

And so, we were joined as bride and groom, as a "threefold cord"[401] in the unity and holiness of the Spirit of the LORD whom called and quickened us according to His plan, for His purpose and pleasure. Naked and unashamed, we were joined as one flesh.[402] And we delighted in one

---

[394] Rom 4:17 (God gives life to the dead and calls those things which do not exist as though they did); John 11:43 (Christ calls Lazarus to come forth from the grave); Isa 46:10 (God declares the end from the beginning, and from ancient times things that are not yet done).

[395] Gen 1:9-10; Job 38:8-11; Jer 5:22; Amos 9:6.

[396] Gen 1:14-18; Job 38:19.

[397] Gen 1:26-27, 2:7, 2:18, 2:20-23.

[398] Job 38:2—Who is this who darkens counsel by words without knowledge?

[399] Ex 3:14-15—The God of Israel, of Abraham, Isaac, and Jacob declares himself as: "I AM WHO I AM."

[400] For I am God, and there is no other; I am God, and there is none like Me (Isa 46:9); Before Me there was no God formed, nor shall there be after Me (43:10); Indeed before the day was, I am He (43:13).

[401] Eccl 4:12—A threefold cord is not quickly broken.

[402] Gen 2:24-25.

another,[403] as we delighted to do His will.[404]

And we didn't waste any time! Thanks be to God, who had not only canceled my debt in full, but paid it as well, through an unexpectedly generous donation of $10,000![405] Yes, that's four zeros! One rendezvous to Hanalei Bay, Kauai for our honeymoon, and we were back in Colorado packing, storing, and shipping our life to the Hawaiian Garden Island. Five months later our cool bare feet touched down on the golden sand... "Aloha!" I finished up my Bible college degree at last, and I even got to study abroad in Israel for a summer, thanks to a generous blessing from another faith-filled couple. But before we could grow fins, we sailed back to the mainland, with our eyes fixed on the Pacific Northwest and my intention of attending seminary. After navigating the coast up from San Diego we sailed into the San Juan Islands where a community of believers welcomed us into port (Anacortes, WA). Not long after shivering through our first rainy-gray winter, we were ready to return to Colorado's sunny skies

---

[403] Prov 5:18-19—Let your fountain be blessed, and rejoice with the wife of your youth... Let her breasts satisfy you at all times; and always be enraptured with her love.

[404] Ps 40:8—I delight to do your will, O my God, and Your law is within my heart.

[405] After five years of laboring in prayer under an increasing personal debt, God miraculously provided a check for $10,000 shortly before our marriage. This provision was the fulfillment of a promise God had given to me, which also became instrumental in strengthening my bride-to-be's trust and faith in the Lord and me. Interestingly, with the consummation of marriage, I have watched God release long-awaited blessings in my life; apparently, He foreordained us to walk into His manifest fulfillment together. This anticipated and extended waiting in several of these areas has only served to increase the joy and victory at His arrival—all glory to God!

and bask at base camp. The San Juan Mountains called us home once again, like a *threefold cord not quickly broken!*

THE PLACE OF FAITH

A year later I finished up my first seminary degree,[406] and we launched out for the Mediterranean! Shod in my red and blaze-orange Brooks "Launch" runners,[407] Alisa and I took wings to the City of God, and on to Greece at last! By faith, we made our first trip to Israel together, then followed it up with a stint to the Greek Isles for our first swim in the "Emerald Jewel!" To finish our trip in true celebratory style, after making my trek to Phoenix Harbor (Finix), Crete, Alisa had determined to run her first marathon. Hence, what better of a race to immortalize than the first marathon ever run, from Marathon to Athens, Greece. And, it just so happened to be the 2,500 anniversary of the 26.2 mile run, or 42.195 kilometers, as we learned en route! And yes, it was on Halloween, my spiritual birthday! How could we not launch out by faith and follow the Captain of our destiny. So, we launched: we toured the Promised Land, we sailed the seas, we harbored in Finix, we ate olives, we sunned our buns, and we ran

---

[406] After graduating with my A.Th. from Calvary Chapel Bible College in December, 2008, I received my B.A.R. in Biblical Studies (emphasis in Apologetics) from Faith Evangelical Seminary in October, 2010.

[407] While speaking about "Launching us out" God provided these *phoenix-esque* (red/orange) runners with a secret message embossed on the sole: *Fuel the Fire!* View Brooks Launch at: http://talk.brooksrunning.com/2009/07/09/brooks-launch-inside-scoop-for-shoe-geeks/.

the marathon—true to the Champion of our course,[408] to the glory of the First and the Last.[409] We launched!

Of course, in the back of our minds, we had anticipated transitioning into the place of becoming "fruitful" unto the Lord once we returned from Greece and settled in over the next year. God wasted no time, however! With suitcases sprawled on the floor and laundry still hung out to dry, we conceived our first little seed! No doubt, 2010 marked a year of "firsts," and a decade at that. I can only think now of how God instilled in me the continued discipline to write my first book. And, as though the year seems to have been left open-ended, I can only praise Him for the innumerable *firsts* yet to be apprehended…

"Ahoy! Slow down, mate! One just sailed by!"

❧ ❧ ❧

Last fall in Israel I was blessed with an opportunity to preach God's Word as we sailed upon the Sea of Galilee. That was a first! No, I didn't get to walk on water! Swim, but not walk! And hopefully, it will not have been my last time to sail and preach on Jesus' Galilee.

While drifting along off the shore south of Capernaum, I felt moved to teach out of this familiar passage from Matthew concerning Peter stepping out of the boat to "come to Jesus":

---

[408] Ps 19:1-5—The heavens declare the glory of God… like a bridegroom, like a champion rejoicing to run his course.

[409] Rev 1:8, 1:11, 1:17 (I [Christ] am the Alpha and Omega, the First and the Last); Isa 41:4, 44:6, 48:12.

Lord, if it is You, command me to come to You on the water. So He said, "Come." And when Peter had come down out of the boat, he walked on the water to go to Jesus. (Matthew 14:28-29)

At its core, I see Christ calling His disciple into a relationship dependent upon faith. We see that Peter did walk on the sea; we also see that he began to sink when his faith was overcome with fear. We also see Jesus extending His hand to Peter, even as he begins to sink. There are a few things we do not observe: we don't see James, John, or any other disciple walking on the water "coming to Jesus," and we don't see Jesus approach with His fishing net in hand and jump into the boat with a few handshakes and nods to the boys, inquiring where "we'll" be casting nets this morning. This is not what we see. We see one man stepping out of his boat to come to Jesus. We see a miracle. We see wind. We see a man begin to fear and falter. We see a Savior reach His hand out to a man who got out of his boat and obeyed Christ's call to come to Him. We see Christ call Peter into a place of faith, and we see Christ meet Peter in that place—that's what I see.

Let me ask you a question: "What do you see?" I mean, what's the boat you're in? How is Jesus coming to you in the early morning night watch? And, what is He calling you to do? Perhaps I should say it this way, what "place of faith" is Christ calling you to step out into and "come to Him?" Or, where do you see Christ moving in your life, and how is He reaching His hand out to lift you up from sinking? You are not alone; we're in this rocking boat together, as were Christ's disciples, as do these questions reverberate in my innermost core. My brother's searing words cut to the quick, "[W]hatever is not from faith is sin" (Romans 14:23). My heart trembles as the Holy Spirit shines forth the light of truth into my unbelieving, fear-filled soul. I can only respond: "Lord, I believe; help my unbelief!"[410]

So, why haven't I gotten out of the boat? What am I still doing sitting on the edge dragging a toe on the water's surface, calculating, strategizing, and planning my first step? Why haven't I jumped! Why haven't I dived in! Why haven't I launched out! I can see Him now, coming to me on the water, "Lord if it is You, bid me to come." "Come, my son! Launch out! Don't hold anything back, son! Come to Me; here I AM!"

Can you see Him? Is He calling your name? Is He motioning with His arms and waving His hands? Is He staring you in the eye, looking straight through you? Is He smiling with a penetrating certainty? Do you know He's for real; I mean, do you really know Him? Do you know Jesus is waiting for you right now, bidding you to "come to Him?" He longs to meet you in a place of faith! Jesus gave Himself wholly, holding nothing back, to join hands and dwell with you. He said He would be in you, as the Father is in Him, so He would be in you![411] Go to Him now! Hold nothing back! Launch out—go to Jesus! Let today be the first time you have given yourself, all of

---

[410] Mark 9:24.
[411] John 14:20, 15:4, 17:21.

you, into the outstretched arms of a passionate, loving Savior, who gave His life entirely for you! Let His blood cleanse your secret faults. Let His truth free you from your hidden fears. Let His grace lift you up out of sin's despairing void. Jesus came in the fullness of grace and truth![412] Let faith move you today! Step out of the boat!

How?

By faith. "Faith is the substance of things hoped for, the evidence of things not seen" (Hebrews 11:1). Faith is how! There is no other way; there is no other means! "For by grace you have been saved through faith, and that not of yourselves; it is the gift of God, not of works."[413] From faith to faith, "the just shall live by faith!"[414] "The life which I now live in the flesh [body], I live by faith in the Son of God, who loved me and gave Himself for me" (Galatians 2:20). Step out by faith! "Having begun in the Spirit,"[415] keep in step with the Spirit. Use the faith God has deposited in your heart.[416] For, "without faith it is impossible to please Him, for he who comes to God must believe that He is, and that He is a rewarder of those who diligently seek Him" (Hebrews 11:6). God has equipped you with faith! So, step out of the boat! Here's your point

---

[412] John 1:14-17.

[413] Eph 2:5, 2:8-9—Salvation by grace through faith is "not of works, lest anyone should boast."

[414] Rom 1:17; Gal 2:16, 3:11; Hab 2:4.

[415] Gal 3:1-9 (3).

[416] Rom 12:3—God has dealt to each one a measure of faith.

of contact—today is the day! NOW is the time![417] Put your faith into action! Actualize! Go for it! By faith! He awaits your arrival… Jesus is waiting for you in the place of faith.

A Passing of Tides

With the passing of tides, renewal and opportunity for new life wash in. In the wake of a wildfire, green shoots flourish in mountain ash. A phoenix rises from its fabled flame. Christ's followers are endued with His Spirit after His ascension.[418] And, as one generation passes, another rises, free to reach farther, to soar higher in hopes of bringing the heavens down to earth. In hopes of planting a new tree of life, evidenced by the glory and testimony of a holy God.

My remaining grandparents passed away between 2009 and 2011.[419] My grandfather was the first to rest, and my grandmother followed. As I have reflected on their passing, I have found great peace and release to move forward in the call God has bestowed upon my life and family. Our heavenly Father has called us to advance the cause of Christ in the earth by making disciples of all nations and bearing much fruit unto God's glory. This is our highest goal, abiding in Christ; this is our chief cornerstone, loving one

---

[417] Heb 3:7, 3:13-15 (Today, if you hear his voice, do not harden your heart); 2 Cor 6:2 (Now is the accepted time; behold, now is the day of salvation).

[418] Acts 1:8-9, 2:4.

[419] These grandparents were on my father's side; my mother's parents passed when I was a freshman (mother), and when she was a teen (father).

another![420] To this end, I have determined to stand:[421] "As for me and my house, we will serve the LORD" (Joshua 24:15). So be it.

❧   ❧   ❧

I stood with my back to the entrance of the old red barn facing west. The last familiar views of my childhood were soon to pass me by. To no soul's concern, the white paddock gate stood open, swinging back and forth in the breeze. There was no horse to lift his head flicking his mane, trotting a step or two while he looked me in the eye. Doc had passed, and with him a generation. Laughter, tears, and stories uncountable to be told, still to remain in the hearts of many near and far; and others, too many others to be known or found out. The horses, the barn, and the track passed too... The trainers, the races, the whips, the boots and hats, and the sugar cubes too... The cigars, smoke rings, and old musty books... The black leather handbag, the brown glass bottles, the patients, the house calls, the train wrecks... The women, the temper, the dogs, the pick-ups and the Cadillacs... The hay bails, the go-kart, the watermelon seeds, and the barbecued ribs... Every man, every woman, every neighbor and community had their say when my grandfather died... This is mine.

---

[420] Mat 28:19-20 (Jesus' Great Commission for making disciples given to the church); John 15:1-17 (Jesus calls His disciples to abide in Him, the vine, and bear fruit by loving one another).

[421] Eph 6:11, 6:13, 6:14—Take up the whole armor of God that you may withstand in the evil day... Stand therefore!

It was as if God had reached out into the universe and gently paused the earth, and the tides and seasons were free to shift. The world was moving in a slow peaceful rhythm; a new order was taking form before my eyes. My heart swelled with life's release. Free from tears past, my mind was clear, my spirit light. A new day had dawned. A new sun had risen in the east. The night was less alone; the stars appeared brighter. And God, He had not changed. He was only near. Near in the same presence and being. Not more; not less. At moments more visible or clearly seen, but no less, nor more Him or real. Changeless in the changing of times, His comfort dwelled in the place of unknown. My heart gave thanks. My Spirit rejoiced.[422] The passing of tides had come, a new day set forth beneath the sky. Masts erect; sails were hoisted. And the sea shone brilliantly as we set out from shore. Nowhere known to go, nowhere known to be… a new day had dawned, setting out to sea.

❧   ❧   ❧

Truthfully, I'm not really sure why I got saved on October 31, the day my grandfather was born into this life… the day Martin Luther set Christendom on fire… the day of All Hallows' Eve, more commonly known as—Halloween? And, I suppose it doesn't really matter in the end, save that my Sovereign Lord has called me on. I could write much, say much, and I have thought "a great much" over the years. I could theologize, psychologize, and heck, I

---

[422] 1 Thes 5:16, 5:18—Rejoice always, in everything give thanks; for this is the will of God in Christ Jesus.

could probably even hypnotize! But in the end, a new day has dawned, and with it a *passing of tides*. God's grace has washed away all my sin, and behold He makes all things new. I am a new creation. The old has passed and the new has come.[423] At last, *A New Generation* has come.

So, here's to you, Doc, "The gloom of my bachelor days is flecked with the cheery light / Of stumps that I burned to Friendship and Pleasure and Work and Fight." Heralded in the oft and distant past, by generals and clergymen alike, "Open the old cigar-box, let me consider a space / Open the old cigar-box, let me consider a while / Open the old cigar-box, let me consider anew."[424] And until the days pass between the tides, and until the parting of sleepless starry eyes; my mind shall rest, my heart too, while I make watch and keep tune... Hear old friend, thy Helmsman cries: "Behold, I make all things new!" This trumpets He who is Faithful, He who is True, *"Behold, I make all things new."*[425]

---

[423] Ps 51:2-12; 2 Cor 5:17.

[424] Both quotes taken from Kipling's poem "Betrothed," from *Departmental Ditties* (1886); read at: www.readbookonline.net/readOnLine/2738/.

[425] Rev 19:11 (Faithful and True), 21:5 (I make all things new).

AFTERWORD: WHERE NOW?

IN CONCLUDING OUR JOURNEY TOGETHER, I am compelled to ask, "Where do we go from here?" At this juncture in *Phoenix Road*, perhaps it is more important where we are going, and where you are going, than where I am headed, or even where I have been, for that matter.

Assuming that you have parted ways with the "Stayer" by now, and have chosen to follow the "Goer's" road of faith… "Where is it you are going exactly?" What's the next step God has for you on your Phoenix Road? After all, if you have believed and trusted in Christ by faith, then you too are traveling redemption's road. So, where is your Redeemer leading you? Have you asked Him? He is waiting for you: "Call to Me, and I will answer you, and show you great and mighty things, which you do not know" (Jeremiah 33:3). So, trust Him, follow His lead… Discover the unknown. Go!

What about me? Well, I've got my own road before me, with several bends and twists yet to navigate. A few billboards have caught my eye, and I'm currently idling along a nearby wayside. As I press on to do my Father's will[426] I trust He will direct my steps, and yours![427] Perhaps our roads will intersect one day soon!

❧ ❧ ❧

As I bring these pages to a close, a few thoughts from our travels still circle through my mind. And, as I reflect on the shifts in our country's culture since my Younger Years, I am left unsettled looking into the future... Where are we going? To say nothing of our current economic downturn, or the seismic tremor sensed in the global West. Or, without gazing my attention toward the Middle Eastern Epicenter, *Phoenix Road* would not be complete without a discerning look at the hour we find ourselves in. Earthquakes, tsunamis, hurricanes, wars, acts of terror, bombings, domestic shootings[428]—all have become the normalcy of today's age, broadcast hourly over the net on our favored news pages. Shock value has ceased. America's superpower-status has weakened. Much has and can be theorized about the decay of societies great and small: the decline of family, rampant sexual immorality, the corruption of leaders, and narcissistic individualism. These realities all necessitate observance and thought, and great

---

[426] Similarly, Luke 12:42-48 characterizes the parable of the servant and the master—Blessed is the servant who does his master's will.

[427] Ps 143:8 (Cause me to know the way in which I should walk), 23:2-3 (He leads me in the paths of righteousness For His name's sake).

[428] The Bible's prophetic timeline concludes Christ's return with heightened natural disasters and outbreaks of war: Matt 24:6-8; Mark 13:7-8; Luke 21:9-11.

knowledge is to be gleaned from cultures past. Not to mention, the wisdom and blessing[429] available to the reader of humanity's most authoritative text—*The Holy Bible!*

But today, while my ink still dries, I cannot but call into account the spiritual bankruptcy plaguing our nation and many of our local churches this very hour.

> Has a nation changed its gods, which are not gods?
> But My people have changed their glory for what
> does not profit. Be astonished, O heavens, at this,
> and be horribly afraid; be very desolate, says the
> LORD. For My people have committed two evils: they
> have forsaken Me, the fountain of living waters, and
> hewn themselves cisterns—broken cisterns that can
> hold no water. (Jeremiah 2:11-13)

The twenty-first century is a postmodern ground zero. The decline of morality and Judeo-Christian ethics has left us in a global upheaval of catastrophic magnitude, shaking[430] the very pillars of heaven. Every threshold is being tested beyond capacity. Constructivists are busily at work reframing reality, housing their blueprints (or fingerprints rather) within subjectivity's "story." But why not, when humankind is an evolving adaptation of apery? Who or what is left to contain the limitless bounds of ego's inverted

---

[429] Rev 1:3—The Bible promises blessing upon the reader, hearer, and keeper of Revelation's message.

[430] Hag 2:6, 7—Once more (it is a little while) I [the LORD] will shake heaven and earth, the sea and dry land; I will shake all nations.

godism?[431] With relativism clouding our vision, who is able to see through the smog of a pluralistic worldview? Interest groups have long derailed our systems of government, education, health care, and corporate business. Who is yet entertained by media's reeling spin? How long can culture hold the helm before running amok? America, has she defiled her beauty?[432] Where is Christ's sweet and fragrant aroma?[433] Where is life, liberty, or freedom?[434] Why should a *holy* God bless America?[435] Rather, how hasn't He?

When a culture is deteriorating from the inside out, how long is tolerance a virtue? When democracy defaults, partiality drives politics, lenders prosper with users' increasing debt, customer service is outsourced, consumerism self-consumes, the digital highway bypasses the neighbors, and when families must forfeit to foreclosure… is now when culture is to be trusted?

Is now when the Word of God is to be cast off, or out?

---

[431] A direct result of Lucifer's fall (Ezek 28:12-19; Isa 14:12-22), and Adam's rebellion in the garden (Gen 3).

[432] Defiled or polluted: Jer 2:23—"How can you say, 'I am not polluted, I have not gone after the Baals' [foreign gods/idols]?"

[433] 2 Cor 2:14-16—It is God's desire to diffuse the fragrance of Christ through us in every place!

[434] Implicitly, I'm asking where Christ is in our midst? See references: John 14:6 (I [Christ] am the way, the truth, the *life*); 2 Cor 3:17 (where the Spirit of the Lord is, there is *liberty*); Ps 146:7 (the LORD gives *freedom*), John 8:32 (the truth [Christ is the truth—John 14:6] shall make you *free*).

[435] Understandably, I am not anti-patriotic, nor am I ungrateful for the blessings God has gifted the United States with. Rather, I am passionately advocating for Americans' (and all peoples') citizenship to be anchored in the Kingdom of Heaven (Phil 3:20), not a land established or upheld with hands (2 Cor 5:1; Heb 9:11).

Is the "way of the world" really convincing? admirable? or, life-breathing? what about life-giving? Is a stress-strung society really "evolving"? Should anxiety escalate in a people progressing in life, happiness, and equality? Rather, isn't it exhausting, discerning between good and evil? Has it not become increasingly uncommon to hear the truth, to find what is pure, and to observe what is lovely?[436]

Are "We the People" the nation we are (or once were) acclaimed to be? Or, are we holding on at the mercy of peril's hand: It appears that objectivity's arm awaits amputation. Absolutes have been castrated. Poor Lady Justice has been liberated! With regaining her sight, however, her scales have tipped to the highest bidder. Truth? Pilate's reply still resounds: "What is truth?"[437] Reality ceases to align with what *is* true, or what *can be* known. Theory has trumped fact! Science and technology's expansion are infinite! Man has overcome his limited nature! At last, he kicks no more—God is dead.[438]

❧   ❧   ❧

Is now the time to redefine, reinterpret, or reconstruct that which was real, that which once comprised reality?

---

[436] Phil 4:8.

[437] John 18:38 (Pilate's response to Jesus).

[438] Nietzsche, Friedrich. *The Gay Science* (1882); Sections 108, 125 (The Madman), and 334.

Or, is now the time to reverse our thinking?[439] The time to: embrace reality, uphold truth, accept objectivity, affirm absolutes, acknowledge know-ability, and embody the image of God (Imago Dei) inherent in being human...

> To everything there is a season, a time for every purpose under heaven:
> A time to be born, and a time to die;
> A time to plant, and a time to pluck what is planted;
> A time to kill, and a time to heal;
> A time to break down, and a time to build up;
> A time to weep, and a time to laugh;
> A time to mourn, and a time to dance;
> A time to cast away stones, and a time to gather stones;
> A time to embrace, and a time to refrain from embracing;
> A time to gain, and a time to lose;
> A time to keep, and a time to throw away;
> A time to tear, and a time to sew;
> A time to keep silence, and a time to speak...[440]

Phoenix Road is such a time as this. Today is a time to speak. Today is the day. Today is the hour. Your salvation

---

[439] Repent: to change one's mind. "Repentance (*metanoia*, 'change of mind') involves a turning with contrition from sin to God; the repentant sinner is in the proper condition to accept the divine forgiveness." (F. F. Bruce. *The Acts of the Apostles* [Greek Text Commentary], London: Tyndale, 1952, p. 97.)—from Blue Letter Bible at: www.blueletterbible.org/lang/lexicon/lexicon.cfm?strongs=G3340.

[440] Eccl 3:1-7; side note: Pete Seeger wrote "Turn! Turn! Turn! (To Everything There Is a Season)" in the late '50s, and The Byrds cover topped the charts at # 1 in December of 1965.

is at hand. "Your redemption draws nigh."[441] Now it is near time to rise.[442] "Now is when the dead will hear the voice of the Son of God; and those who hear will live."[443] Today is the day of the Bright and Morning Star.[444] Today a new day emerges from an eastern shore... Today *your* Phoenix is rising.

---

[441] Luke 21:28 ("nigh" borrowed from KJV).

[442] Rev 1:3; Matt 24:33; Isa 26:17; Ezek 30:3 (the day/time is near); 1 Thes 4:16-17 (the dead shall rise, those alive will be caught up).

[443] John 5:25—Most assuredly, I [Jesus] say to you, the hour is coming, and now is..."

[444] Rev 22:16—Jesus is the Bright and Morning Star!

Postscript:

And they said to one another,
"Did not our heart burn within us while He talked with us on the road, and while He opened the Scriptures to us?" *Luke 24:32*

…Till we meet again on *Phoenix Road*.

CHRONOLOGY OF TRAVELS

1   *2007–08* Kauai, HI

     2008 Jerusalem, Israel; Ephesus, Turkey

     2009 Oceanside, CA; West Coast; Anacortes, WA; Montrose, CO

2   *1975–86* Eastern Wisconsin (WI *below*); Acapulco, Mexico

3   *1986–88* WI; Summit County, CO; Canada

4   *1989–91* WI; Summit County, CO

5   *1991–94* WI; Summit County, CO; Park City and Cottonwood Canyons, Utah; Mt. Hood, OR

6   *1991–94* WI

7   *1994–96* Colorado; Montana; Canada; West Coast; WI; Summit County, CO; C.W. Canyons, Utah

8   *1996–97* WI; Steven's Point, WI

     1997 Alaska; Canada; West Coast

9   *1997* WI

10 *1997–98* WI

     1999 West Coast; Murrieta Hot Springs, CA

11 *2000* Bali, Lombok, and Sumbawa, Indonesia; Millstatt, Austria; Rome, Italy; Bakersfield, CA; Telluride, CO; WI

     2001 Bali and Java, Indonesia; Australia; Oceanside, CA; Boise, ID; Portland, OR; WI; Ireland; Paris; Seville and Barcelona, Spain

     2002 WI, Oceanside, CA

12 *2002* Boise, ID; Telluride and Montrose, CO

     2003 Montrose and Ouray, CO

2004 Bakersfield and Murrieta Hot Springs, CA; Montrose, CO

2005–06 Montrose, CO; Baja, Mexico

2006–07 Louisville, CO

13 *2007* Montrose, CO; Kauai, HI; Louisville, CO

2008 Kauai, HI; Jerusalem, Israel; Bodrum and Ephesus, Turkey

2009 Anacortes, WA; Montrose, CO; WI

2010 Montrose, CO; Israel; Petra, Jordan; Corinth, Finix-Crete, Santorini, and Athens, Greece

2011 Montrose, CO; Oceanside, CA; WI; Phoenix, AZ; Boulder, CO

SONGS FROM PHOENIX ROAD

"Spirit in the Sky" by Norman Greenbaum (Reprise, 1969)
"Free Bird" by Lynyrd Skynyrd (MCA, 1974)
"The Devil Went Down to Georgia" by
Charlie Daniels Band (Epic, 1979)
"Another One Bites the Dust" by Queen (EMI, 1980)
"Rebel Yell" by Billy Idol (Chrysalis, 1983)
"Too Tough to Die" by Ramones (Sire, 1984)
"I Fought the Law" by Dead Kennedys
(Alternative Tentacles, 1987)
"Sympathy for the Devil" by The Rolling Stones (Decca, 1969)
"Scarred but Smarter" by Drivin' n' Cryin' (Island, 1986)
"I Believe" by R.E.M. (I.R.S., 1986)
"Running to Stand Still" by U2 (Island, 1987)
"Fast Car" by Tracy Chapman (Elektra, 1988)
"Closer to Fine" by Indigo Girls (Epic, 1989)
"Learning to Fly" by Tom Petty (MCA, 1991)
"Quick Sand" (David Bowie cover) by Dinosaur Jr. (Sire, 1991)
"Spaceboy" by Smashing Pumpkins (Virgin, 1993)
"Accident Prone" by Jawbreaker (DGC, 1995)
"Randy Described Eternity" by Built to Spill (Warner Bros, 1997)
"Fool on the Hill / Nature Boy" (eden ahbez cover) by
Peter Cincotti (Concord, 2003)
"Rain King" by Counting Crows (Geffen, 1993)
"Redeemed" by The Snax (Screaming Giant Records, 2000)
"Be Thou My Vision" by Pedro the Lion
(Made in Mexico, 1999)

"The Transfiguration" by Sufjan Stevens
(Sounds Familyre, 2004)
"Upward Over the Mountain" by Iron and Wine
(Sub Pop, 2002)

*Bonus Track: "Jericho Road" by Damien Jurado
(Secretly Canadian, 2014)

READINGS FOR THE ROAD

Devotion-Classics

The Calvary Road by Roy Hession (CLC, 1950)

The Cost of Discipleship by Dietrich Bonhoeffer (Simon & Schuster, Touchstone Edition, 1995)

The Greatest Fight in the World by Charles Spurgeon (Pilgrim Publications, Reprints, 1990)

In a Pit with a Lion on a Snowy Day by Mark Batterson (Multnomah, 2006)

The Making of a Man of God by Alan Redpath (Revell, 1962)

My Utmost for His Highest by Oswald Chambers (Unabridged Edition; free digital version at: http://utmost.org/)

Pilgrim's Progress by John Bunyan (A. J. Rowland, Phoenix Edition 1897)

The Pursuit of God by A. W. Tozer (WingSpread Edition, 2006)

Apologetics

Apologetics for a New Generation by Sean McDowell (Harvest House, 2009)

The Case for Christ by Lee Strobel (Zondervan, 1998)

5-Minute Apologetics for Today by Ron Rhodes (Harvest House, 2010)

Mere Christianity by C. S. Lewis

True For You but Not for Me by Paul Copan (Bethany House, Revised edition, 2009)

The Universe Next Door by James W. Sire (Intervarsity Press, Fifth Edition, 2009)

INDEX

(Note: Page references denoted *fn* identify a subject's corresponding *footnote*, for further information.)

A

absolutes, 299-300

abundant life, 36, 95*fn*, 272-73

abuse,
  sexual, 23, 35
  substance, 82, *see also* addiction

accountability, 24, 138, 261

addiction, 36, 75, 78, 89, 99, 145, 149

adopted/ion, by God, 47, 185*fn*, 234

afterlife, 100

alcoholic/sm, 49, 61-62, 69, 74, 81-83, 142-43, 266, *see also* addiction

altar, 174, 178, 181-82
  God's, 186

amen, 249*fn*

American Indians, 28, 99, *see also* Native American

angel/ic, 75, 95, 154, 184*fn*, 196, 247
  of light, 101, 165, 179*fn*, *see also* demonic (host, medium, spirit), Satan
  of the LORD, 75, 154*fn*, 177*fn*, 269*fn*
  cherub, 96, 179*fn*

anger, 24-25, 71, 74-75, 80, 84, 105, 177, 182
  rage/d, en-, 24, 177, 182, 246

animal/ism, 54, 134*fn*, 136, 151, 159, 186, *see also* birds
  bear, spirit of, 141, 150-53, 255
  crow, 54-55, 167-68*fn*-69, 177
  eagle, 135, 150-51, 153, 157-58, 174, 206-07
  snake, 179
  tiger, 159, 177

animism/istic, 98-99, 103, 221

anxiety, anxious, 160, 173, 182, 191, 233*fn*, 275, 299

apologetics, apologia, xiii-xiv, 97, 195, 259*fn*, 286*fn*, 309

appear/s/ed, 29, 31, 34-35, 44, 47, 87, 168, 170-71, 177, 179, 190*fn*, 192, 299

appearance, 43
  dress, 39, 214

Assisi, Saint Francis, 2, 223*fn*

astrology, 125

atonement, 167*fn*, *see also* substitute

authority/ative, 27, 55, 80, 119*fn*, 157, 161, 164, 170, 174-75, 190, 202*fn*, 210, 243*fn*, 297, *see also* power
  God's, Jesus', 55, 190

B

baptism, *baptizo*, 204-06*fn*, 234

belief, believe, xiii, 43, 46, 73, 85,

94, 98, 101, 103, 133, 135, 219^{fn}
deceive with, 99
everlasting life obtained by, 25, 73, 90^{fn}, 123, 184^{fn}-85, 295
promise received by, 123, 184^{fn}, 290
system of, 100, 103, 131
unbelief, 52, 55^{fn}, 60^{fn}, 63, 72-73, 104, 133-34, 289
believer, spirit-filled, 5^{fn}, 84-86, 95, 118, 129, 160^{fn}, 174^{fn}, 185^{fn}, 190^{fn}, 195-96^{fn}, 208^{fn}, 219^{fn}
Bible, The Holy, 297
biblical numerology, 91^{fn}
bird/s, 171, 206, 239, see also animalism
black, -winged, of the air, 54^{fn}-55, 167^{fn}-68^{fn}-71
crow, raven, 54^{fn}-55, 167-68^{fn}-69
eagle, 135, 150-51, 153, 157-58, 174, 206-07
hummingbird, 255
Phoenician, 3
white-winged, 187^{fn}
blackout, consciousness, 74, 76
blind/ness, 53^{fn}-54, 66, 106, 116^{fn}, 119^{fn}, 170, 179^{fn}, 193^{fn}
bondage, 48^{fn}, 71, 85
born again, 92, 185^{fn}, 196-97, 208
of the Spirit, 196^{fn}, 269^{fn}
boundary/ies, 37, 40, 165, see also existence ("shatter all…")

C
calling, spiritual, 8, 112, 133-36, 145, 150, 157, 161-62, 174, 203, 208, 214, 268, 289

Chinaski, H., the band, 203^{fn}
Christian, a/the, 83-85, 99, 139, 190^{fn}, 257, 260, see also believer
non-, 84, 88, see also belief (unbelief)
persecution of, 220
Christian, culture, life, xiii, 1, 83-84, 165, 199, 216, 220, 248, 267, 297
subculture, Christianese, 201
Christianity, 42, 72, 137, 158, 160-61, 214
post-, 47, 55, 297, see also Post-
church, the, 38-43, 57, 107-08, 137, 186, 189, 195, 198-99, 201^{fn}, 203-04, 215, 218, 220, 223, 227, 240, 260-62, 282-83, 297
-Age, 66
head of, Christ, 57, 107, 201^{fn}, 215, 282-83
persecution of, 220
community, 107, 202, 260-61, 202^{fn}, 274, 285
condemn/ed/ation, 81, 102, 201, 277^{fn}
confess/ion, 84, 106, 184, 197-98
confirmed, 40-44, 48, 178
constructivism/ist, 297
reconstruct, 299
contradiction/s, 38, 134
self-defeating, 96
Cornerstone, Christ the, 158^{fn}, 201^{fn}, 215, 291
stumbling block, 158^{fn}, 161
Cornerstone, festival, 201, 270
counterfeit, 175^{fn}, 179^{fn}, see also deceive, deception, Satan

created being, 96-97
creation, 99, 102, 103^{fn}, 116, 119-
    20, 139, 150, 160, 171, 199,
    204, 255, *see also* nature
  God of all, 212^{fn}
  groans, 119
  voice of, 171
  worship of, 54, 93, 102-03^{fn},
    150-51, 158-61, 163-64,
    166-67, 170, 174-75^{fn}, 178,
    199, 207, *see also* worship
creative visualization, 95
Creator, God, 66^{fn}, 93, 96, 103,
    136, 176, 199, 204, 210-
    12^{fn}, 282^{fn}
  creator, 98, 134, 150-51, 157,
    161, 163, 174, *see also*
    Father Sky
  Maker, 176^{fn}
crucified, with Christ, 85, 185^{fn},
    207
cult/s, 137^{fn}, 155^{fn}
culture, xiii, 9, 28, 37, 99, 137,
    237, 260, 296-98, *see also*
    Christian (culture, sub-)
curse, the, sin's, 83, 103, 149

D
dark, 62, 72, 84, 94, 137, 141,
    179^{fn}, 180-81, 284
  -ness, 50, 166, 168, 173, 175,
    180-81, 194^{fn}, 241
Darwin, 97
deceive/d, deceit, 66, 99, 172^{fn},
    193^{fn}, *see also* Satan
deception/ive, 119, 170, 172
delivered/ance, 86^{fn}, 189, 190^{fn}-
    91, 236, 272^{fn}
demonic, 54, 166, 169, 190^{fn}, *see*

also Satan
attack, assault, 108, 185 *see also*
    spiritual (battle)
authority/ies, principalities, 27,
    28^{fn}, 157, 161, 164, 170,
    173-75,
Beast, 190^{fn}-91
haunt/ings, 66, 100, 180, *see*
    also ghost
host, 165, 167, 173, 193^{fn}
images, 180, 185
influence, 16^{fn}, 98, 169, 193^{fn}
man, 131, 157, 160, 175, 186,
    190-91
medium, 165
outbreak, 171
possession, 16^{fn}, 52, 54^{fn}, 179,
    189-90^{fn}-93, *see also* Satan
    (possessed), spiritual (process)
shadowed beings, 180
spiral, vortex, 179
spirit/s, 27^{fn}, 51-52^{fn}, 100, 125,
    151, 157, 159, 161, 163-65,
    168, 170, 172-75, 179-80,
    182-83, 185, 189, 190^{fn}-91,
    196, *see also* shamanism,
    spirit guides
voice, audible, inner, 157, 164,
    171, 175, 177-78, 185-86
demonology/ist, 191
depression, 49, 125, 140, *see also*
    isolation
despair, 101^{fn}, 108, 290
destiny/ed, 112, 146, 162, 164,
    286, *see also* predestined
Devil, *see* Satan
direction/al, worship of, 131, 134,
    163^{fn}, 174-75^{fn}
discern/ment, 25, 55, 86, 97,

159-60^{fn}, 165, 194^{fn}-95, 200^{fn}, 271^{fn}, 296, 299
disciple/ship/ing, 1, 33, 36^{fn}, 101, 200, 215, 228^{fn}, 288-89, 291, 292^{fn}
discipline, 138-39, 144, 162, 276, 287
divination, 135-36^{fn}, 169, see also witchcraft
divorce, 23, 59^{fn}, 62, 92, 158
doubt/s/ful, 63, 201^{fn}, 277, see also belief (unbelief)

E
ego, 75, 95, 297, see also self
election, 95, 135, see also sovereign
enlightenment, 92
  transcendental, 100, 158
environmental, 94, 139, 174
eternal/ity, 25, 70, 86^{fn}, 108, 123, 185, 187, 277, 284
  God's nature, being, 4^{fn}, 145, 173, 212, 185, see also Father (Everlasting), First Cause
  Jesus' nature, 4^{fn}, 119^{fn}, 173
  life, 66^{fn}, 70, 194^{fn}
  salvation, 66^{fn}, 186^{fn}, 194
  Spirit, Holy, 185
everlasting, life, 25, 184, see also eternal (life)
evil, 50-51, 55, 86, 134, 136, 170, 200^{fn}, 292^{fn}, 297, 299
  discern, how to, 86, 200^{fn}, 299
  root of, 28
exist/ence, 63, 93, 102, 155, 186
  God's, 4, 22, 43, 284^{fn}
  issues, 63, 93, 101^{fn}, see also paradox of life

"movement beyond my", 158
"shatter all forms and boundaries of", 155^{fn}, 162, 184
spiritual reality, 28, 43, 98 169, 190-92, 284^{fn}, see also reality (spiritual)
truth, 118
experience/tial, 9, 10, 95, 101, 131, 135, 150, 153, 157-61, 163-65, 171, 173, 177^{fn}, 190^{fn}-93, 196-97, 204-05, 207, 262
  driven by, 204-05

F
faith, by, 2, 5^{fn}, 84, 86, 207, 220^{fn}, 235-36, 239^{fn}-40, 254^{fn}, 268, 275, 286, 290-91, 295
  defend/ense, the, xiii, 65, 97, 203, 259^{fn}
  good fight of, 70-71
  Jesus', author of, 195
  "obedience to the", 144^{fn}, 198^{fn}, 234, 236
  place of, 288-89, 291
  race of, 253, 265^{fn}, 267, 272, 277
  saving, 3, 42, 80, 173, 184, 185^{fn}, 195, 290^{fn}
  shield of, 173
  without, 123, 289, 290
Faithful, and True, Christ, 106, 221^{fn}, 277, 294^{fn}
Father, 25, 56^{fn}, 73, 84-85, 133, 194^{fn}, 206^{fn}, 211-12, 246, 296
  Christ's, 12^{fn}, 34^{fn}, 73, 101, 219^{fn}, 228^{fn}, 289
  Everlasting, Time, 4^{fn}, 66^{fn}
  heavenly, 6, 13, 47^{fn}, 185, 205,

207, 228, 233-34, 238-39^{fn}, 274, 291
of lies, 108^{fn}, 193^{fn}, *see also* Satan
of lights, 282
Sky, creator, 98, *see also* Creator (creator), Native American
Son, Holy Spirit, 56^{fn}, 185
fear/ful, viii, 11, 78, 100, 134-36, 151, 158, 161, 168, 171, 177, 191, 288-90
love casts out, 76
of the LORD, 77, 209
fight/ing, 24, 61, 70, 79 *see also* violence
good fight, of faith, 70-71, 73
fire, "a great", 3, 4, 186^{fn}-87, 189
burning, heat-energy, 159, 177^{fn}, 182
consuming, 4, 57, 186-87
flame, Christ's, 186-87
First Cause, God, 96, 277
First Love, Christ, 102, 271^{fn}-72
flesh, 71-73, 80, 83^{fn}, 86, 125, 131, 167^{fn}, 173, 196, 206-07, 251, 271^{fn}, 277, 290, *see also* man (natural)
battle with, 71-73, 86, 91, 145, 189
Christ's, 183, *see also* word (became flesh)
fleshy/natural-ruled, 85-86, 106, 159
lusts/desires of, 52, 83^{fn}, 85^{fn}
one flesh, 251, 284
sinful, 33^{fn} 80, 83^{fn}, 86, 180
vs. spirit, 83^{fn}, 91
force/ful, energy, 160, 164
free, set/make, 36^{fn}, 85^{fn}, 104, 145, 207, 290, 298^{fn}

"love", 37
"spirit", 48^{fn}
freedom, 298^{fn}, *see also* liberty
from captivity, 36^{fn}, 104, 194^{fn}
from sin, 73, 85^{fn}-86, 145, 290
in Jesus, 36^{fn}, 212, 257, 290
in nature, 23, 112, 159, 231
fringe, outer, 98

G
Generation X, 29
generational, 23^{fn}, 47
genes, genetic, nature, 82, 86
ghosts, 100 , *see also* demonic
God's image, 95^{fn}, 97^{fn}, 300
good,
and evil, 55, 86, 134, 200^{fn}, 299
news, the, 15, 22, 52, 198^{fn}
pleasure, God's, 271^{fn}-73
work/s, 41, 105, 208^{fn}, 235^{fn}, 290^{fn}, *see also* religion
Good Shepherd, 103, *see also* Great Shepherd
grace/ious, 42, 130, 144-46, 172, 184, 198-99, 202, 214-15, 228, 232, 235-36, 256, 262, 290, 294
abounds/ed, 50, 72^{fn}, 235^{fn}
abundant, 44^{fn}, 235^{fn}, 274
"Amazing", 235
and truth, 35, 223^{fn}, 244^{fn}, 290
but by the, 145^{fn}
gift of, 185^{fn}, 235^{fn}-36, 290
God of all, 145
immeasurable, 235^{fn}
is sufficient, 50^{fn}, 72^{fn}, 232^{fn}, 235^{fn}, 256
much more, 50
of life, 283^{fn}

saving, through faith, 42, 185[fn], 290[fn]

Great Physician, The, 17[fn], 25, 86, 194[fn]

Great Shepherd, 232[fn], 248

Great Spirit, 98, 125, 135, 158, 160, 163, 168, 178, *see also* Native American

guilt, sin's, 50, 56, 71, 103-04

H

heal/ing, health/y, 3, 36[fn], 61, 77, 95[fn], 144, 162, 164, 170-71, 174, 246[fn], 261, 266, 271, 277, 298, 300, *see also* power

hear, listen to, 25-27, 38, 56, 84, 105, 151, 175, 249[fn], 299

faith comes by, 207[fn]

God's voice, 59, 98, 129, 197, 269[fn], 272[fn], 281, 291[fn], 301

heaven/ly/ward, xiv[fn], 16, 57, 73, 163-66, 169, 173, 175-76[fn], 184, 187, 194[fn], 206, 210, 212[fn], 235, 287[fn], 297[fn], 300, *see also* Father (heavenly)

cast out, Lucifer, 96[fn], 175[fn], 179[fn]

host of, 103[fn], 184[fn]

kingdom of, 241[fn], 298[fn]

high place/s, 102-03, 158, 175 *see also* tree (oak)

Higher Power, 91-92, 112, 130

hippie, Era, 46-47, 62

holistic, 95, 207, 261

Holy Spirit, the, 1, 42, 48, 84-86, 97, 107, 119, 190[fn], 195-96, 245, 289, *see also* power (Holy Spirit's)

anointing, endowed, 204, 206

Christ's, 119, 173, 194[fn], 196[fn]

Comforter, 196[fn]

convicts, 85[fn], 289

Counselor, 35-36, 196[fn], 283

Encourager, 196[fn]

filled with, indwelt, 84-86, 158, 173, 190[fn], 195-96

fire of, 187[fn]

fruits of, 191[fn]

gifts of, 160[fn], 191[fn], 204[fn]

God's Spirit, 48, 97, 158

Guide, 196[fn]

Helper, 84[fn], 196[fn]

knowledge, Spirit's, 160[fn], 197

living water, 195-96, 219[fn], 297

moved by, 9, 42-43, 182, 184, 196, 204, 210, 233, 245, 287

personal, 85[fn], 196[fn]

regenerated/ion by, 160[fn], 196, *see also* regenerated

Spirit, of God/LORD, 50[fn], 55, 97, 194[fn], 212, 283-84, 298[fn]

Teacher, 97, 196[fn]

temple of, 174[fn], 190[fn]

trinity, 56[fn], 185

wise, 185, 282[fn]

homosexuality, 35

gay, 37

lesbian, 62

hope, viii, 29, 36, 72-73, 98, 107-08, 129, 253[fn], 290

anchor of, 108[fn]

-less/ness, 73, 107-08, 140, *see also* despair

living, 72-73,

of glory, 73

hypocrisy/tical, 38, 41, 100

fake, phony, 39, 42

I

I AM, Jehovah, 179[fn], 282[fn], 284[fn], 289

I am statements, Jesus', 118[fn], 144[fn], 184[fn], 194[fn], 272

"I Am being", 118, 155[fn], 179

idol, idolatry/ous, 102[fn]-03, 110, 186[fn], 223[fn], 298[fn]

illuminate/d, xiv[fn], 1, 98, 119, 165

illusion/ive/ory, 55, 66, 95-96, 98, 118, 167, 170, 179, 223

denial, 95

dis-, 53, 120

sin's, 119

incense, offering of, 98, 125, 134, 158, *see also* smudging

indigenous, peoples, 166-67[fn], *see also* native, Native Am.

intercede/cession, 25[fn], 85[fn], 105[fn], 161[fn]

isolation, practice of, 49, 101, 130, 140, 171

J

Jehovah, YHWH,

Jireh, 239, 263[fn], *see also* provision

Shammah—THE LORD IS THERE, 10, 77, 187[fn], 204, 214, 240, 262, 268, 273

journey, spiritual, xiv, 1, 25, 50, 54, 97-99, 121, 150, 157, 159, 165, 195, 253, 271, 295, *see also* path, quest

justified,

by Christ's blood, 52

by faith, 80

K, L

law, letter of, 50, 80[fn]-81, 285[fn]

and sin, 50, 80, 84

Levitical, 103

legalism, 41, *see also* religion, good (works)

"let go", loose grip, 162, 255-56

liberty, 36[fn], 50[fn], 194[fn], 212, 298[fn]

life,

abundant, 36[fn], 95[fn], 272-73

Christ is, 53[fn], 73, 118[fn], 129, 184, 194[fn], 199[fn], 207

Christian, 84, *see also* Christian (culture, life)

eternal, everlasting, 25, 66[fn], 70, 184, 194[fn]

fruitful, 52

God gives, 43, 85, 129, 239, 284[fn]

Lord of, 4

new, 84, 185[fn], 208[fn], 272[fn]-73

public vs. private, 171

lifestyle, 27, 36, 51, 100, 154, 276

light, 95, 163-66, 177

angel of, 101, 165, 179[fn], *see also* Satan

being of, 158

Father of, 282

-force, 164

God's, emanate, 51, 98, 166, 184-85, 284, *see also* illuminate

of truth, 289

of the world, Christ, 165-66[fn], 194[fn], 273[fn]

otherworldly, 99

radiant, 163

unapproachable, 149

walk in the, 208[fn]

white, 163, 170, *see also* power, magic

logic/al, 96, 106, 170, 173, 228

rationality, 77

Lucifer, 56, 96, 172, 175[fn], 179[fn], 298[fn], *see also* Satan

spirit of deception, 172[fn]

Luther, Martin, 38, 40-43, 223[fn], 293

M

MacLaine, Shirley, 137[fn]

magic/ian, 167, 186[fn]

black, 170

white, 170

man, woman, 1, 24[fn], 43, 65[fn], 71-73, 83[fn]-86, 91-92, 94-95[fn]-97[fn], 103, 106, 114, 131, 135, 186, 192[fn]-93, 206[fn], 235, 251, 271, 283-84, *see also* woman, self, flesh

inner, 11, 196, 206[fn]

natural, 24[fn], 55, 94, 97, 100-01[fn]

new, 84, 185[fn], 206-07, 235, 253

old, 24[fn], 71-72, 84-85, 186, 206, 235

sinful, 24[fn], 71, 83[fn]-85, 136

manipulative/ion, 23, 35

Martin, Walter, *The Kingdom of the Cults*, 137[fn]

mediator, 57, *see also* substitute

medicine, *see also* shamanism, divination, animalism

cards, animal, 134, 136, 186

bag, 166

man, 130-31[fn]

wheel, shield, 131, 153, 168, 178, 186, *see also* Native American

meditate/ion, 1, 13, 25, 90, 102, 150, 163, 169, 171, 217, 237, *see also* philosophy, nature, isolation

contemplate/ive, 104-05, 179, 224[fn]

wilderness, in the, 22, 25, 101

medium, 165

mentor, spiritual, 90, 135, 162, 172, 270

metaphysical, 94

mind, 41, 52, 86, 94[fn], 138, 155, 158, 163-64, 173, 186, 193[fn], 256, 259, 276, 293, *see also* psychological

battle of, 102, 105, 107-08, 128, 138, 171, 173, 175, 180, 182, 185

change one's, 300[fn]

double-, 201[fn]

of Christ, 193[fn]

renewing of, 94[fn], 186-87, 193[fn], 272

"-space", 171

Morning Star, Christ, 3[fn], 15[fn], 186, 301[fn]

Mother Earth, creatress, 98, *see also* Native American

womb, rebirth, 162, 164, 166 *see also* sweat lodge

music, *see also* Cornerstone (festival)

emo, -rock, 138-39

Independent, indie, -rock, 29, 138[fn], 226, 202[fn]-03

punk, -rock, 24, 29, 32-33, 39-40, 46-47, 80, 107, 138

mystery, 73[fn], 93, 175, 178, 180[fn]

mystic/ism, 214, 224[fn]

N
name, change of, 47[fn], 216, 233[fn]-34, 248
  new, 234-35[fn]-36
narcissistic, 296, *see also* self
native, 158, 163, 217, 220-21, 227, 230, *see also* indigenous
Native American, spirituality, 95, 98, 136[fn], 158, 162-65[fn], 168
natural, 118-19, 134[fn], 190[fn], 196, 204[fn], 296[fn]
  earthy, 136
  insight, 42
  instinct, 151
  man, 24[fn], 55, 86, 94, 97, 100-01[fn], *see also* man
  super-, 163-65, 171, 190[fn]-91[fn], 205
  un-, 174
  world, 22
nature, 25-27, 46, 48, 101, 139, 144, 168, *see also* creation
  "back-to-", 47-48, 50, 54, 66
  being, my, 52, 82, 190[fn]
  characteristic of, 52, 55, 56[fn], 60[fn], 82, 83[fn], 86[fn], 95-96, 165, 190[fn], 202, 299
  Christ's, 56[fn], 119, *see also* eternal (Jesus')
  destruction of, 94, 168
  God's eternal, 66[fn], *see also* eternal (God's), Father
  of created beings, 96
  of the Devil/Lucifer, 96, *see also* Lucifer
  of self, 95, 299, *see also* self
  outdoors, in the, 22, 25-27, 48,

101, 141, 144, 166, 168, 206
  physical, 60[fn]
  sinful, *see* sinful man
  spirit-, Jesus', 119
  threat of, 168
  wilderness, solitude of, 22-23, 25, 27, 101, 108, 141, 168
naturism/tic, disrobed, 159[fn]
neglect, 24
New Age, 65-66, 90, 94, 137, 153[fn], 165
new creation, viii, 82, 185[fn], 294
Nietzsche, God is dead, 55[fn], 299[fn]
nonconformity, 100

O
objective/ity, 66, 169, 299-300
occult/ist, 137[fn], 205
offering/s, 98, 150, 158, 163, 168, 181[fn], 219, *see also* incense
old man, 24[fn], 71-72, 84-85, 186, 206, 235, *see also* man, sinful man
omni-,
  "-personal-God", 197
  -potent, 96
  -scient, 197
Om, 91, *see also* Oneness
One/ness spirituality, 91, 98-99, 103, 118, 158-60, 179, 190[fn], *see also* "I Am being"
opportunity, "window of", 233
outcast, 32-33

P
pagan, neopagan, 46, 102, 131, 134[fn], 136, 170, 186[fn]
paradox, "of life", 93
path, spiritual, 48, 92, 98, 125,

134, 150, 158, 161, 165, 174, 195, 229, 274, 296^{fn}, *see also* journey, quest
peace/ful, viii, 2, 12, 16, 101, 178 184, 189, 191, 274, 291, 293
lack of, 23, 71
of God, 2, 184, 191^{fn}
persecution, of Christians, 220
Phoenix (Finix), Crete, 261-62^{fn}, 286
philosophy/ies, 50, 83, 90, 139, *see also* meditation
daydream, 48
muse/ing, 50, 53, 169
of nature, 46, *see also* nature
of rebellion, 29-30
thinking, thought, 62, 102, 137, 199, 300, *see also* suicidal
pilgrimage, 141, 274, *see also* path, quest, journey
pluralism, 86, 134^{fn}, 298, *see also* relativism
pornography, 34^{fn}
possessed, *see* demonic (possession)
Post-,
Christian/ity, 47, 55, 297
modern/ism/ity, Era, 29, 47, 65, 92, 137, 297
power/ful, em-, 28, 42, 54, 85, 128, 131, 160-61, 164, 170, 173, 180, 196, 204-06, 245, 255, 257, 271
God, Savior, 81, 185^{fn}, 193^{fn}, 197
gospel's, 81, 193^{fn}-94, 199
healing, 95, 162, 164, 170-71, 174
"Higher-", 91-92, 112, 130
Holy Spirit's, 85, 185^{fn}, 204, 206, 245, 257

-less, 80, 85, 181
white, 54, 134^{fn}-36, 151, 157-61, 163-64, 168, 170, 174, 175^{fn}, 180, 196 *see also* healing, magic
pray/ers, *see also* intercede
answered, 144, 227, 229, 254^{fn}, 257, 262, 269, 272, 285^{fn}
Christ's, 101^{fn}, 105^{fn}
for blessing, viii, 195, 206, 232^{fn}, 255
for help, 105, 214, 245, 275
for sufficiency, 199, 206, 216-17, 226, 232^{fn}, 237
for wisdom, 195, 206, 218, 221, 224-26, 239, 254
house of, 202
others', vii, 25^{fn}, 160-61, 184-85, 189, 200, 206, 249^{fn}
pagan origin, of, 98, 103, 163, 165^{fn}, 168, 174, 177
relational, with Christ, 217, 222, 224-25, 237, 259
predestined, 95, *see also* sovereign
preference, of self, 91, 200-01
prince, *see* Satan (prince, of air)
prophecy/sied/tic, 33, 43, 111, 159^{fn}, 206, 216, 225, 236, 247, 254, 256-57, 267
Christ, related to, 43, 194^{fn}, 198^{fn}, 201^{fn}, 296^{fn}
propitiation, 90^{fn}, *see also* substitute, atonement
provision, provider, God as, 227, 239, 243, 263^{fn}, 285^{fn}, 286^{fn}
psychoanalysis, 192
psychological, 24, 51, 245, 293
breakdown, 171, 173, 175
game, 51, 245

mind, 94[fn], 105, 107-08, 128, 138, 171, 173, 175, 193[fn], 300[fn], *see also* mind
psyche, 51, 80, 99, 171, 173, 193
theories, 24, 192
thinking, 105-07, *see also* meditation, suicidal
punk, -rock, 24, 29, 32-33, 39-40, 46-47, 80, 107, 138, *see also* music

Q

quest, 93, 102, 130, 132, 140, 144, 196, *see also* journey, path, pilgrimage

R

reality/ies, xiii, 66, 70, 73, 77, 118-19, 123, 155, 170, 173, 296, 299-300
    align with, 123, 299
    Creator of, 193
    escape, 83, 144, 149
    illusive, not, 118-19
    labyrinth of, 98
    reframing, 297
    space-of-mind, 171
    spiritual, 28, 118-19, 170, 173, *see also* existence (spiritual)
    unseen, 193[fn]
rebel/lion/ious, 29-30, 51, 56, 59, 117, 298[fn]
reckon, 85-86, 185[fn], 236[fn]
redeem/er, un-, 51, 207, 282[fn], 295
redemption, viii, xiii-iv, 36, 159, 186[fn], 195, 234, 295, 301
Reformation, 38, *see also* Luther
refuge, 220
regenerated/ion, 160[fn], 196, *see also*
born again, transformation
rehab/ilitation, 81, 91, 138
reincarnation, 94, 100
relativism/ist, 65, 134[fn], 298
religion/ous/sity, 41, 83, 92, 119, 131, 137, 158, 223[fn]
repent/ance, un-, 54, 183, 184[fn], 204, 300[fn]
reproduce, after their kind, 96-97[fn]
resurrect/ion, 4, 60[fn], 72-73, 84, 119[fn], 144, 173, 185[fn], 206[fn], 234
    Christ is the, 73, 84, 119[fn], 144[fn]
reveal/ed, God, 55, 118-19, 179[fn], 197, 199, 212[fn]
revelation, 43[fn], 52, 73, 97, 119, 134, 172, 178, 234, 297[fn]
riches, of Christ, 73, 235[fn]
rock, Christ the, 136[fn], 158[fn], 161
run, away, on the, 24, 68-70, 149

S

sacrifice, Christ's, *see* substitute
salvation, 52, 84, 172, 269[fn], 290[fn]-91[fn], 300, *see also* saved
    eternal, 66[fn], 186[fn], 194
    from sin, 84-86, 167[fn], 290
    gift of, 185[fn], 236, 290
    gospel of, 180[fn]
    "helmet of", 27, 107[fn], 173
    work out, 86[fn], 209[fn], 236[fn]
Satan, 16, 23, 51, 54-56, 76, 93, 106, 108, 170-73, *see also* Lucifer, demonic
    accuser, 193[fn]
    adversary, 93, 106, 145, 193[fn]
    angel of light, 101, 165, 179[fn]
    counterfeit, 175[fn], 179
    cunning, 172

deceiver, deceiving spirit, 54^{fn}, 101, 172^{fn}, 193^{fn}

Devil, 27, 53-54, 93, 108^{fn}, 172-73, 193^{fn}

illusive being, 170, 179

lies, father of, 108^{fn}, 185, 193^{fn}

lion, roaring, 27, 93, 101

murderer, 108^{fn}

possessed, governed by, 16^{fn}, 52, 54^{fn}, 107, 174^{fn}-75, 179-80, 189-90^{fn}-93

prince, of air, 27, 51, 101

serpent, of old, snake, 26^{fn}, 179

"Sons of", 51-53, 55, 57

spirit being, 170

tempter, tempted by, 108, 170

violent affection, of, 172

wicked one, 172-73

worship of, 170

satanic, 52

save/ed/ing, 33, 34^{fn}, 51, 81, 171, 194, 215, 227, 246^{fn}, 272, 293, *see also* salvation

baptism, does not, 206^{fn}

by grace/faith, 173, 185^{fn}, 290^{fn}

from wrath, 52

uttermost, to the, 81^{fn}, 194^{fn}

Savior, 4, 81, 119^{fn}, 185, 288, 290

seduction/ive, 66, 167, 178-79

self, 72, 85-86, 91, 93-96, 101, 107, 260-61, *see also* ego, flesh, man

absorbed, consumed, 39, 41, 49, 296, 298

behavior of, 85-86

bondage of, 71

conversing with, 160

destructive, 50, 72, 74, 104-06, 143-44, 241

determination, 75, 260

exaltation, 56, 96

"find my-", 90, 92, 99

governed will, 24^{fn}

introspection, 50, 93-94

-less, 60, 152, 200-01, 282, 289-90

limited nature of, 95, 299

motivated by, 24, 74, 86^{fn}, 162

preferences of, 91, 200-01

realization, reawakening, 95-96

worship of, 91, 96

sex, 34, 37

sexual,

abuse, 23, 35

appetite, 34, 37

immorality, 36, 83, 296

innuendos, 37

sexuality,

biblical, 35^{fn}

homo-, 35, 37, 62

nature, and, 159^{fn}

strangleholds of, 36

shaman/ism, 130, 134^{fn}-35-36^{fn}, 151, 164-65^{fn}, 168, 174, *see also* animalism, witchcraft

shekinah (Hb.), glory, 177^{fn}

shift, 55, 63, 167, 293, 296, *see also* spiritual (shift)

sin, 36, 50, 71, 76, 78, 80, 83-86, 89, 103-04, 106, 119, 134, 136, 147, 289, 300^{fn}

behavior, practices of, 50, 83, 85-86, 100^{fn}, 144

choice of, to, 83

curse of, 83, 103, 149

dead in, 27, 51, 83-84

despairing void, 290

escape, way of, 56^{fn}, 106

freed from, 73, 84-86, 119^{fn}, 145, 167^{fn}, 236^{fn}, 290, 294
hamartia (Grk.), 132
slaves of, 85, 145, 174, 258
sinful man/"nature", 24^{fn}, 33, 71, 78, 80, 83-85, 89, *see also* man (natural, old, sinful), flesh (sinful)
sinner, 56, 83-84, 184^{fn}, 235, 300^{fn}, *see also* sinful man
skateboard, 29, 46, 48, 107, 109^{fn}-10, 117-18^{fn}, 154, 210
smudge/ing, practice of, 98, 125, 134, 158, 168 *see also* offering, Native American
snowboard, 20, 74, 109-12, 115-17, 122-28, 130-31, 133
solitude, 3, 22, 101 , *see also* nature (wilderness)
Son of Man, 119^{fn}, 194^{fn}
Sons of Satan/disobedience, 27, 51-53, 55-56
sovereign/ty, 48, 84, 95, 135, 160, 232, 270, 293
spirit, God is, 50^{fn}, 55, 56^{fn}, 84, 94, 97-98, 119, 193^{fn}, 211-12 *see also* Holy Spirit
broken, contrite, 128^{fn}, 183^{fn}, 215
of prophecy, Jesus, 43
spirit guides, 134^{fn}-35, 151, 153, 158, 168, 174 *see also* animalism, shamanism
spirit-walk, 151
spirit world, 164
spiritual, the, 55, 90-91, 97, 100, 118-19, 136-37, 150, 154, 160, 171, 196, 215, 236
armor, 107-08, 166, 172-73, 199, 292^{fn}

bankruptcy, 297
battle, 27, 28, 91, 106-08, 134, 145, 172-73, 181, 189, 199, 201, *see also* mind (battle of)
calling, 133-36, 145, 150, 157, 161-62, *see also* calling
condition/s, 17, 23, 25, 194
discernment, 97, 160^{fn}, 165, *see also* discernment
experience, 158, 161, 163-64
game, not a, 92-93, 96, 106
gift/s, 160, 204^{fn}, 236, 254^{fn}, 270
influence, 169
Integration/Disintegration, 190^{fn}
journey, *see* journey, quest
mentor, counselor, 90, 135, 162, 172, 270
process, 165, 170, 190^{fn}, 234, 256
quest, *see* quest
realm, 160, *see also* existence (spiritual), reality (spiritual)
shift, 159-60, 167, 175, 179, 181, *see also* shift
spirituality, 54, 66, 90, 93, 95-96, 98, 100, 110, 125, 130, 137, 144, 160, 164, 255
Eastern, 3, 95
steal, to, 49, 149, 223 *see also* theft
subculture, *see* Christian (culture)
substitute/ionary, Christ, 90^{fn}, 103-05, 119^{fn}, 167^{fn}, 196, 215, 256, 263^{fn}
suburbia, ideal, 29, 62
suicide/al, 50, 62, 105-07, 144, *see also* self (destructive)
sacrifice, self, 102-05, 183^{fn}, 215
thinking, 50, 105, 107, 144
supernatural, 163-65, 190^{fn}, 205
supreme, Being, God, 212

survive/al, mode, 71, 104, 186
sweat lodge, 162-65[fn], 174, 176,
    see also Native American
symbolism/ic, 55-56, 91, 98, 125,
    131, 163[fn], 168[fn], 170, 174,
    178, 181[fn], 187[fn], 206[fn]-07,
    234, *see also* tattoo
syncretism/tic, 100

T
tattoo, 71, 98-99, 125, 131
temptation, 83, 106, 144, 213
theft, thievery, 49, 62, 83
    burglary, 49
    shoplift, 50
    steal/stole, 49, 149, 223
theories, 24, 97
Three-Step Method, 86, 90
tolerance, 298
torment, 76, 183, 201
torture, 180, 182-83
trance, -like, 159, 183
transcendental, 100, 158
transform/ation, xiv, 47, 50, 94[fn],
    190[fn], 193[fn], 215, 235-36,
    246, 271
treatment, 81, 82-83, 86, 89, 90,
    110, 135, 194
tree, 9, 59-60, 100, 141
    oak, grove, 25, 48, 101-04, 108,
        112, 167-68, 176
    of life, 98-99, 291
    worship of, 102[fn]-03[fn], 168
triathlon, 265-67, 273[fn]-74[fn]-
    75[fn]-76
Trinity, The Holy, 56[fn]
    in practice, 185
    triune, God, 136
True Vine, Christ, 228[fn]

trust, 35, 40, 144, 159, 239, 249[fn],
    256, 266, 275-76, 285[fn],
    296, 298
    in Christ, 25, 123, 185, 220,
        239[fn], 295
    worthy of, 63, 123, 198, 256
truth, 35, 36[fn], 42, 83, 93, 104,
    195, 208[fn]
    absolute, 299-300
    conflict with, 38, 40, 63, 93
    grace and, 35, 223[fn], 244, 290
    I am the, Christ, 36, 118[fn]-19,
        184, 298[fn]
    knowledge of, xiv, 34[fn], 36[fn], 43[fn],
        118-19, 129
    objective, 66, 169, 299-300
    relative, 134[fn], *see also* relativism
    Spirit of, 85[fn], 196[fn], 289
    word is, of, 198[fn], 207

U
unbelievable, 55[fn], 63, 72-73,
    289, *see also* belief (unbelief)
universal, order, 98, 104, 131,
    160, *see also* Oneness
unnatural, 174, *see also* natural
unworthy/iness, to live, 102-03

V
violate, God will not, 246[fn]
violence, 24, 60, 62, 74, 177, 220,
    246, *see also* fight
vision/s, 150, 157-58, 161, 163,
    177, 180, 182-83, 186, 197,
    see also trance
    of glory, 184

W
walk, the believer's, 85, 98, 145,

185[fn], 198, 199, 208[fn], 296[fn]

Wicca, 134[fn], *see also* witchcraft

will/ing, act of, 11, 26, 56, 59, 62, 94, 130, 132, 134, 139, 162-63, 168, 179-80, 189, 190[fn], 271, 272[fn]

   God's, Spirit's, 73, 85[fn], 196[fn], 285[fn], 293[fn], 296[fn]

   Lucifer's, Devil's, 175[fn], 193[fn]

   self-governed, 24[fn], 94, 128

   to live, 78, 127

   volitional, 179, 190[fn]

wisdom, wise, 59, 66[fn], 77, 97, 185, 194[fn]-95, 208[fn], 239, 282[fn], 297

witchcraft, 30, 134[fn], 136[fn], *see also* divination, shamanism

   practice of, 174

woman, 7, 42, 73, 84, 95[fn]-96, 106, 148, 157, 189, 206[fn], 221, 225, 230, 247, 251, 254, 257, 271, 283-84, *see also* man

Wonderful Counselor, 35-36, 196[fn], 283

word/Word, God's, 26, 33, 54, 97, 107[fn]-08, 192, 199-200, 203, 214, 218, 221, 249[fn], 254, 269, 277, 287, 298

   armed with, 107[fn]-08, *see also* spiritual (armor)

   became flesh, 66[fn], 118, 192[fn]

   cleanses, washes, 282

   directs, 98, 114, 123, 237, 296[fn]

   discerns the heart, 271[fn]

   exposition of, 203, 225[fn], 273

   faith comes by, 207[fn]

   is living and active, 199[fn]

   is Spirit and life, 199[fn]

   is/of truth, 198[fn], 207

   of His power, 193[fn]

   of prophecy, 33, 43, 194[fn], 198[fn], 206, 224-26, 236, 254, 256-57, 267, 296[fn]

   of righteousness, 200[fn]

   promise of, 277

   spiritual food, 200[fn]

   spoke through, His, 214

   study of, 6-7, 13, 175, 198, 202-03, 218, 221, 229, 234, 264, 268

   timely, 219

Word of God, Jesus, 56[fn], 66[fn], 198[fn]-99, 208, 215, 298

worldview, xiii, 86, 298

worry, *see* anxiety

worship/pers,

   experience-driven, 205

   in Spirit and truth, 211-12

   Lucifer receives, 56[fn], 96, 175[fn]

   of creation, pagan, 54, 90, 93-94, 98, 102[fn]-03[fn], 131, 150-51, 158-64, 167, 170, 175, 178, 199

   of God, Jehovah, Jesus, 158, 189, 201-02, 204-07, 211-12, 218, 227

   of idols, 102-03[fn], 150-51, 159, 166-67, 170, 174-75[fn]

   of man/woman, 96

   of Satan, 170

wrath, 52-53

   not appointed to/saved from, 52

X, Y, Z

ABOUT THE AUTHOR

Born in November 1975, Jon Kelly originated in the Midwest. Like many explorers, a steady migration westward carried him to the peaks of the Rockies and finally washed him out on the Golden Coast. As a child, Jon passionately lived and breathed the outdoors. 80s punk rock and nonconformity shaped his teen years, while a broken home, anger, and alcohol eventually drove him back to the wilderness in search of himself—his purpose and the Author of his existence. *Phoenix Road* is Jon's unexpected story of redemption; his first published work.

Jon Kelly holds two undergraduate degrees in theology and is currently pursuing his Master of Philosophy in Religion. Today, Jon resides with his wife and spirited daughter in southern California, whilst longing for Colorado's San Juan Mountains—"his writer's paradise!"

Jon would like to personally thank you for your purchase of *Phoenix Road* and he invites you to share a brief, objective review of your reading experience at amazon.com, goodreads.com, or your favorite book or media site.

PHOENIX ROAD FUND

Phoenix Road Fund was created to aid believers called to the work of the ministry who might not otherwise reach their highest potential. The vision for the fund was birthed out of prayer for a brother Jon met on the island of Kauai in 2008—God had graciously redeemed him from a destructive lifestyle, but an overwhelming debt had placed a heavy burden upon his call to ministry.

Phoenix Road Fund desires to alleviate such burdens through financial assistance, education, and discipleship, with the goal of seeing believers released to serve God freely. It is only appropriate to Jon to extend the grace that he also received from Christ and other key individuals along his path.

Inherently, the fund serves to continue the vision of *Phoenix Road*; therefore, a portion of each book sale goes directly to Phoenix Road Fund. Thank you for your support and partnering with redemption's road in the lives of others…

Find out more at: phoenixroadfund.org

The Sun of Righteousness shall arise with healing in His wings. Malachi 4:2

www.ingramcontent.com/pod-product-compliance
Lightning Source LLC
Chambersburg PA
CBHW020459100426
42813CB00030B/3041/J